To Nigel & Louise

It was an honor to cross paths. May God richly bless you both.

Love Brenda

HOLY SPIRIT SPEAKS

50 Days to Hearing the Voice of God Workbook

BRENDA NASH, PhD

WESTBOW PRESS
A DIVISION OF THOMAS NELSON
& ZONDERVAN

Holy Spirit Speaks: 50 Days to Hearing the Voice of God Workbook by Brenda Nash, Ph.D.

First Edition

Copyright © 2018 Brenda Nash, PhD

All rights reserved. No part of this book may be used or reproduced by any means, graphic, electronic, or mechanical, including photocopying, recording, taping or by any information storage retrieval system without the written permission of the author except in the case of brief quotations embodied in critical articles and reviews.

Unless otherwise noted, Scripture quotations are from the Holy Bible, New Living Translation, copyright © 2007. Used by permission of Tyndale House Publishers, Inc., Wheaton, IL 60189. All rights reserved.

Scripture quotations marked NIV are from the Holy Bible, New International Version of the Bible. Copyright © 1973, 1978, 1984, 2011 by Biblica, Inc. Used by permission.

Scripture quotations marked ESV are from the Holy Bible, English Standard Version, Copyright © 2001 by Crossway Bibles, a division of Good News Publishers. Used by permission.

Scripture quotations marked KJV are from the King James Version of the Bible.

Scripture quotations marked NKJV are from the New King James Version of the Bible. Copyright © 1979, 1980, 1982 by Thomas Nelson, Inc., publishers. Used by permission.

Scripture quotations marked AMPC are from the Amplified Bible, Classic Edition. Copyright © 1954, 1958, 1962, 1964, 1965, 1987 by The Lockman Foundation. All rights reserved.

Scripture quotations marked AMP are from the Amplified Bible. Old Testament copyright © 1965, 1987 by the Zondervan Corporation. The Amplified New Testament copyright © 1954, 1958, 1987 by the Lockman Foundation. Used by permission.

WestBow Press books may be ordered through booksellers or by contacting:

WestBow Press
A Division of Thomas Nelson & Zondervan
1663 Liberty Drive
Bloomington, IN 47403
www.westbowpress.com
1 (866) 928-1240

Because of the dynamic nature of the Internet, any web addresses or links contained in this book may have changed since publication and may no longer be valid. The views expressed in this work are solely those of the author and do not necessarily reflect the views of the publisher, and the publisher hereby disclaims any responsibility for them.

Any people depicted in stock imagery provided by Getty Images are models,
and such images are being used for illustrative purposes only.
Certain stock imagery © Getty Images.

ISBN: 978-1-9736-3124-8 (sc)
ISBN: 978-1-9736-3125-5 (e)

Print information available on the last page.

WestBow Press rev. date: 08/01/2018

Acknowledgments

I did not purposely set out to write a workbook. At least, not at first. It is a product of ten years worth of journal entries, trial, and error, as I had to navigate my way through establishing a visible, living relationship with an invisible living God. Therefore, my first acknowledgment is to my Father God, the King of my life, the lover of my soul, who found me while I was steeped in sin and brokenness. He encompassed me with His extravagant love; who taught me how to hear His voice and follow Him. He is my constant companion, my anchor amidst the storms of life, my 'go to' when everyone else is busy, and the ear that never tires hearing from me. I love You, Lord. You are my Rock. You have entrusted me to steward this project, and I pray it succeeds in all You desire. I am a rose, Your white rose, whom You have transformed into a daisy, now blowing and multiplying these seeds into the wind. May they fall on the soils of those hearts whom You are going to plant, grow, nurture and water them in. May You develop 'hearing ears' in Your children and advance the Kingdom of God.

To my home church, Church of the Rock, and my spiritual fathers; Pastor Mark, Pastor Keith, and especially Pastor Aubrey. Their commitment to Jesus is awe-inspiring. Their leadership as pastors models the very heart of Jesus as Shepherd over His flock of sheep. Feeding us. Leading us. And teaching us. It is because of them, and Pastor Aubrey's persistent belief in God's hand upon my life, directing me with his godly counsel, that I am where I am today. I thank you all from the bottom of my heart.

To my beautiful, faithful friends in Christ, Helen Taupe, Karyn Pearson, Joye Creaser and my prayer team. First, during the beginning stages of the development of this book, each woman has contributed time and a little piece of themselves, whether in thoughts, ideas or partial edits; though I apologize, ladies, things have changed dramatically. Secondly, to my prayer team who consistently has lifted this book, our family and my ministry up in prayer. I love our friendship. I love their constant support and encouragement. I am thankful and humbled to have all of you be a part of this workbook and my journey in this life.

To my incredible, faithful and supportive husband Brian. The one who took on chores and at times, all the financial responsibilities to make this dream possible. First, my dream of becoming a counselor and accepting God's call on my life, as well as in all the long, excruciating hours it takes to write, edit and publish a workbook. Sweetheart, your constant support to my walk in Christ has blessed me more than I could ever put into words. I love you, hun. You are everything to me, and I am forever grateful for your love. I am so thankful I get to do life with you!

To my four handsome, compassionate young adult sons; Matt, Dylan, Austin, and Travis. And to their beautiful, and ever so gentle, loving girlfriends; Shelly, Jackie, Rachel, and Breanna. I am so proud of each of you. Your loving kindness towards my deep spiritual walk with Christ is both admirable and comforting. I love you all to the moon and back. Mama Nash thanks you from the bottom of my heart for your constant support!

Finally, to my editor, Jevon Bolden. Her insight, wisdom and astronomical editing skills and ideas are beyond my ability to put into words. I could not appropriately captivate her expertise through mere statements. I can say that she has made my first experience both enjoyable and memorable. Thank you, Jevon, for being such a pleasure to work with, and allowing my voice and heart to penetrate throughout every page while showcasing your intelligence and competence. I am indebted to you for making this project all that it is!

Contents

Acknowledgments v
Introduction xi

Lesson 1: God Still Speaks Today
    Day 1   The Conversation Begins 1
    Day 2   The Conversation Continues 4
    My Story: Learning to Listen 8
    Day 3   How Badly Does God Want to Speak to You? 10
    Day 4   God Is the Same Yesterday, Today, and Forever 18
    Day 5   Hear God for Today 23

Lesson 2: God Speaks Through the Bible
    Day 6   Hearing God Through the Bible 29
    Day 7   The Logos and the Rhema 33
    Day 8   Cultivating Intimacy with God 38
    My Story: Encounters with the God of the Bible 42
    Day 9   Praying the Scriptures 45
    Day 10 Developing a Hunger for the Word of God 50
    My Story: The Word Brings Growth 56

Lesson 3: God Speaks Through the Holy Spirit
    Day 11 The Inner Witness 59
    Day 12 The Sound of the Inner Witness 62
    Day 13 The Testimony of the Inner Witness 66
    My Story: The Inner Witness Confirms Prophetic Words 69
    Day 14 The Power of the Inner Witness 70
    Day 15 The Inner Witness Is Our Encourager 74

Lesson 4: God Speaks Through the Still, Small Voice
- Day 16 What Is the Still, Small Voice?..81
- Day 17 The Voice of Authority...86
- *My Story: A Literal Move of God*...89
- Day 18 God Speaks Spontaneously, Unmistakeably, and with Purpose.....................91
- Day 19 The Wisdom of God...95
- Day 20 God's Wisdom Is Greater...100
- *My Story: Trusting His Word for Me*...104

Lesson 5: God's Voice, Satan's Voice, and Your Voice
- Day 21 Not Every Thought Is Your Own...109
- Day 22 The Characteristics of God's Voice...112
- *My Story: Whispers of Love*...116
- Day 23 The Voice of Our Soul...117
- Day 24 The Voice of the Enemy..121
- Day 25 Practicing Discernment..130

Lesson 6: God Speaks Through People and Circumstances
- Day 26 God Speaks Through People...139
- *My Story: The Voice of God Through the Writings of Another*........................142
- Day 27 The Nature of Prophecy..144
- Day 28 God Speaks Through Prophets..147
- Day 29 God Wants Us to Prophesy..151
- Day 30 God Speaks Through Circumstances and Object Lessons....................155

Lesson 7: God Speaks Through Visions and Dreams
- Day 31 God Speaks Through Visions..161
- Day 32 What Do Visions Look Like?..165
- *My Story: A Vision of Trouble*...169
- Day 33 God Speaks Through Dreams...171
- Day 34 What Do Prophetic Dreams Look Like?..174
- *My Story: Warning, Instruction, and Freedom*...179
- Day 35 Testing the Spirits Regarding Visions and Dreams.............................182

Lesson 8:   Actions That Block Us from Hearing God
    Day 36   Distractions 187
    Day 37   Lack of Rest 193
    My Story: The Energizer Bunny Running on Empty 196
    Day 38   Disobedience and Sin 199
    Day 39   Exalting Human Reasoning Over the Wisdom of God 202
    Day 40   Ignorance to How or What God Is Speaking 205

Lesson 9:   Attitudes That Block Us from Hearing God
    Day 41   Pride and a Rebellious Spirit 211
    Day 42   Unforgiveness and Bitterness 215
    Day 43   Doubt 218
    Day 44   Depression 221
    Day 45   Worry and Fearfulness 225
    My Story: Death to Self Brings Life 230

Lesson 10: Grieving and Quenching the Holy Spirit
    Day 46   Grieving the Spirit of God 235
    My Story: Letting Go of Others, Holding on to God 238
    Day 47   What Is a Hardened Heart? 240
    Day 48   The Road to a Hardened Heart 244
    Day 49   Quenching the Spirit of God 247
    Day 50   Softening a Hardened Heart 249

Appendix A: How to Troubleshoot Problems with Hearing God 255
Appendix B: Learning to Judge and Test What You Hear 259
Notes 261

Introduction

Although I grew up knowing there was a God and went to church on holidays, if truth be told, I possessed very little knowledge about who God was. Despite the fact that I had my perceptions and ideas, thoughts and imaginations (which by the way stemmed from a vain appetite of who I wanted God to be), nothing was concrete; nothing satisfied my longing for absolute assurance or peace of His reality. In essence, I guess I have always needed the facts. Still, I remember I had this insatiable thirst on the inside of me that yearned for—even *craved*—a relationship, not a religion, with a living God, One I could talk to and who would talk back. I possessed this indisputable discernment that something or someone existed outside of this physical realm.

I was equally determined and motivated by this faith to find Him. As such, I devoted my time to practicing one religion after another—hoping to encounter a living God that would finally convince me of His existence. If there truly were a God, shouldn't He be able to reveal Himself? Shouldn't He be able to let me know that He is present? Surely this isn't too hard for an all-powerful God? Is it? While on this journey, I ascertained nothing more than burdensome religion and man-made traditions. I repeatedly discovered my peace was dependent upon my good works or my good deeds—both of which were miserable failures. Thus, discouragement and exhaustion overwhelmed me. My search for peace was just too tiring and fake.

Additionally, as time passed, my life frantically spiraled out of control. Barely surviving and at the end of my rope so to speak, I desperately prayed a prayer that changed my life forever. It was not that the prayer had any power, but the One who tuned His ear to the bleeding of my heart did. Let me give you a condensed version of my life seventeen years ago.

I remember that cold, blistering winter night like it was yesterday. It was February 2002, and I was about to engage in my usual evening ritual: I'd put the kids to bed, invite a friend or a couple of friends over, play some cards, have a few drinks, and smoke a couple of joints. But this night was different. As I took a hoot, suddenly I could feel this bizarre heat rise from the pit of my stomach, and like a volcano, it erupted up my chest toward my head. Instantly I felt both dizzy and fearful.

"What in the world is happening?" I thought. Panic began to tighten its grip, choking the life right out of me. Casually but nonchalantly, as I did not want anyone to know the panic I was feeling, I removed myself from where we were sitting and proceeded toward the door. I imagined fresh air would calm me down and help settle this unwavering fear. But it was to no avail. I paced and paced and paced as the symptoms only worsened. Dizziness, heart palpitations, and now nervous tremors ravaged my body and tormented my mind. "Perhaps a bath might help," I thought. Nope. Nothing. Nada. For hours, I battled this sense of foreboding. By this time, everyone had left, and I felt very much alone.

"Surely anxiety doesn't last this long," I worried. "Or with this much vengeance. Does it?" Terrified, and crying out for my life, almost bargaining with God, who I wasn't even sure I believed in. "God, if You save me, I promise to serve You."

I recall the tangible manifestations were so bad that I honestly thought I was dying. I never knew the heart could pound so hard and beat so fast—and for so long. I was in a state of absolute, uncontrollable panic.

Out of sheer agony and despair—and a grueling seventeen hours later—I plopped down on my bed like a limp ragdoll. At the time, I was defeated in every sense of the word. I genuinely cried out to God as my body continued to pulsate, "God, if You are real, I want to know You—the true God. Please show me what I need to do spiritually, physically, emotionally, and mentally to be well."

Spiritually, I was empty, confused, lost, and fed up, quite frankly. After many attempts, every religion I had practiced was empty. As for my current fad, New Age, it too wasn't working. Practicing tarot cards and following my spirit guides to a supposed better life only led me down more destructive paths, which I blindly followed time and time again.

Physically, I shuffled between bulimia and anorexia. I barely weighed one hundred and ten pounds soaking wet (and that was after having four children).

Emotionally, I mirrored a yo-yo, internalizing anger one day and spewing it out the next. I was up and happy one minute, sad and melancholic the next. I suffered emotional exhaustion, sleepless nights, and days of endless chores. Add to this distress four energetic boys and a husband who was a truck driver, which consequently left me with most, if not all, of the household responsibilities. Let me also confess we had declared financial bankruptcy.

Mind you, our marriage was in the same state of ruin. Several times we'd split up, only to reconcile for the sake of our children. As such, I felt stuck in a loveless marriage.

Furthermore, mentally I battled bipolar disorder, which sowed its seeds and sprouted roots the day I lost my mother at the innocent and raw age of eighteen. Unfortunately, she lost her fight to breast cancer. Fear, anxiety, anger, depression, worry, and stress were common emotions that raged within on a daily basis.

Because I was unwell in all four of those areas, my heart pleaded again, "God, if You are real, I want to know You—the true God. Please show me what I need to do spiritually, physically, emotionally, and mentally to be well."

Immediately after praying that prayer, I saw an indirect light in the corner of my bedroom. Still trembling and tremoring, racing thoughts and racing heart, this light kept getting bigger, illuminating the entire room until it consumed me. I could feel this light, this presence, rest atop my head first, then slowly and gently make its way down my body, ceasing and settling every tremble, every tremor, every fearful thought, even calming the heart palpitations. It was miraculous. Somehow, I felt loved. I felt heard. I felt God and the warmth of His embrace. There was a stillness in my being. In an instant I went from seventeen hours of cruel and relentless torment to instant peace and total body calmness. I was experiencing a peace I had never known, a peace that was supernatural and that surpassed any understanding.[1]

For days after that encounter, I searched for the familiar symptoms of my bipolar disorder, but there was nothing. I had this undeniable peace and inexpressible joy. All I could do was sing and pray, pray and sing. What was happening to me? And who was this God? What was His name? The only thought I had during that encounter was, "I AM the God of the Bible," which no less triggered a desire to go out and purchase a Bible. From that day forward I have been on a spiritual journey with a supernatural God.

That night in my room I was healed mentally, emotionally, physically, and spiritually. That evening a living God came into my room and breathed His life into me. I am forever changed. Bipolar disorder—gone. Bulimia and anorexia—gone. Fear and anxiety—gone. Dissatisfaction with my marriage—gone (although this was a process)! That night I discovered a real God who loved me and desired to interact with me, as He still does to this day. I learned that the God of the universe wants to communicate with me. I can share my heart with Him, and He shares His heart with me. I discovered that He longs to love, guide, lead, instruct, comfort, care, provide, and counsel me.

What do you long to hear God say to you? Do you need a word of encouragement? Answers to problems you are facing? Breakthrough? Do you just need to know He is there or that He sees you? If so, you've come to the right place. I believe that the Spirit of God speaks today, and I know you can learn to tune your heart in to the frequency of heaven to hear Him clearly.

As an avid seeker of God and a licensed clinical Christian/pastoral counselor, I long to see the body of Christ hear God for themselves. I truly desire to see God's children well emotionally, mentally, spiritually, and then ultimately physically—and that begins with an intimate relationship with God where communication with His Spirit is active. That's why I wrote this book, to teach you that God loves you and desires to commune with you. As you read it, you too will discover that God speaks, but more importantly, you will learn how you can posture yourself and respond to His voice and leading in childlike faith. So, buckle up and hold tight, because you and I are going for a ride!

I'm asking you to commit the next fifty days to pursuing the voice of God. The ten lessons in this book cover everything you need about how to orient your spiritual ears to hear God speaking to you. Each lesson, or chapter, is broken up into five sessions. You'll read the session for that day and then answer the reflection questions at the end. I encourage you to write your answers down. The exercise of writing out your responses will cause your brain to process the information in a different, deeper way than if you just thought about them. It will also make it easier for you to recall your thoughts when or if you gather in a small group to share.

Also at the end of each session is a prayer. Like writing out your reflections, prayer is crucial to hearing the voice of the Spirit. Though there are many ways to hear from God, prayer is the primary way we speak to Him, and as such, it is an essential part of our relationship with the Father. I encourage you to pray what's written in the book, but I also encourage you to feel free to continue to pray as you feel led.

Many believers find that as they are learning to listen for the voice of the Holy Spirit it is easy to dominate the conversation, so to speak. The Listen prompt at the end of sessions 1 through 4 of each lesson will give you an opportunity to ask the Lord a question and then pause with expectancy as you wait to hear from Him. Do not be discouraged if you don't receive a response during that time or at all. Instead, as you continue about your day, thank the Lord that you know He wants to speak with you and tell Him you are ready to receive from Him.

On the last day of each lesson (and also at the end of some other sessions in between) you will find exercises that will give you the opportunity to apply what you are learning about hearing from the Holy Spirit. This practice is essential. Don't skip it! These exercises are designed to teach you how to be sensitive to the voice of the Spirit, and they are an important part of developing and strengthening your spiritual hearing.

Finally, even though our relationship with God is personal and individual, none of us are called to live in a vacuum. In fact, the opposite is true: God has called us to participate in Christian community and to engage with those in our circle of influence who need to encounter the saving love of Christ. Healthy, affirming relationships with other believers will strengthen and encourage you when you need support and accountability and can help to lovingly steer you back on a godly path if you miss the mark. Because of this, I highly recommend going through this study with a trusted, believing partner or a small group, though you are welcome to complete this study on your own. If you do choose to work with a group, it would be helpful to meet weekly to discuss your daily reflections and to go through the last exercise and prayer from each section together. Also consider asking one question from each lesson as part of your discussions.

Are you ready to get started? It's time for you to begin your fifty-day journey to hearing the Holy Spirit speak.

Lesson One

God Still Speaks Today

Day 1
The Conversation Begins

This is what the LORD says, he who made the earth, the LORD who formed it and established it—the LORD is his name: "Call to me and I will answer you and tell you great and unsearchable things you do not know."

—Jeremiah 33:2–3, NIV

Since the beginning of creation, God has revealed He is a God who communicates with mankind; however, this communication begins with understanding that He is God and He is a Person, not a religion or mere force. A religion is an organization made up of "persons adhering to a particular set of beliefs and practices."[2] Religion can't speak. It can't hear. Moreover, God is not a force. Again, He is a Person. He is a Spirit being capable of having an intimate relationship. A *relationship* is "a connection, association or involvement."[3] Strong connections require communication. Thus, God is a Person and a spirit Being who speaks and desires relationship with people. We see this planned union begin in the Book of Genesis when God first created man and woman:

> Then God said, "Let us make human beings in our image, to be like us. They will reign over the fish in the sea, the birds in the sky, the livestock, all the wild animals on the earth, and the small animals that scurry along the ground." So God created human beings in his own image. In the image of God, he created them; male and female he created them. Then God blessed them and said, "Be fruitful and multiply. Fill the earth and govern it. Reign over the fish in the sea, the birds in the sky, and all the animals that scurry along the ground." Then God said, "Look! I have given you every seed-bearing plant throughout the earth and all the fruit trees for your food. And I have given every green plant as food for all the wild animals, the birds in the sky, and the small animals that scurry along the ground—everything that has life." And that is what happened. Then God looked over all he had made, and

he saw that it was very good! And evening passed and morning came, marking the sixth day.

—Genesis 1:26–31

Do you see what just took place? Man's identity—his very being—was birthed in the heart of almighty God.

Imagine: God had made the earth and all of its beauty, and still He was not quite satisfied. Therefore, God created man in His image and likeness so that man could co-labor with Him in fulfilling His will on Earth. However, for God and man to co-labor together, there must be communication. How incredible is that? According to the above Scripture, God desired an interdependent relationship with man to rule, reign, and fill the earth. Ephesians 2:10 confirms this truth: "For we are God's masterpiece. He has created us anew in Christ Jesus, so we can do the good things he planned for us long ago."

This union in "doing the good things He planned for us long ago" requires a relationship and ongoing communication with God and man. Otherwise, how will we know what to do or what He planned? Sure, there are the general plans and purposes of God, but what about for each of us specifically? We are not going to find that out through reading the Bible or being a part of organized religion. Rather, direct communication from God to each heart is indeed a necessity if we are to each fulfill our God-given destinies.

Reflect

1. What experiences have shaped your perception of God? Do you see Him as a Spirit being capable of having an intimate relationship with you?

_____
_____
_____
_____

2. Do you feel like a co-laborer with God? Why or why not?

_____
_____
_____
_____

3. What have you felt in your heart that God wants to do with your life and talents? Take some time now and write out some things you've felt you were meant to do from a young age, big and

small. Are there any goals or plans that seem out of your reach? Why or why not? If you've never had any impression about what God's specific plan or purpose may be for your life, spend a few minutes in prayer asking the Holy Spirit to reveal this to you. Don't be discouraged if you don't get an answer right away. You can continue to ask this question as your spiritual hearing gets better.

_____
_____
_____
_____

Pray

Father, thank You for telling me that I could call out to You and that You would answer me and show me great and unsearchable things. Thank You, Lord, that I have been made in Your image and that You desire to have intimate fellowship with me. Lord, I want to hear Your voice. I ask that You teach me how to listen for You and to hear You speaking clearly to me. I come to You with an open mind ready to hear all that You want to say to my heart today. Give me ears to hear and a heart that is receptive. In Jesus's name I pray. Amen.

Listen

Ask the Lord to tell or show you how much He loves you. Spend a few minutes silently and expectantly awaiting a response.

If you don't hear from Him during that time, that's OK! Close your time of listening by thanking the Lord for His desire to speak with you and continue about your day. Every so often you can praise the Lord or even restate your question and then pause again to allow Him to respond.

This practice is one way of praying "without ceasing," as Paul called it (1 Thess. 5:16–18). Inviting the Lord into your inner monologue and focusing your thoughts around Him and toward Him during the day are excellent ways of cultivating your relationship with the Lord and developing a receptive heart to hear from Him.

If you start to wrestle against discouragement that you haven't heard anything at the end of your time of listening or even as the day goes on, replace those feelings of dismay with praise to God for loving you and for His written Word, which clearly tells us His thoughts toward us and provides direction.

Day 2

The Conversation Continues

> My people, my chosen, the people I formed for myself that they may proclaim my praise.
>
> —Isaiah 43:20–21, NIV

As we continue reading, we understand that His *voice* echoed in the skies when He *declared* light to penetrate through the darkness and day to break the night. Even when God brought forth animals, He *said*. It causes such love in my heart to know that everything that I am surrounded by—the trees, the vast sky, the beautiful, fragrant flowers—all came into existence by the word of the Lord. All of the creation entered into being by the words spoken from the mouth of God. God *said*, and it was.

When it came to mankind, God did not simply speak man into existence. Instead, He formed Him with an intimate, involving touch. Like a potter with His clay, He reached down to Earth and formed man from the dust of the ground. God then brought Adam to His mouth and breathed into his nostrils the breath of life—His own breath—and man became a living being. (See Genesis 2:7.) Can you see that image? Envision, if you will, the Father's large hands gently picking up man and bringing him toward His mouth, then breathing His very life inside of man. We not only came from the dust of the earth but from the very breath of God Himself. I love that image. Man was distinctly woven by the Potter's hands. *Selah.* (Really think about that for a moment.)

Shortly after that, God and man began to speak directly one to another. That is nothing short of a personal and intimate union. It reveals the love of the Father for man and His desire for ongoing intimacy, which—no less—involves heart-to-heart communication.

As we continue to study Scripture, we find numerous examples of God continuing to speak to mankind in various ways. It begins in Genesis with Adam and Eve in the Garden and stretches through the end of the Bible in the Book of Revelation. God spoke to and through the prophets in the Old Testament and to the disciples in the New Testament through Jesus Christ. The Scriptures declare:

> Long ago God spoke many times and in many ways to our ancestors through the prophets. And now in these final days, he has spoken to us through his Son. God promised everything to the Son as an inheritance, and through the Son, he created the universe.
>
> —Hebrews 1:1–2

But God didn't want conversation and relationship to end after Jesus left the earth. No, before Jesus died and rose again, He promised to send us His Helper, the Holy Spirit, who would teach us all things and tell us of things to come. (See John 14:16–17; 16:13–14.) For the Holy Spirit to show us and tell us, He must be able to speak to us. That also means we are equipped to hear His voice and that we must listen.

As we examine the Scriptures further, we will see that God paints an unambiguous picture of His relationship to His children as One who not only listens to our prayers but speaks. And He speaks in many ways: when we pray, as well as through dreams, visions, and many, many other means. In fact, not only does the Word of God say that the Holy Spirit will teach us and tell us of things to come, but it also says that when we look all around us creation itself reveals the invisible attributes of God, thereby leaving all of mankind without excuse. (See Romans 1:16–20.) As such, His Word declares that each of us can know God and hear Him.

Take my husband, Brian, for example. He can hear and know God when he sees a sunset or a sunrise. His heart gets excited, and the glorious view reminds him of God's majesty, just as Psalm 104 ascribes praise to God for His creation. Brian relates to God and feels close to Him while he is outdoors. Fishing for Brian isn't just about casting a line and reeling one in, though that is always exciting as well. He says that the stillness of the water with the sun reflecting off of it reveals the hand of God in such a way that it causes him to reflect on God and worship Him in silence. His description of how he is moved to commune with God through observing nature reminds me of Psalm 46:10: "Be still, and know that I am God; I will be exalted among the nations, I will be exalted in the earth" (NIV).

I, on the other hand, am not prone to hearing God through creation. My husband and I could be driving somewhere, and he will see beauty in creation that I just don't see. He'll often stop and snap a picture. It astounds me when I see the image he has captured, because suddenly I see it differently! I couldn't perceive what he saw with his eyes and felt in his heart until I saw a photograph, and sometimes even then I don't always see it in the way that he does. I'm just not captivated in the same way, and that is OK.

I am a seer. Most often God speaks to me through visions, images, and pictures in my mind (we will discuss visions in greater detail in a later lesson.) When I press into Him and ask Him for an interpretation, I then hear Him speak to me in words. Sometimes it is not until I step out in faith and share what I saw that God reveals the meaning. God also connects with me by "downloading" revelations of Scripture or particular words. These revelations are released through words of knowledge, wisdom, and prophecy. And at other times, He gives me great insight into His Word.

I will share more on each of these ways that God speaks in later lessons, but I wanted you to see that He has equipped each of us to hear and experience Him differently. In His infinite wisdom, He has chosen to speak to us uniquely.

Reflect

1. Take a moment to meditate on the image of God forming man out of the dirt and breathing His very breath of life into man's lungs. What does it mean to you to know that you are filled with the breath, the Spirit, of God? How does that affect your perception of your worth and worthiness to communicate with Him?

_____
_____
_____
_____

2. If you have heard God speak to you and/or felt His presence, describe the circumstances and the environment of that encounter. How did you know He was present and/or speaking to you? If you have had this experience many times, are you able to identify a pattern with respect to how, when, or where you might be most in tune with His Spirit?

_____
_____
_____
_____

3. If you have never heard God speak to you or sensed Him near to you, consider when or where you feel most at peace, most "at home." Could this be a place or context in which it might be easier for you to hear God?

_____
_____
_____
_____

Pray

Father, I am so excited to know how intimate You desire to be with me. This image of Your large hands cupping man and holding him close to Your breath comforts me. It brings me joy knowing that You are always listening when I pray, and now You desire for me to hear what You have to say. Lord, I want to know how You have uniquely created me to hear You. Show me or tell me what that looks like. Teach me all there is to know and learn about hearing You speak. As I take this journey of listening to You speak, help me to be faithful. Help me to be diligent. And help me to take the time that is necessary to complete this workbook. I pray this in Jesus's name. Amen.

Listen

Ask the Lord to tell or show you why He wants to communicate with you specifically. Spend a few minutes silently and expectantly awaiting a response.

If you don't hear from Him during that time, that's OK! Close your time of listening by thanking the Lord for His desire to speak with you and continue about your day. Every so often you can praise the Lord or even restate your question and then pause again to allow Him to respond.

My Story
Learning to Listen

For days after my encounter with the living God, I felt peace, joy, and excitement. I was in awe of the One who healed me supernaturally and who loved me unconditionally. This God met me where I was at—steeped in sin, sorrow, brokenness, and shame. Yes, as the Bible says, I was dead in my trespasses. (See Ephesians 2:1.) Yet, this God revealed Himself to me. He had pursued me. When I drew near to Him, He drew near to me. All throughout my search in various religions, I had never had an encounter like this. I was always on the lookout but would come up empty handed.

In spite of my awe and enthusiasm, I knew little about God. I was filled with a desire to know Him more. Someone had to have the answers to who this God was. In search of more information, I called a relative who was more knowledgeable about the Bible than I was. Once I explained my experience with her, she instantly suggested that I get a Bible and told me we would go to her church together. She promised me it would not be what I was used to. It would not be traditional but very charismatic—whatever that meant. Because I trusted her, I listened and went.

The minute I held my New King James Version of the Bible in my hands, I felt so excited. I remember running up to my bedroom and slumping on the bed just raring to tear into it. If you think about it, this in and of itself is supernatural. For a person to change so radically from someone who drank, partied, and was depressed and discontent to someone who hungered to read the Bible could only be explained by God transforming me from the inside out. This is the power of love in action!

I recall verbalizing all the questions I had about New Age, divination, and speaking to the dead, more to myself yet out loud, like one who talks to themselves while completing some task. I was neither thinking nor imagining that I would get some answers. Notwithstanding, I heard inside me say, "Read Leviticus 19."

"Leviticus? What is that? Is that even in the Bible?" I mused.

I curiously yet frantically turned to the table of contents at the front of my Bible, only to find that Leviticus did indeed exist. How about 19? To my surprise, it did too! I remember feeling goosebumps throughout my entire body. "How bizarre," I thought. "How did I know this?" It couldn't be me talking to myself, because I didn't know anything about the Bible. How could I? I had never read it. There was no way I could know that Leviticus 19 existed. It had to be God talking to me. Could it be God?

At that point I was confused and a little weirded out but still enthralled by this phenomenon. But what caused tears to fall from my eyes was when my eyes zeroed in on verses 26–31. In these verses, it actually said, "You shall not practice divination or soothsaying ... Give no regard to mediums and familiar spirits; do not seek after them; to be defiled by them: I am the L<small>ORD</small> your God" (NKJV).

I couldn't stop weeping. To say I felt overwhelmed by these words of scripture and the reality of what was happening was an understatement. Before my salvation I had always believed that reading tarot cards for others and being led by my spirit guides as a medium was loving and helping others. I had believed that we all loved the same God but that He just may have various names according to other religions. However, these Scriptures laid down a defining line of demarcation, a line in the sand so to speak—so much so that it sent shivers down my spine. The God of the Bible was separating Himself from all other gods and declaring His identity—I AM—and He was personally speaking to me about His rejection of practicing divination and New Age in general.

All day long and for months after, I experienced God like this. I could hear Him on the inside of me. It was evident and precise. Wise and all-knowing. It wasn't just reading the Bible. I would ask a question, and then I'd listen. Silently, I would hear, "Read," and then a specific Scripture reference. The instructions were very, very specific. Each time, as I fumbled through the Bible, not only would it be in the Bible but it would undoubtedly be the answer to my question. Subsequently, I'd bawl like a baby, overwhelmed and in awe that the God of the Bible—no, the God of the universe—was indeed speaking to me! To me. He was indeed telling me where to look in His Word for the answers to my questions.

At times I was worried about my sanity. I had never heard of anyone hearing God—spirits, yes, but not God Himself. I felt afraid, but the peace and joy I felt, coupled with the undeniable nature of these experiences, motivated me to continue on in my walk with God. Soon, though, there was no doubt in my mind; it was time to go to this church my relative had mentioned, because I needed reassurance that I wasn't going crazy.

Day 3

How Badly Does God Want to Speak to You?

> For I am convinced that neither death nor life, neither angels nor demons, neither the present nor the future, nor any powers, neither height nor depth, nor anything else in all creation, will be able to separate us from the love of God that is in Christ Jesus our Lord.
>
> —Romans 8:38–39, NIV

God's desire for communication with us is reinforced through Jesus Himself. After all, God sent His Son, Jesus, to Earth to repair the breach in relationship caused by sin. So where did sin come from? Where and how did this breakdown in communication first occur?

The short answer is this: Sin is the transgression of divine Law, and it entered the world with the sin of Adam.[4] After God created Adam and Eve, He gave them every tree to freely eat, except the tree of the knowledge of good and evil. Unfortunately, Satan entered the picture. He lied to Eve and told her the fruit of that tree was good to eat, and she believed him. Once Eve saw that the tree was good for food, was pleasant to her eyes, and could make her wise, she ate it. She also gave some to Adam, and he ate. Thus, sin was committed, and God's relationship with mankind—a union formed by His own hands and His own breath in the Garden of Eden—was now broken, distant, and nonexistent. This was the beginning of the breakdown of communication.

Imagine just for a moment—and I want you to stop and pause right here—how it must have broken God's heart when man, who He created for the purpose of relationship with Him, was suddenly separated from Him because of sin. As we saw in our study of the Scriptures on Day 1, this was the very purpose for which God created them: relationship and communication. In addition to being holy, righteous, and just—all of which are individual attributes—God is also very loving, an attribute that implies and even requires relationship. Remember the first image we shared, how God carefully crafted man from the dust of the earth and gently brought him to His mouth and breathed life into him? That is a delicate picture of unconditional love. With that image we see the longing of His heart for intimate relationship and communication. It also helps us understand the degree to which God was heartbroken that His relationship, intimacy, and communication with man was now ruptured through sin.

Because God is holy, righteous, and just, He also knew that this breakdown in communication and relationship could not be the only consequence of Adam and Eve's sin. Sin needed to be punished, and as Judge, God would not forego or excuse this sentencing. Romans 5:18 explains, "Adam's one sin brings condemnation for everyone." That is, because of the Fall, all of mankind for all time would bear the consequences of sin. Each of us has a sin nature, exposing us to temptation and making us prone to committing our own sin against God.[5]

Thank God that is not the end of our story. Otherwise, we would all be doomed. In His infinite love, God provided mankind with a way out. Until it was time for a more perfect, permanent solution, He gave the Law so that His people could avoid the pitfalls of sin and, when they erred, atone for their wrongdoing through the substitutionary sacrifice of an animal. Romans 5:20 tells us, "God's law was given so that all people could see how sinful they were. But as people sinned more and more, God's wonderful grace became more apparent."

Even while the Law was still in effect, God set in motion a plan for redemption through His Son, Jesus, so that mankind could be restored to the fullness of relationship with Him. Instead of rejecting us or sentencing us to a punishment we deserved, God came down from heaven in the form of Jesus, fully Man yet fully God.[6] He suffered temptation and all the same evils in this world as we do, yet He remained sinless.[7] Jesus spent three and a half years in ministry preaching the gospel and sharing the good news about God's plan for restoring His relationship with mankind.[8] He was determined to share the truth about the love of God and the destruction of sin, all the while aware that He would suffer the ultimate punishment of sin. Jesus would experience the most excruciating and humiliating form of death on the cross, taking our punishment for sin upon Himself so that we could make a choice and accept His gift of salvation by grace through faith in Christ. Jesus's work on the cross—His willing sacrifice of Himself for all of mankind's sins simultaneously—fulfilled the Law instantly.[9] Romans 5:18–19 tells the rest of the story:

> Yes, Adam's one sin brings condemnation for everyone, but Christ's one act of righteousness brings a right relationship with God and new life for everyone. Because one person disobeyed God, many became sinners. But because one other person [Jesus] obeyed God, many will be made righteous.

Jesus's willing obedience to the cross enables man to be reconciled back to this holy, righteous, and just God to continue this intimate union with Him!

Let that sink in for a moment. God Himself came down from heaven to relate to us—face to face—just as He did when He carefully crafted Adam and breathed His breath of life into him. God Himself, in the Law, told men and women that sin destroys and separates them from God for all eternity. But because He loves people and desires an eternal relationship with us, Jesus came to take the punishment for our sin upon Himself. Hence, our relationship and communication with Him are restored!

> But God showed his great love for us by sending Christ to die for us while we were still sinners. And since we have been made right in God's sight by the blood of Christ, he will certainly save us from condemnation. For since our friendship with God was restored by the death of his Son while we were still his enemies, we will certainly be saved through the life of his Son. So now we can rejoice in our wonderful new relationship with God because our Lord Jesus Christ has made us friends of God.
>
> —Romans 5:8–11

Romans 10:13 puts it concisely: "Everyone who calls on the name of the Lord will be saved."

Our intimate union with Him mattered to God to the point of His death and resurrection. Would you not agree that is how badly God desires to commune with us? That alone should convince you of God's desire to fellowship with and be intimate with you! I encourage you, if you want to know the heart of God, study the life of Jesus. He is God in the flesh in pursuit of a loving relationship with us.

"My Sheep Hear My Voice"

Still not convinced? During His ministry on Earth, Jesus told a parable that perfectly illustrates how His work on the cross saves us from spiritual death through sin and makes clear His desire for restored relationship. The Book of Luke recounts the parable of the lost sheep this way:

> Tax collectors and other notorious sinners often came to listen to Jesus teach. This made the Pharisees and teachers of religious law complain that he was associating with such sinful people—even eating with them! So Jesus told them this story: "If a man has a hundred sheep and one of them gets lost, what will he do? Won't he leave the ninety-nine others in the wilderness and go to search for the one that is lost until he finds it? And when he has found it, he will joyfully carry it home on his shoulders. When he arrives, he will call together his friends and neighbors, saying, "Rejoice with me because I have found my lost sheep." In the same way, there is

more joy in heaven over one lost sinner who repents and returns to God than over ninety-nine others who are righteous and haven't strayed away!

—Luke 15:1–7

We are the sheep Jesus was talking about in this parable. Because of our sin, we were separated from God and were wandering, lost, through the world. However, God sought us out and rescued us so that none of us would die separated from His love and presence for eternity.

Jesus used this metaphor about the sheep (us) and the shepherd (Him) often in His earthly ministry.[10] In John 10:27 Jesus used this same terminology to reveal His heart and thereby the heart of God: "My sheep hear my voice, and I know them, and they follow me" (ESV). Jesus is the Shepherd who laid down His life for His sheep, and since those who believe in Jesus are His sheep, this scripture should give us confidence that we can and will hear His voice and that He knows us. What a promise!

John 10:3–4 says, "To him, the doorkeeper opens. *The sheep hear his voice*, and he calls his own sheep by name and leads them out. When he has brought out all his own [sheep], he goes before them, and the sheep follow him, for they *know His voice*" (ESV, emphasis added). Beloved, if you have accepted Christ as your personal Lord and made Him the Savior of your life, you *are* aware of His voice, even if you aren't conscious of it. Don't be afraid any longer that you don't know His voice. That fear will only make it harder for you to identify when and how He is speaking to you.

If we are commanded to follow Him, then it makes perfect sense that we hear His leading. Furthermore, if we were created in the image of God, then it stands to reason that we were wired to hear Him, that is, to communicate with Him spirit to Spirit, our spirit to His Holy Spirit. It is not God up there in the heavens and us down here as if we are trying to hear God from a distance with our natural ears; instead, God is in us if we are born again, thereby enabling us to hear His whispers from within.

These verses from Luke 15 and John 10 are a few among many indications of God's desire to have an intimate and personal relationship with us. They are evidence that when we become His by trusting in Jesus, He will speak to us, and we will know His voice. Notice that these scriptures are written in present tense, not past tense, so there is no refuting that God wants to speak to all His disciples, including you and me.

We are equipped to know and hear God's voice. Perhaps this is the first time you have heard that you can hear God, so there is some exciting training ahead for you as you learn to be sensitive to the voice of the Spirit. Some of us may be out of practice. Still others of us could be distracted by the noise of life; thus, God's voice is drowned. Whatever may be causing us not to hear God, we must remember that our lack of hearing Him does not mean that His desire to speak to us has changed. Neither does it mean that He isn't speaking. We just need to learn how to hear from Him so we can get reconnected.

In Pursuit of His Creation

Not only is it important to establish that God still speaks, but it is equally imperative to understand that God *wants* to talk to us. God is never too busy, there is no problem too small for His attention, and we are never a botheration to Him. Instead, our Father in heaven desires to speak and commune with us.

Throughout Scripture, from beginning to end, we see God's desire to speak and relate to mankind. With Adam and Eve, as illustrated earlier, we first observe God's heart for intimate connection as He formed man with His own hands in His image, in His likeness, and then gently breathed His breath into man's mouth, connecting them spirit to Spirit. God generously provided food, work, and a helpmate for Adam, revealing His love for mankind. Through the scriptures given in Genesis, we see how communication between man and God was possible.

As we journey through the Old Testament and read about the fathers of our faith from Abraham to Joshua, we see God pursuing these men and speaking to them about their divine purpose. God sought out Abraham and promised to make him "into a great nation ... a blessing to others" (Gen. 12:2; see vv. 1–4). With Joshua, God encouraged him and gave him principles to apply to walk in the blessing. Three times God commanded him to "be strong and courageous" (Joshua 1:6–7, 9; see vv. 1–9), and He promised Joshua, "I will not fail you or abandon you" (v. 5). These accounts show us that God desires us to know His will for our lives and that He will give us direction and encouragement as we follow the path He has ordained for us.

In the Book of 1 Samuel we first learn that hearing God is not limited to adults, but children can learn to hear God as well. (See 1 Samuel 3:4–9.) Jesus reiterated this in the Gospels when He rebuked men from keeping the children from coming to Him. His atoning sacrifice was to restore God's relationship with all, not just a select few spiritual elites and not just with grown-ups.

In the New Testament, the story of the woman at the well is a powerful example of God's redemptive love and desire for fellowship. (See John 4:3–29.) In this account, we see Jesus actively pursuing communication with a Samaritan woman, though the Scriptures tell us that at the time "Jews ... [did] not associate with Samaritans" (v. 9, NIV). In that day and culture, not only did Jews and Samaritans tend to dislike each other, but Jewish men did not address strange women—and yet Jesus did both. He initiated conversation against the proper protocols because He had a *divine appointment* in mind with this Samaritan woman. Jesus crossed the religious border, moral border, gender border, and even racial border when He spoke to this woman because she mattered to Jesus. In His eyes, she had value and worth. That's why verse 4 uses the words "had to go through Samaria" to describe the route Jesus took that day; there were certainly other ways of getting to His destination, but only that road could lead Him to her. The implication in that phrase is that Jesus purposely went.

Throughout the entire conversation between Jesus and this Samaritan woman, we see wisdom in operation. Jesus passionately spoke love toward her, as well as acceptance, belonging, freedom, and hope using truth, prophecy, and purpose. By the time she left the presence of Jesus she had been transformed. In fact, she became the first woman evangelist! That is the power of grasping the revelation that God is passionately pursuing your heart and longing for communication with you.

Paul's biography conveys the same message. (See Acts 9:1–31.) Before Paul became an apostle he was known as Saul, a religious zealot who persecuted and killed Christians. While Saul was en route to Damascus one day to round up and arrest any Christians he might find there, the risen Christ appeared to him on the road and revealed Himself to Saul. He shone a light all around him and spoke forgiveness and destiny into Saul's heart. Then He told Saul to go to the city and await instructions. Saul was temporarily blinded by the bright light from heaven, and his traveling companions had to lead him by hand to his destination. When Saul arrived, he discovered that God had already sent a Christian named Ananias to find Saul and pray for him. This is why I call my born-again experience a Paul-on-the-road-to-Damascus encounter. Just like Paul, light shone in my room, and also like Paul, I was radically transformed.

Ananias must have been terrified. He even told God, "I've heard many people talk about the terrible things this man [Saul] has done to the believers in Jerusalem! And he is authorized by the leading priests to arrest everyone who calls upon your name" (Acts 9:13–14). But the Lord sent him anyway and equipped him with the courage he needed to find Saul, lay hands on him, and pray for his healing and salvation. When he did, Paul regained his sight and immediately accepted Christ as his Savior. He was baptized that very day, changed his name, and became Paul, a mighty preacher of the gospel of Christ and the author of much of the New Testament. Through Paul's and Ananais's stories, again we see God's passionate pursuit of relationship with His creation, mankind, and the lengths to which He will go to share with us and equip us for our divine calling and destiny.

Finally, the account in Acts 10:9–15, 19–20 of the vision God shared with Peter demonstrates not only His desire to perfect and redeem individuals but also His heart for relationship with all people everywhere. In this scripture, God gave Peter an object lesson through a vision that changed both his personal approach to ministry and the course of history. That vision birthed Christianity as a movement for anyone who would believe. No longer was salvation only for the Jews but for all.

These are just a few examples from the Bible. From cover to cover, on page after page, the Word of God is full of accounts of God's desire to pursue, lead, guide, and speak to mankind. We must not allow the evil one to convince us that God has ceased speaking because we have the Bible or, worse yet, because He doesn't want to commune with us. The truth is, He is the wonderful Counselor. Counselors advise. They listen, instruct, empathize, guide, and lead people to a place of health and well-being. This is exactly the heart of Jesus. From Genesis to Revelation, chapter after chapter, we read, "And God said to …" Why would His desire to speak and relate to mankind stop after the accounts of the apostles? That would make no sense. And why would we think that He only speaks to us through the Bible? Can anyone have a living, breathing relationship with a book?

No! (Of course, the Bible is a necessary tool in aiding us in the spirit of truth and steering us from the spirit of error, and we will discuss this further in the next chapter. My point here is simply this: the reality remains that a relationship is between two people, not between a person and an object.)

Now that we know God is constantly in pursuit of His creation with a desire and longing to speak and relate to mankind, the more important questions may be, Are we listening? Are we stopping long enough to hear His voice? We must learn to stop talking and listen.

Reflect

1. Have you surrendered your life to Christ, making Him your Lord and Savior? If so, how does Christ's work on the cross make it possible for you to communicate with God and have a relationship with Him? If not, why not? What obstacles are keeping you from embracing the free gift of salvation and fellowship God is extending to you now?

_____
_____
_____
_____

2. As you look back over your life, what experiences can you think of that demonstrate that God was and is still pursuing a relationship with you?

_____
_____
_____
_____

3. Read back over the list of stories from Scripture in the last section that demonstrate God's desire to communicate with us. How did God speak to Adam and Eve, Abraham, Joshua, Samuel, the Samaritan woman, Paul, Ananias, and Peter? Did He communicate with each of them in similar or different ways?

_____
_____
_____
_____

Pray

As stated earlier, an important prerequisite in hearing and knowing God is that one must be born again and have the Spirit of God in him/her. So if you haven't believed in your heart and confessed with your mouth that Jesus Christ is the Lord and came to this earth to pay the punishment for your sin and mine, then you will not hear the God of the Bible.

This means acknowledging that not all gods are the same. Contrary to what you may have heard or believed, Jesus is the one true and living God. I didn't say that; God did in His Word. You can go read it for yourself! (See Jeremiah 10:10; 1 Thessalonians 1:9; Isaiah 45:5; Hosea 13:4.) God the Father has distinguished Himself from all other gods by coming down to Earth in the flesh of Jesus Christ, and He revealed in His Word that no one comes to Him except through Jesus. (See John 14:6.) Until you believe this in your heart and confess this with your mouth, you are eternally separated from Him. But if you desire not only to be saved forever but to hear from the true God from this moment forward, then pray the following prayer with all sincerity of heart:

Dear heavenly Father,

I come to You with a desire to know and hear Your voice. I believe in my heart and confess with my mouth that Jesus Christ is Lord. I believe that You are the one true God, and I acknowledge that I have sinned and done many wrongs in this life. I realize I need a Savior for the forgiveness of my sins, and I thank You that all my sins have been dealt with on the cross. Jesus paid the price for all my sins to be forgiven. I receive this gift of grace through faith in Jesus Christ. Thank You for loving me enough to die for me. Thank You for loving me enough to forgive me for everything I've ever done wrong. Thank You for loving me enough to accept me just as I am and that I don't have to earn this new relationship with You.

Teach me now how to be intimate with You and how to hear Your voice. I desire to follow You. Fill me now with Your Holy Spirit and all that is required to walk in the fullness of power and boldness. I thank You, Lord. In Jesus's name I pray. Amen.

If you prayed this prayer, welcome to the family of God! Now it's time to start learning about Him and hearing from Him.

Listen

Ask the Lord to give you a word of direction for your day. Spend a few minutes silently and expectantly awaiting a response.

If you don't hear from Him during that time, that's OK! Close your time of listening by thanking the Lord for His desire to speak with you and continue about your day. Every so often you can praise the Lord or even restate your question and then pause again to allow Him to respond.

Day 4

God Is the Same Yesterday, Today, and Forever

Then, after doing all those things, I will pour out my Spirit upon all people. Your sons and daughters will prophesy. Your old men will dream dreams, and your young men will see visions.

—Joel 2:28

Hebrews 13:8 declares, "Jesus Christ is the same yesterday, today, and forever." If He is the same yesterday, today, and forever, then that means He hasn't changed. If He hasn't changed, then we can reason that He still speaks today. Because we know that whatever is in the Bible is true, we can consider Hebrews 13:8 as just another piece of evidence that God desires to and does communicate with us.

However, though God remains the same, His methods of speaking to mankind have changed somewhat from the Old Testament to the New Testament era. In the Old Testament era God usually spoke through the prophets as the Holy Spirit came upon them. Because of the separation that took place between God and mankind after the Fall, God was unable to converse intimately with all of His creation, as He had with Adam and Eve in the Garden, so He chose a small group of men and women called prophets to be His mouthpiece in nearly every generation leading up to the birth of Jesus. These prophets were specially anointed by God to share His messages with His people. In the New Testament era, however, people had Jesus with them in the flesh, that is, face-to-face. Some of His disciples recorded His words to us during His life and ministry—an account that made it into the Bible in the form of the four Gospels—and after His death, God sent the Holy Spirit to believers to restore personal, individual communication between Him and us. Because of His indwelling presence, one with us and living on the inside of us, we can speak with Him, Spirit to spirit, at any time.

Let's take a closer look at the function of prophets and the way in which their role has changed due to the advent of the Holy Spirit.

Old Testament

Throughout the Old Testament God occasionally spoke directly to His people, as when He appeared to Moses face to face, as an angel of the Lord to others, or through various miracles, such as the revelation to Moses through the burning bush or to the children of Israel through the cloud by day and fire by night. (See Exodus 33:11; Numbers 12:8; Deuteronomy 34:10; Genesis 16:7; 22:11, 15; and Judges 6:11–22.) However, God most often spoke to and through His prophets, who became known as God's messengers. He anointed and appointed them to be His voice. As the Holy Spirit came upon them, they spoke for God.

The Prophet's Role in the Old Testament

Prophets were known as a voice for God or one who heard the voice of the Lord and delivered His word to the people. Though prophets always spoke for God, the specific role or purpose of the message varied. The purpose or function of the prophet's work was to give words of direction, correction, warning, impending judgment, and sometimes to exhort the people and move them to action. In fact, God's heart, communicated through the prophet, was always to encourage people to remain faithful to Him, to follow Him, and to keep the Law before their eyes. Obedience was for their good, for blessings and protection. Again, it was always about relationship and intimacy. Prophets usually but not always addressed a nation.

We must understand that in the Old Testament the Holy Spirit never permanently indwelt a person but rather came upon them temporarily to carry out commands from God and to speak on His behalf. Although God was ever present, He did not indwell people until the Day of Pentecost in the New Testament (see Acts 2), which Joel prophesied about six hundred years earlier. (See Joel 2:28–29.) This limited who could hear Him. That is why in those days they needed prophets.

To be a voice for God, prophets first had to hear. These prophets were equipped by God's Spirit to hear His voice. God chose to speak to prophets as the Holy Spirit came upon them and gave them utterance. They then had a responsibility to be obedient and to relate those words back to mankind. In a sense, the prophet was a chosen, temporary mediator between man and God until it was time for Jesus, our Intercessor and Mediator, to come and break the curse of sin.

New Testament

When Jesus willingly submitted Himself to death on the cross, He became the atonement for our sin—the sin that once separated us from God and, ultimately, from hearing Him. Through this substitutionary work at Calvary, Christ became the ultimate Mediator between man and God, repairing the breach in our relationship with Him. Because of Christ's resurrection, the Holy Spirit indwells believers upon the born-again experience, and because of the indwelling presence of the Spirit of God speaking to us Spirit to spirit, we can all hear God for ourselves.

Remember, it was the Holy Spirit who equipped the prophets in the Old Testament to hear God. Therefore, if we are born again, God speaks to each of us directly and individually through His Spirit. Jesus is the High Priest with a new and better covenant, a covenant that allows everyone—not just prophets—to come boldly into the throne room of grace to seek God in time of need and to hear His voice. (See Romans 8:14; Hebrews 4:16; 8:6; 10:15–22.)

Although God still speaks through prophets today, the difference is that we no longer need to seek out a prophet to hear from God. Because of Christ, prophets aren't the only ones who can understand God.

The Prophet's Role in the New Testament

Though the role of the prophet remains the same as in the Old Testament in that the prophet speaks those words given to him by God, the function of the prophet differs in the Old and New Testaments. As we have seen, because of Christ's role as High Priest and His death and resurrection, God has given us all direct access to approach God any time we want. In fact, Jesus said that it was better that He go so the Holy Spirit could be sent so that all could come to God to speak to Him and hear from Him through the indwelling presence of His Spirit as a result of faith in Christ:

> Nevertheless I tell you the truth. It is to your advantage that I [Jesus] go away; for if I do not go away, the Helper will not come to you; but if I depart, I will send Him to you. ... However, when He, the Spirit of truth, has come, He will guide you into all truth; for He will not *speak* on His own authority, but whatever He hears He will *speak*; and He will *tell* you things to come. He will glorify me, for He will take of what is Mine and *declare* it to you.
>
> —John 16:7, 13–14, NKJV, emphasis added

Again, this scripture reveals that the Spirit of God will teach us the truth by speaking and telling us of things to come. He will take what is Christ's and declare it to us directly, without the need for an earthly mediator. Isn't this exciting? The God of the universe desires to disclose His heart to us.

So if we do not have to be a prophet or go to a prophet to hear what God is saying, what purpose do prophets serve? Today, the prophet may be part of the eldership of the church and serves to equip the saints for the work of the ministry. (See Ephesians 4:11–12; 1 Corinthians 12:28–31.) This includes building and establishing the church in discipleship (Eph. 2:20); speaking and releasing words of edification, comfort, and exhortation (1 Cor. 14:3; Acts 15:32); and by bringing direction and confirmation through God's Word, as the Lord leads. The prophet today teaches the body of Christ to hear God for themselves. Because we can all prophesy and are exhorted to desire to prophesy (1 Cor. 14:1, 39), someone must teach them how. (This begins with learning to hear His voice. Before you can speak the words of God, you first must learn how to hear Him.)

Furthermore, in God's goodness, He may send us a prophet to bring words of confirmation to encourage us in our faith and ability to hear God. Also, there are things God chooses to entrust to a prophet that He doesn't tell others. Because God and His Word are unchanging, Amos 3:7 (NKJV) is no less true today than it was under the Law: "Surely the Lord GOD does nothing unless He reveals His secret to His servants the prophets." But again, even these messages are for the profit of the body of Christ, though they reflect a clear calling on the prophet's life.

Reflect

1. Some among many, many examples of God speaking to and through His prophets in the Old Testament are Numbers 11:24–25; Deuteronomy 18:15–22; Isaiah 6:1–8; Jeremiah 1:4–19; Amos 3:7; and Ezekiel 2:1–8. Read each of these passages and write down your observations about the different ways in which God spoke to and used prophets to carry out His will during Old Testament times.

_____

2. What has been your personal experience with prophets and the prophetic? Has it been positive, negative, or nonexistent? Explain.

_____

3. In your own words, why is it that we do not need to rely on prophets any longer in order to hear from the Lord? Include at least one Scripture verse that supports your answer.

_____

Pray

Father, thank You that You are the same yesterday, today, and forever. Thank You that I have direct access to approach You anytime I want. How comforting to know that You desire to speak to all mankind, and that includes me. Lord, I want to know You. I want to hear Your voice. I desire deep intimacy with You. Develop in me a hearing ear. Increase my sensitivity to You. Teach me Your truth. Give me eyes to see, ears to hear, and a heart that is receptive to the leading of Your Spirit in my life. I pray this in Jesus's name. Amen.

Listen

Ask the Lord give you a word of encouragement for today. Spend a few minutes silently and expectantly awaiting a response.

If you don't hear from Him during that time, that's OK! Close your time of listening by thanking the Lord for His desire to speak with you and continue about your day. Every so often you can praise the Lord or even restate your question and then pause again to allow Him to respond.

Day 5

Hear God for Today

For all who are led by the Spirit of God are sons of God.

—Romans 8:14, ESV

Each of us likely has many perceptions of prayer, and each of these types of prayer is necessary and purposeful. So often we think of prayer merely as intercession, where we pray for others for extended periods of time, or we see prayer as petitioning, which is making requests of God either for ourselves or others. At other times, we think of prayer as bearing all our present emotions, especially painful ones, and then walking away once we feel the burden lifted. On the other hand, we can even walk away from prayer feeling like it was nothing more than a duty, an item to check off our to do list, or a stress relief tactic. But in each of these examples of prayer, did you notice who was doing all the talking? On whom is the focus placed? If this is all we do in prayer, chances are we are not truly seeking God daily.

Now, I am not saying that these kinds of prayers are wrong. Not at all. In fact, each has their place and all are needed, but a healthy relationship requires that both people are communicating. That's why the essence of all prayer is a simple conversation with the Father. Not only does God enjoy listening to our hearts, but He wants to reveal His. It's like playing tennis. It would be no fun hitting the ball if someone wasn't on the other side hitting it back. In his book *The Circle Maker* Mark Batterson writes:

> The reason many of us miss the miracles is that we aren't looking and listening. The easy part of prayer is talking. It's much harder listening to the still small voice of the Holy Spirit. It's much harder looking for the answers. But two-thirds of praying hard is listening and looking.[11]

Listening to God in prayer takes time, energy, silence, focus, stillness, and much patience! Even daily practice is necessary to get accurate with it. It would have been so much easier talking with Jesus face to face, flesh to flesh, but since His death and resurrection we all must learn to communicate with Him, our spirit to His Holy Spirit.

Though the process of learning to listen to God may challenge our flesh, we can always be confident of this: When we pray, God promises that He will answer! He not only desires to talk with us, but He desires to do so today:

> *Call to me* and *I will answer* you and *tell you* great and unsearchable things you do not know.
>
> —Jeremiah 33:3, NIV, emphasis added

> Your ears *shall hear* a word behind you *saying*, "This is the way, walk in it."
>
> —Isaiah 30:21, NKJV, emphasis added

> Now I know that the LORD saves His anointed; He *will answer* him from His holy heaven with the saving strength of His right hand.
>
> —Psalm 20:6, NKJV, emphasis added

> Draw near to God and *He will* draw near to you.
>
> —James 4:8, NKJV, emphasis added

So, you see, we are instructed to come to God, to pray to Him, and to call out to Him. God commands us to draw nigh, to listen, to hear, and to be with Him today.

All throughout Scripture we read phrases like, "He who has ears to hear, let him hear" (Mark 4:9, NKJV; see also Luke 8:8, NIV); "Today when you hear His voice, don't harden your hearts" (Heb. 3:15; 4:7; see also Ps. 95:7; Heb. 3:7); and "He who has an ear, let him hear what the Spirit says to the churches" (Rev. 2:11, 17, 29; 3:6, 13, 22, NKJV; see also Rev. 2:7). Notice the words *today* and *says* in these passages; they are both in the present tense. We mustn't be satisfied with yesterday's bread or last year's revelation. Neither must we be content with someone else's crumbs or the preacher's "bam bombs." ("Bam bombs" are what I call those words spoken from the pulpit that hit you like a ton of bricks. A lightbulb goes on, and it is like you are hearing that truth for the first time.) God desires to tell us new things, lovely things, things for today. Every day is a fresh day with God. Therefore cry out to God with expectation, "Give us this day our daily bread!"

God Leads Us by His Spirit

Let's recap: So far we have learned that God still speaks. He desires an intimate dialogue with us, not a monologue where we do all the talking. We've also discovered that God is the God of the Bible, and He is the same yesterday, today, and forever. It is up to us to believe that He desires an intimate relationship with us today. Our part is to accept and engage.

> We have seen this day that God speaks with man; yet he still lives.
>
> —Deuteronomy 5:24, NKJV

Though there are many ways in which God speaks to His people, it is only through His Holy Spirit, who dwells in every born-again believer, that we are able to hear His voice. In John 14:16–17, 26 Jesus promised:

> And I will pray the Father, and He will give you another Helper, that He may abide with you forever—the Spirit of truth, whom the world cannot receive, because it neither sees Him nor knows Him; but you know Him, for He dwells with you and will be *in you*. ... But the Helper, the Holy Spirit, whom the Father will send in My name, He will *teach* you all things, and bring to your remembrance all things that I have *said* to you.
>
> —emphasis added

Through this scripture we see that the indwelling presence of the Holy Spirit within will teach us all things and bring to our memory things that Christ has said to us by His Word. We do not hear Him with our physical ears as an audible voice (though this is not impossible for God and some testify that they have) but rather with the ears of our heart inside of our being.

Are you ready to start listening?

Reflect

1. Over this next week, read Hebrews 7–9; 10:12–22. Meditate on and consider what these scriptures are revealing. In short, what did you learn?

_____
_____
_____
_____

2. How can we be confident that God still speaks?

_____
_____
_____
_____

3. How can we be assured that God *desires* to speak to us?

_____
_____
_____
_____

4. How do we hear God?

_____
_____
_____
_____

Pray

Write out your own prayer letter of adoration or gratitude to God. Tell God how you feel, what your thoughts are towards Him. Be honest. Be genuine. No matter where you are at spiritually with Him. He knows anyway. That is how we develop intimacy. Feel free to share with Him what you really want out of this journey you are on with Him. Tell Him everything.

Exercise

Ask the Lord to reveal His love and devotion back to you. Ask Him to tell you how He feels about you and what His thoughts are toward you. Journal your impressions. You may be shown a picture or image, be led to a specific scripture, or perceive thoughts accompanied by words. Write whatever comes to mind. Share what you heard Jesus say to you with someone whom you know hears from God so they can discuss it with you. If you are following this study in a group, judge these words together when you gather.

Lesson Two

God Speaks Through the Bible

Day 6

Hearing God Through the Bible

In the beginning was the Word, and the Word was with God, and the Word was God. He was in the beginning with God. All things were made through Him, and without Him, nothing was made that was made.

—John 1:1–3, NKJV

The Bible, or the Holy Scriptures, is the Word of God and is the key to intimacy with Him. It is the inspired, written record or history book of what approximately forty different authors have heard, seen, and spoken. It spans about fifteen hundred years "and is profitable for doctrine, for reproof, for correction, for instruction in righteousness, that the man of God may be complete, thoroughly equipped for every good work" (2 Tim. 3:16–17, NKJV). This means that all Scripture is God-breathed and was given to chosen vessels, like His apostles and prophets, directly by God under the inspiration of the Holy Spirit. This alone makes it desirable to read.

From Genesis to Revelation, the Bible records and reveals many things. It records how creation took place, the history of man and how he came into being, as well as his genealogies and various events he has had to endure. We also learn about the Law (the Old Covenant, recorded in the Old Testament), prophecy (both prophecy that has come to pass and prophecy which is yet to come), and God's supernatural power, which supersedes natural law. It records myriad signs, miracles, and wonders. We also discover God's plan of redemption through Christ for mankind and witness in its pages the establishment of the new covenant of grace. Within its pages, it contains story after story that reveals Jesus Christ as God, as the Word, who is God.

Moreover, the Holy Scriptures teach us right from wrong through God's eyes. When Paul wrote that the Bible is "for reproof, for correction, [and] for instruction in righteousness," he was saying that the Scriptures make clear God's moral standards so that we may walk in righteousness and live in the fullness of all that God planned for us (2 Tim. 3:16, NKJV). The Scriptures are a tutor in showing man what sin is, for man would not know what sin is without understanding God's moral standards (Rom. 7:7; Gal. 3:24). Thankfully, however, God "has not dealt with us according to our sins, nor punished us according to our iniquities" (Ps. 103:10, NKJV), and the Bible shares with us the hope we have in Jesus, who atoned for our sin, forgives our iniquities, and sanctifies us for right living.

Every book, chapter, and verse of the Bible paints a picture of our holy, just, and righteous God and His plan for us. First Corinthians 2:12 tells us:

> And we have received God's Spirit (not the world's spirit), so we can *know* the wonderful things God has freely given us.
>
> —emphasis added

The word *know* in this scripture is the Greek word *eidō*, which means "to perceive by any of the senses; to look at, behold; to experience any state or condition; to know, i.e. get knowledge of, understand, perceive."[11] How do we get to know God in this way? By reading His biography, which is His Word, the Bible.

God's Word tells us everything we need to know about God, Jesus Christ, and the Holy Spirit: who He is, what His nature is like, His character (fruit), and what His will is. To learn who God is and what He says, we read the Bible. The Word of God is more than just a book; it is a gateway to deeper, intimate relationship with God.

The Bible is our plumb line by which we should measure and test everything we hear from within, all that we hear in prayer. In fact, any word that we hear outside of God's Word will never contradict what is written in the Scriptures. God will not speak contrary to what He has already spoken in the Bible. As spirit beings, we are equipped to hear into the spirit realm. This is not limited to Christians. If we are not acquainted with the Word of God, chances of hearing lying spirits and doctrines of demons—and being led astray by them and other spirit beings—is indeed a possibility. If a word we receive doesn't line up with the Bible, then we throw it out. For example:

- If you are married, God will not "divinely connect" you with another man/woman. Why? Because that is adultery, and God is against adultery. In fact, lusting after someone other than your spouse is also committing adultery, adultery of the heart. (See Deuteronomy 5:18; Matthew 5:27–28, NLT.)

- If you are in debt and struggling financially, God will not instruct you to borrow more money for another expensive pleasure, no matter how much of a good deal or "blessing" it is. Why? Because God is against debt. He is not going to bless you or give you favor to go into debt. He tells us in His Word to "owe no one anything except to love one another"

(Rom. 13:8, NKJV). Another translation says it this way, "Let no debt remain outstanding, except the continuing debt to love one another" (NIV). He also says that "the blessing of the LORD makes a person rich, and He adds no sorrow with it" (Prov. 10:22). There is sorrow when in debt because one becomes enslaved to its lender. (See Proverbs 22:7, NIV; James 4:3–4, NKJV.)

- God will not instruct you not to attend church or not to be part of a church family, because His Word says not to forsake the gathering together of the saints. (See Hebrews 10:24–25, NKJV.)

- If you hear or receive a vision that instructs you to renounce Jesus and follow after another god, then clearly it is not from God but a deceiving spirit. Likewise, a true prophet of God will warn you not to follow after other gods. (See Deuteronomy 13:1–5; Jeremiah 35:15.)

God will not tell you to do anything that contradicts His Word. Period. That is why it is imperative that before you begin to hear from God, you must learn to know God in His Word. How will you know it is Him if you don't know what He is like?

We can certainly read, meditate on, and even study the Bible rationally with our minds, learning many facts about God and what He says to be true, yet still not know Him intimately. We can even learn that God is love and that He loves us, but if we don't experience that love with a God-encounter, such as hearing Him reveal His love Spirit-to-spirit, then there is a possibility that we will never fully believe in that love. We are going to unlock the difference between an intellectual relationship with God—like reading the Bible with our mind only—and an intimate relationship with the Spirit of God, who uses His written Word as a means of teaching, enlightening, guiding, and directing us. This is the difference between conformation to a set of rules or expectations (religion) and the transformation of our heart and mind (relationship).

Reflect

1. Why is studying the Bible one of the best ways to develop a relationship with God?

_____

_____

_____

_____

2. Why is it important to become well acquainted with the Bible when we start to listen for His voice? What are the potential pitfalls of hearing and accepting words of instruction, reproof, or prophecy without knowing the Scriptures well?

_____
_____
_____
_____

3. What does the Bible tell us about God's nature and plans for us?

_____
_____
_____
_____

Pray

Father, thank You for Your Word. Thank You that there is great insight into who You are, what Your will is, and what is acceptable in Your sight. I ask You, Lord, to give me a hunger and thirst for Your Word. Help me to read Your Word and to invite Your Holy Spirit to give me revelation of what I read. I want to understand what is of You and not be led astray. I desire to hear Your Spirit. Quicken me daily to seek You through Your Word. In Jesus's name I pray. Amen.

Listen

Ask the Lord to bring to your memory or lead you to a scripture verse or passage to encourage you today. Spend a few minutes silently and expectantly awaiting a response.

Day 7

The *Logos* and the *Rhema*

All Scripture is inspired by God and is useful to teach us what is true and to make us realize what is wrong in our lives. It corrects us when we are wrong and teaches us to do what is right. God uses it to prepare and equip his people to do every good work.

—2 Timothy 3:16–17

The Bible is sometimes referred to as the *logos*, which simply refers to the written Word of God. However, when the Holy Spirit breathes into it, giving it life and application to our life and situation specifically, that revelation or specific "word" from the Lord comes a *rhema* word for us. Only by the Spirit can the *logos* Word, which applies to all men and women, become a *rhema* word for you and me as individuals. Mark and Patti Virkler put it this way:

Both *Logos* and *Rhema*

The Scriptures can be *logos* if I approach them simply for content. [When I receive them as revelation from God, they can be called *rhema*. When God speaks a Scripture to me, it comes as *rhema*.] If God bids me to note the content of the Scripture, I am then treating it as *logos*. The Scriptures originally came as *rhema* to the writers (2 Pet. 1:21). Since they had content, they were also *logos*. The Scriptures are quickened to us by the Spirit and thus become a *rhema* to us in the same way that they were to the original writers. As we ponder the *rhema*, it becomes *logos*, since we shift from emphasizing its manner of coming to its content.

We Need Both *Logos* and *Rhema*

The content of the Bible (*Logos*) is necessary because it gives us absolute standard against which to measure all "truth." It is our safeguard to keep us from error, and our instruction for life.

Rhema is also necessary because it emphasizes the way the Bible was initially given—through individuals actively interacting with God—and the centrality of divine communication with man to the Christian message. It emphasizes the fact that God spoke and continues to speak to His children. We need to see that the men and women throughout the Bible model a way of living which involves ongoing contact with the God who created them. If the Bible tells us anything from Genesis to Revelation, it tells us that God desires to actively communicate with His children, and that we should expect to hear His voice and see His vision as we walk through life."[12]

In other words, when the Holy Spirit speaks to us through the Bible—and it is one of the principal ways He speaks to His people—the general *logos* message is transformed into a *rhema* word of revelation for our life. The *rhema* word we hear, or the voice of God in our heart from within, will always be grounded in His *logos*.

This transformation of the Scriptures is possible only because the Bible is a living, breathing document. It is more than simply words on a page. John 1:1–3 says, "In the beginning was the Word, and the Word was with God, and *the Word was God*. He was in the beginning with God. All things were made through Him, and without Him, nothing was made that was made" (NKJV, emphasis added). Revelation 19:13 gives us a picture of Jesus "clothed with a robe dipped in blood" and tells us, "His name is called The Word of God" (NKJV). Jesus is the very embodiment of the Word spoken out from the mouth of God. Thus, everything people heard from the mouth of Jesus Christ when He walked the earth was the Word of God (Luke 5:1). Sometimes when He taught it was *logos* for content and teaching purposes. Other times we read that when Jesus spoke the Word, the bellies of those who heard Him burned within them or their eyes were opened. Has that ever happened to you?

We see a clear example of this in the New Testament. Luke 24:13–35 records the story of two disciples who encountered the risen Christ while walking to a village called Emmaus. They were conversing back and forth about the recent uproar over Jesus in Jerusalem. Jesus had been well known by His miracles, His teachings, and His claims to be the Son of God and the great I AM, but He had been crucified a few days earlier. It was now reported that He was alive again and that His grave was empty. The Bible tells us that while these two disciples were reasoning together, Jesus

Himself drew near to them and walked with them, but the Bible also says that their eyes were restrained so that they did not know Him.

Jesus played along with them, skillfully drawing out what was in their hearts regarding who He was by asking them, "What kind of conversation is this that you have with one another as you walk and are sad?" (v. 17, NKJV). The disciples were astounded that He didn't know the things that were happening. They even questioned if He was really the only "stranger in Jerusalem" not to know "the things which happened … in these days" (v. 18, NKJV). Undaunted by their shock, Jesus again asked "what things" they were talking about (v. 19). It was there that the disciples revealed all that was in their hearts regarding what they believed about Jesus and who they thought He was:

- They knew He was Jesus of Nazareth, who was a prophet (v. 19).
- They knew He was mighty in deeds (miracles) and word (teachings, v. 19).
- They knew He had been crucified (v. 20).
- They were hoping that it was He who was to redeem Israel (v. 21).
- They knew certain women had gone to claim His body, but He was gone and the tomb was empty (v. 22–24).
- They knew of the vision of angels, who said He was alive (v. 23).
- The did *not* seem convinced that this same Jesus was the promised Messiah.

After hearing their explanation, Jesus lamented that after all He had "suffered" (v. 26, NKJV) they still weren't confident that He was the Messiah. Do you know how He convinced them of who He was and how they would truly know Him? Did He perform another miracle? Did He give them an outward sign? No. Instead the Bible says that "Jesus took them through the writings of Moses and all the prophets, explaining from all the Scriptures the things concerning himself" (v. 27). Imagine, Jesus was right there—face to face, flesh to flesh. As God incarnate, He could have chosen any other way to reveal Himself, yet He chose to "expound to them in all the Scriptures the things concerning Himself" (v. 27, NKJV). For the disciples to truly *know* Jesus, He taught them using the Scriptures first because it is the Scriptures that reveal the real Jesus.

Luke says in verse 32 that after Jesus explained who He was in terms of the Scriptures, "And they said to one another, 'Didn't our hearts burn within us as he talked with us on the road and explained the Scriptures to us?'" These responses are characteristic of when God speaks a *rhema* word through His written word.

You see, we use our mind to engage in the content of the *logos* Word to understand who God is, what His will is, what His ways are, and all that He desires. However, God's *rhema* word reveals His truth to us in such a way that it becomes life in our hearts, changing from head knowledge to heart enlightenment. It is a God-encounter. This is exactly what happened to me. Right after I was born again, the Lord Himself led me and taught me through His Word. It was as if the Word of

God had come alive in my spirit. Sometimes it seemed like the words just jumped out at me and leapt off the pages of my Bible!

You may or may not experience this same response to hearing God speak to you through the Scriptures. Some people are moved to tears or get goosebumps; others have no such reaction. However, you can and should expect to hear the Holy Spirit give you a *rhema* word as you read the Bible. In fact, I encourage you to practice inviting the Holy Spirit to open your eyes to revelation in God's Word. Before you open up the Word, ask the Holy Spirit to make the Word of God clear to your heart. It may come as a prompting to read a certain scripture, or His voice may "sound like" a fresh take on a verse or passage you have read many times before. Whatever the form, listening for the voice of God by reading His Word is one of the best ways to start training your spiritual ears to hear His message to your heart today.

Reflect

1. In your own words, what is the difference between the *logos* and the *rhema*?

_____
_____
_____
_____

2. What does it mean that Jesus is the Word of God? What, specifically, does this mean for you and God's promise to speak to you?

_____
_____
_____
_____

3. Have you ever felt the Holy Spirit leading you to write a certain passage of Scripture, or have you found yourself surprised that a specific verse or passage seemed to apply directly to your life? What was the passage? Reflect on the experience. Could this have been the Holy Spirit giving you a *rhema* word?

_____
_____
_____
_____

Pray

Father, learning the difference between your logos *Word, and a* rhema *word can be a bit overwhelming. I ask that You teach me and give me understanding of Your Word as* logos *to aid in my studies, but I also desire that Your Spirit speak* rhema *words to the deepest parts of my heart and life. Lord, I desire spirit-to-Spirit communication with You. I pray this in Jesus's name. Amen.*

Listen

Ask the Lord to bring to your memory or lead you to a scripture verse or passage to direct or guide you today. Spend a few minutes silently and expectantly awaiting a response.

Day 8

Cultivating Intimacy with God

> Dear friends, let us continue to love one another, for love comes from God. Anyone who loves is a child of God and knows God.
>
> —1 John 4:7

In 1 John 4:7, the word *know* is the Greek word *ginōskō*, which means "to learn to know, come to know, get a knowledge of perceive, feel; Jewish idiom for sexual intercourse between a man and a woman."[13] Because the context of this word is connected to the Jewish idiom for sexual intercourse between a man and a woman, it implies a deeper, more intimate knowledge than the word *eidō* ("know," used in 1 Cor. 2:12), which we discussed in Day 1 of this lesson.

For example, we can read an autobiography of someone who has written a book about themselves. We can learn where they were born, what things are important to them, and what interests they have because it is a book that describes their life story and history. Reading this book helps us learn all about them, but reading from a book won't let us hear what their voice sounds like or even if they have an accent or not. On the other hand, if we go for coffee together with them our knowledge gets a little more personal.

However, even the depth of this knowledge is dependent upon their openness and vulnerability. Perhaps, in the beginning, the conversation would be more superficial. Let's be honest: we are just getting to know one another. However, if we continue in this relationship and we are open and sincere, with both people engaging openly and honestly, we will go deeper. We will learn more intimate details about each other. This is the difference between head knowledge and intimate knowledge. The more time spent with a person, the more we will truly get to know them. Eventually, once a deep relationship is established, we could go to the mall together or stand at a distance from one another with loads of people in between and still easily find one another because of our familiarity with each other's voices. This type of closeness would make us familiar with the words each of us uses, the pitch or tone of voice, and any accents that may be particular. Just the sound of that person's voice would lead me directly to him or her, and vice versa.

So, it is with God. We can read His Word to know about Him, and we can sit in His presence and learn to hear His voice. God speaks, but we must be listening, and we must move from knowing (*eidō*) God to knowing (*ginōskō*) God. He hasn't changed. He is the same yesterday, today, and forever! But this knowing takes time.

Therefore, when we read the Word, we must come to the Scriptures asking the Spirit of God in us to speak to us through His Word so that the words do not become dull and dead but rather give life, "for the letter kills, but the Spirit gives life" (2 Cor. 3:6, NKJV). Many are familiar with the aphorism: "All Word and no Spirit, we dry up; all Spirit and no Word, we blow up; both Word and Spirit, we grow up!"[14] God's Word can be viewed or received as His love letter to us or as His autobiography. It can also be seen as a history book or a book of promises and blessings. The Word of God is all of these things, but how we approach the Word determines our growth from it or lack thereof. Let me ask you:

1. When you read the Word, what are you looking for? Content? Instruction? History? Knowledge? Doctrine? If these are your goals, there are many resources and tools to help you unlock and understand context and the meanings of both Greek and Hebrew words as well. Remember, the Word of God is profitable for doctrine and is given by inspiration of God. Make a commitment to read and study the Word, and your knowledge of God will increase along with your understanding of its content, history, and doctrinal pillars.

2. Do you approach His Word as though the King has something loving to say to you? Through meditation of Scripture, you can ponder a verse that speaks His love to you. You can think about it and ask the Spirit of God to help you believe and understand it. This will also help you memorize it. Reading the Word of God for encouragement, edification, or to receive His love while inviting the Holy Spirit to enlighten you will empower you to trust Him and grow in faith and His love. If you find you are still struggling, the Song of Solomon is a great book for meditating on the love of God for us.

3. Do you use His Word to stir up prayer within yourself or to pray for the struggles of others? Using the Word of God to come into agreement with your prayers and petitions will empower you to grow in faith and see His promises manifest. Likewise, using the Word as a sword or shield against enemy attacks will equip you for every battle. This can be done using any Scripture or through the many prayers written within its pages.

4. When you read the Bible, do you ask God to reveal something to you about Himself that you have never seen before? For example, perhaps you desire to learn about His character, such as that

He is all-powerful? You can start by studying the names of God. His names reveal who He is and what He can do.

5. Do you tend to see God's Word as rulebook that only condemns you to try harder, regardless of the effort you put into living for Him? Do you see God's Word as only a source of reproof and correction? Are you always looking at yourself and feeling condemned because you've failed, asking, "Do I measure up?" Though God desires obedience, obedience comes out of love for Him and a place of understanding that obedience is for our benefit and protection. God's promises are principles that prevent mishaps and misfortunes, but we cannot lose sight of the fact that Jesus earned our salvation and the blessings for us. We are saved by grace through faith in Christ and not by how good we are or how well we obey His Word. In fact, no one is good or good enough to obey God's entire Word, and that is why we need Jesus! Remember, "There is, therefore, no condemnation to those who are in Christ Jesus" (Rom. 8:1, NKJV).

Because of Jesus's work on the cross, we are no longer under the Law. For us, God's Word contains principles to live by so that we might thrive in this life! I repeat: God's Word was never meant to be strictly a manual that condemns us because it reveals right behavior. Yes, it is a tutor containing glorious protective principles, but through Christ there is no condemnation. Conviction yes, condemnation no. If we fail and are condemned, two things are happening: 1) We've not accepted our flawed humanity, and 2) we are upset because we inwardly desire to be perfect.

6. Finally, the Word of God can also be used as a tool—not a rule book—for instruction, wisdom, correction, and discipline because faith without works is dead (James 2:17). Do you see His commands as His wisdom to bring life, hope, and solutions to your problems? Every command of God, or every promise with a condition attached, is a principle that activates the spiritual laws that God has set in place. In other words, when we obey God's condition, whether we understand or not, we are activating our faith in God, in His ways, not ours. For example, is God asking you to tithe? In Malachi 3:10, we are commanded to tithe, and God promises to pour out blessings so that we will not have room enough to receive it.

The Bible is a delightful guidance counselor filled with wisdom for every aspect of life. The Word of God keeps us from error and guides us into all truth. Whatever wisdom you seek, you will find it in the Bible if you approach it with an open heart to hear the Holy Spirit speak to you from within its pages.

Reflect

1. Take a few minutes to make an honest assessment of your relationship with God. How well do you know Him?

_____
_____
_____
_____

2. Take another few minutes to make an honest assessment of your knowledge of God's Word. How well do you know it? Do you think your level of knowledge of the Scriptures is related to your level of intimacy with God and ability to hear His voice? Explain.

_____
_____
_____
_____

3. When you sit down to read and study the Word, how do you approach that time? What do you expect to read, or hear, within its pages? What do you want to read or hear?

_____
_____
_____
_____

Pray

Father, I pray that You quicken me to read, study, and meditate on Your Word so that I can know You more intimately, so I can hear You more easily. I pray that as I read Your Word it would dwell richly in my heart, bringing to light those things that are contrary to Your nature and character. Let Your Word penetrate the deepest parts of my soul, exposing the lies that have been implanted and harboured in my memories, for Your Word is life, and it is Spirit, bringing renewal and revival, exposing my innermost thoughts and desires. Let all that I do be done for Your glory. I pray this in Jesus's name. Amen.

Listen

Ask the Lord to bring to your memory or lead you to a scripture verse or passage that highlights an attribute of His character. Spend a few minutes silently and expectantly awaiting a response.

My Story

Encounters with the God of the Bible

I am so thankful that when I was first saved I had such a hunger to read the Bible. I ate every word. Just as when God first started communing with me and telling me to read specific passages in response to my questions, He continued to enlighten my quest for Him through His Word. I have stacks of journals that record scriptures that would jump out at me, and I would immediately have a revelation about what that scripture was saying. I was so excited to receive such understanding.

Because I was so young in the Lord, I would run to my pastor and tell him of my revelation. He would clasp his hands, sit back on his chair, and shake his head, saying, "God has you on the fast track. This is so awesome to witness." In fact, after he and I got to know each other, he lovingly said, "You know, when I first met you, I couldn't figure you out. Here you were coming to our foundations class [for new members] as a new believer, yet you understood the Scriptures way past seasoned Christians. That is how I knew how much time you spent/spend reading His Word and communing with Him."

He was right. I would read the Gospels, then pray them back to God. I would journal Scripture and pray/write them over my family. I couldn't get enough of the Bible. But I didn't just read it; I meditated on it. I spoke it. I pondered it. I prayed it. I thought about it throughout the day. I talked to the Holy Spirit about it. And I applied it to my life. Being a doer of the Word and not a hearer only has benefits and blessings far beyond my scope of understanding.

Here is an excerpt from one of my journals from 2003, the year after I was saved. I have included verse references in parentheses to show where I was praying the Scriptures so that you can see an example of what this looks like.

> *Equip me, O God, to do Your good works. Thank You for molding and perfecting me. I praise You, Lord. Teach me Your ways, and I will walk in them. Blessed is the man/woman who trusts in the Lord. He will be like a tree planted by the river, and in due season he will bear much fruit. Make me be the blessed woman who trusts in the Lord,*

and give to me Lord a believing heart, a heart that will stand firm in the Word of God. Create in me, Lord, a new hunger and thirst for righteousness. Burn in me Your Holy Spirit. Lead me and teach me new things from Your Word. Thank You, Lord. I praise You, and I pray this in the mighty name of Jesus. Amen. [See Ephesians 2:10; 1 Peter 5:10; Jeremiah 17:7–8; Matthew 5:6.]

Two weeks later God spoke this to me:

Eat and absorb the bread (My Word) I give you.
    Drink and be filled.
    My Word will not go before Me empty but will accomplish what I desire.
    My thoughts are not your thoughts, and My ways are not your ways. Do not worry what bread you will eat next or how you will share it with others, for I am with you. In My time, you will feed My sheep. You will scatter bread over many lands, and many sheep will taste. And many sheep will trample over it, but I will be with you.
    Take this bread and multiply it in your own heart each day, and much fruit will you bear.

Today, as you read, study, and apply the principles you are learning in this workbook, you are fulfilling prophecy.

At the end of the same year in which God shared this message with me, God taught me another important lesson about praying His Word. I had just discovered Psalm 91, which quickly became one of my favorite passages. I prayed that scripture over my family daily using the same model and style that I shared from my journal. Soon praying it felt natural, and I began to memorize the promises it contained.

One cold, wintery, and blustery day that December when I was going to Tuesday morning prayer at my church I decided to take the shortcut instead of going through the city, which meant taking the perimeter and cutting across an open field. As I approached the open field, I could not see a foot in front of me. The snow was blowing so thickly that I had to travel at a snail's pace. My knuckles were white from gripping the steering wheel in terror. I was almost in tears praying to God, terrified that I would either crash into oncoming traffic or veer right off the road into the ditch.

Then I heard Him say, "Do you believe what you pray? Do you not pray that I charge My angels over you to keep you in all of your ways?" (See Psalm 91:11.)

"Yes, Lord. I do."

"Then pray it again. Speak My Word."

And so, I did. Then suddenly, right before my very eyes, I saw these two angels, as large as my van, who were already posted beside me. I watched them come from the sides of my van and zoom in front of me. Now, I couldn't actually see a full figure or body, but they appeared like a silhouette. Right before my very eyes, the blowing snow began to part. I could not believe my eyes. I looked in absolute amazement.

I kept shaking my head, rubbing my eyes, and whispering to myself, "Is this really happening? Could this be real?" I guess I really didn't fully believe His Word was alive until that moment. That day, I remember looking behind me to see if anyone else could be seeing what I was seeing. But it was only me. I had experienced the parting of the snow, just as Moses experienced the parting of the Sea.

God had opened my eyes, as He did for Gehazi. Gehazi was a servant of Elisha. One morning Gehazi arose early from his sleep and saw an army surrounding the city with horses and chariots. Fear gripped his heart. Elisha comforted Gehazi by telling him that those who were with them were more than what he could see. Then Elisha prayed that God would open up Gehazi's eyes, that he may see, and Gehazi saw into the spirit realm. He saw the mountain was full of horses and chariots of fire all around Elisha. (See 2 Kings 6:15–17.)

As I approached the prayer room I was shaking like a leaf. My knees were so weak I was barely able to walk. I don't know if it was because the roads were so bad or if it was because of what I had just experienced. I immediately talked to my pastor. In his gentle tone, he assured me that what had just happened was a God moment created just for me. God breathed life on His Word!

Day 9

Praying the Scriptures

The unfolding of your words gives light; it gives understanding to the simple

—Psalm 119:130

It's good to approach the Word as content, as history, and as knowledge when you are studying it. If you are struggling anywhere in your walk with the Lord, it is also good to approach His Word for comfort, instruction, wisdom, counsel, love, and direction. And as we have seen, the Bible is one of the primary ways of connecting intimately with God and hearing Him speak to us. However, the Scriptures are so much more than this. The Word is also an instrument to help us pray effectively and powerfully. When we take the sword of the Spirit and pray it back to God, we can be assured His Word will not return to Him void. God assures us that when we pray according to His will, He hears and we can receive (1 John 5:15).

The easiest way to begin to develop a practice of praying the Word of God is to start your time with the Lord by praying to have ears to hear and a heart to understand. In all areas of your approach to the Word, invite the Spirit of God to enlighten you, as I have suggested many times over. Remember, "All Word … we dry up; all Spirit … we blow up; both Word and Spirit, we grow up!"[15] That's relationship—always including the Spirit of God. He has much to reveal to you. He has much to say to you. Listen to what He says through His Word and resist the urge to do all the talking, so to speak. Journal what you hear from the Lord. Trust and believe it is His personal instruction, comfort, and word to you.

Whenever I sit down to study the Word, I also pray first that God would break through any mind-sets, doctrines, false teachings, or beliefs that are not from Him and to grant me the wisdom, knowledge, and understanding of His truth, especially His grace. I want an open mind when I read His Word so that I can hear Him directing me toward specific passages to meditate on and pray over. Ephesians 1:17–19 is one of my favorite passages of Scripture because it is where I learned to ask God to grant me wisdom, knowledge, and understanding of His truth. It reads, "That the God of our Lord Jesus Christ, the Father of glory, may give to you the Spirit of wisdom and revelation in the knowledge of him, having the eyes of your hearts enlightened, that you may know what is the hope to which he has called you, what are the riches of His glorious inheritance in the saints, and what is the immeasurable greatness of his power toward us who believe, according to the working of his great might" (NIV). I then personalize this scripture and pray it back to God:

> *Heavenly Father, my God of my Lord Jesus Christ, the Father of glory, I ask that You give to me the spirit of wisdom and revelation in the knowledge of Jesus. And I ask that the eyes of my understanding be enlightened, that I may know what is the hope of Your calling for my life, what are the riches of the glory of Your inheritance in the saints, and what is the exceeding greatness of Your power towards me, according to the working of Your mighty power. I pray this in Jesus's name. Amen.*

Once you have prayed and prepared your heart to receive from the Lord, you can begin to read. As you read the Word, you give the Spirit of God something inside you to work with. It doesn't matter where or how you start. Some people prefer an organized approach to reading the Bible, selecting a reading plan with daily, prescribed readings to help them cover the entire Word of God in a set period of time, like a year. Others, especially those who have already read through the Bible, may prefer to read chapters or passages as the Holy Spirit leads them.

Whatever approach you choose, read slowly and intentionally. Be willing to pause and meditate on a passage, reading and rereading it to let it sink in. And while you are doing so, converse with Holy Spirit. Ask Him what the scripture means. If something stands out to you, stop and ask the Lord what He wants to say to you through that verse or passage. As He leads, or if there is a clear and obvious connection to your life, use the scripture as a basis for your prayer and praise. Personalize it. There is nothing more beautiful and powerful then when you use the Scriptures as your own words to God or when God's Word is spoken directly to you. As you read psalms or other verses of praise, repeat them—out loud if you can—and make it your own confession of worship and prayer to the Lord. If you read about God blessing someone with something, read the passage and ask the Lord to bless your life in the same way. If you encounter a passage in which a biblical figure commits a sin or makes an error, use that experience to pray that God would protect you from temptation and help lead you in His way and away from poor choices that might hinder your relationship with Him. Don't forget to thank the Holy Spirit as you go for giving you the Word and for His promise to honor His Word.

The Holy Spirit can also use this time of prayer and Bible reading to bring to our attention key lessons about His character, words of encouragement for our life, or to reveal certain scriptures for situations we are facing in order to give us direction, instruction, rebuke, edification, comfort, and so forth. Remember 2 Timothy 3:16–17, which teaches, "All scripture is given by inspiration of God, and is profitable for doctrine, for reproof, for correction, for instruction in righteousness, that the man of God may be complete, thoroughly equipped for every good work" (NKJV). These *rhema words of God* come when we read the *logos Word of God,* which is simply the Bible, and the Holy Spirit of God illuminates that Word to our soul. This is what the psalmist meant when he wrote, "Your word is a lamp for my feet, a light on my path" (Ps. 119:105).

In addition to these new, fresh *rhema* words, God may also bring other passages, stories, or people to your mind as you read though the Scriptures in order to direct your prayers. This may be for your benefit alone, or it may be for you to bless others. In John 14:26 Jesus promised that "the Helper, the Holy Spirit, whom the Father will send in My name, He will teach you all things, and bring to your remembrance all things that I have said to you" (John 14:26, NKJV). These reminders function as a way of enhancing our intercession as we connect with the Spirit of God directly, spirit to Spirit.

For example, have you ever read the Bible and felt like something you read was just made for someone you know? Or maybe the opposite happened and you found that as you prayed for someone, suddenly a Scripture came to mind that was pertinent to the situation or exactly what they needed to hear? That was the Holy Spirit using His Word to give you the opportunity to encourage another person or bringing to your remembrance a Scripture that would edify someone else. When this happens we must be diligent to obey His prompting and allow it to direct our prayers and, as He leads, our actions.

While you are still growing in your knowledge of the Scriptures, feel free to take whatever *rhema* words you hear or directions you sense as you read to someone you know who has a reliable history of hearing from God, who is spiritually mature, who knows the Bible well, and who has good character. Ask them to help you discern if what you have been hearing does, in fact, line up with who God is. Each of us needs wise counselors around us to help teach us in the beginning and later to help us discern if what we are hearing is from God. None of us are exempt from making mistakes or being deceived.

As you make a habit of the practice of praying through the Bible, you will find it easier to hear the Holy Spirit leading and directing you through the Scriptures. Hearing the Spirit of God as we pray in this way is learning to understand Him in us as He brings to life the Scriptures, as opposed to just reading the Word just for knowledge or trying to obey a set of rules in our strength. As this dialogue becomes more frequent during your times of Bible study and prayer, you will learn to discern His voice more readily. You will begin to hear the Spirit of God moment by moment as you go about your day.

Reflect

1. Are you accustomed to beginning your time reading and studying the Bible with prayer? How do you think your study time might change when you begin by intentionally inviting the Lord to speak to your heart as you read?

_____
_____
_____
_____

2. Who can you count on to offer mature spiritual direction and counsel? If no one comes to mind readily, consider reaching out to your pastor and asking for mentoring.

_____
_____
_____
_____

3. Read 1 Thessalonians 5:16–18. How does the practice of praying through the Scriptures affect your understanding of Paul's admonition in this passage to "pray without ceasing"?

_____
_____
_____
_____

Pray

Father, I ask that You may fill me with the knowledge of Your will in all wisdom and spiritual understanding, that I may walk worthy of the Lord, fully pleasing You, being fruitful in every good work and increasing in the knowledge of God. I pray that I would be strengthened with all might according to Your glorious power for all patience and longsuffering with joy, giving thanks to You, Father, who have qualified me to be partaker of the inheritance of the saints in the light. Thank You, Father, that You have delivered me from the power of darkness and conveyed me into the kingdom of Your Son of Your love. Thank You for Your Word, which I can pray and make my own. I pray this in Jesus's name. Amen. [See Colossians 1:9–13.]

Listen

Ask the Lord to bring to your memory or lead you to a scripture verse or passage that addresses an ongoing prayer request or petition you have made to Him. Spend a few minutes silently and expectantly awaiting a response.

Day 10

Developing a Hunger for the Word of God

Blessed are those who hunger and thirst for righteousness, for they shall be filled.

—Matthew 5:6, NKJV

The Bible isn't just words written in a book. No, God's Word is bread, life, spirit, and truth. It is transformative when we commune with the Spirit while reading and we meditate on what is being read. Let's break this down.

In John 6 we read about two of the miraculous signs Jesus performed. He fed over five thousand people with five loaves of bread and two fish, and later that evening He walked on water. The next day the people went looking for Him and found him across the lake from where He had been teaching the previous day. John records their conversation in John 6:26–31:

> Jesus replied, "I tell you the truth, you want to be with me because I fed you, not because you understood the miraculous signs. But don't be so concerned about perishable things like food. Spend your energy seeking the eternal life that the Son of Man can give you. For God the Father has given me the seal of his approval." They replied, "We want to perform God's works, too. What should we do?" Jesus told them, "This is the only work God wants from you: Believe in the one he has sent." They answered, "Show us a miraculous sign if you want us to believe in you. What can you do? After all, our ancestors ate manna while they journeyed through the wilderness! The Scriptures say, 'Moses gave them bread from heaven to eat.'"

The only concern the people had were the miraculous signs, not who Jesus was. The miracle feeding of five thousand captivated them—though it wasn't enough to convince them—and then they desired to perform God's works too. If they had understood why Jesus had performed the signs in the first place, they would have known who they were speaking to. And yet they wanted Jesus to show yet another sign! So, what did Jesus say in response?

> Jesus replied, "I am the bread of life. Whoever comes to me will never be hungry again. Whoever believes in me will never be thirsty. But you haven't believed in me even though you have seen me. However, those the Father has given me will come to me, and I will never reject them. For I have come down from heaven to do the will of God who sent me, not to do my own will. And this is the will of God, that I should not lose even one of all those he has given me, but that I should raise them up at the last day. For it is my Father's will that all who see his Son and believe in him should have eternal life. I will raise them up at the last day."
>
> —John 6:35–40

When the people began to murmur and complain at His response to their request for another sign, Jesus said it again: "I tell you the truth, anyone who believes has eternal life. Yes, I am the bread of life! The Spirit alone gives eternal life. Human effort accomplishes nothing. And the very words I have spoken to you are spirit and life" (vv. 47–48, 63).

In these scriptures Jesus reveals that He is the very Bread of Life. His Word—the words He speaks—is food for our soul. It feeds and renews, revives and refreshes. It nourishes our spirit and gives us life. The fact is, if we want the abundant life, the Word must be our food. We need to have hunger on the inside of us for this bread that is life and spirit and truth. Just as physical food nourishes my body, God's Word, His bread, nourishes my spirit and my soul.

Not only is the Word of God bread for our soul, but though the contents of God's Word are written with ink on paper it is spirit and life. Spirit and life imply active energy. The very words in our Bibles are living and active, "sharper than any two-edged sword" (Heb. 4:12). The Scriptures declare that meditating on the Word can give life to our bodies, health to our bones, joy to depressed spirits, and calm to chaotic minds. God's Word is literally medicine.

The Word of God is also truth. Every word penned in its pages is the truth because Jesus Himself is the truth, and we must worship Him as such.

> Jesus told him, "I am the way, the truth, and the life. No one can come to the Father except through me."
>
> —John 14:6

> For God is Spirit, so those who worship him must worship in spirit and in truth.
>
> —John 4:24

To worship Him in spirit means to be born again; to worship Him in truth means accepting the contents of Scripture in its entirety as given by the inspiration of God as truth—the only truth—whether you agree or not, whether you understand or don't understand.

Because Jesus and the Holy Spirit are One, and because Jesus is the truth, the Holy Spirit is the Spirit of truth. He lives on the inside of every born-again believer. Trust that He will keep you from error as you yield in obedience to His promptings to read His Word, the Word of truth.

> He is the Holy Spirit, who leads into all truth. The world cannot receive him, because it isn't looking for him and doesn't recognize him. But you know him, because he lives with you now and later will be in you.
>
> —John 14:17

> But I will send you the Advocate—the Spirit of truth. He will come to you from the Father and will testify all about me.
>
> —John 15:26

> When the Spirit of truth comes, he will guide you into all truth. He will not speak on his own but will tell you what he has heard. He will tell you about the future.
>
> —John 16:13

Before we can hear God—the real and living God, the one and only true God—we must know Him as bread, life, spirit, and truth through His Word, the Bible. Remember, Jesus Himself expounded the Scriptures the things concerning Himself. The Scriptures are the plumb line to which everything we hear must measure up. If it doesn't line up with Scripture, then I would suggest it is not from God. We must discern what spirit we are listening to, truth or error, and consider the posture of our hearts. Unless you know the Word of God by reading it, meditating on Scripture, and studying its contents to learn who God is, what His nature is, what His character is like, and what His will is generally and specifically, you will not know clearly and without a doubt who or what spirit is speaking to you in prayer or everyday situations.

Neither will you know God's faithfulness. He is faithful to watch over and perform His Word. It is imperative that you gain a good, solid appetite for the Bible and, at first, discipline yourself to daily reading and study of the Word not because you will be a better Christian or because God will be more pleased with you but because you understand that the Word of God empowers you to live this life victoriously, because you understand the benefits of its wisdom when applied to your life, and because you desire to know God intimately, to hear Him reveal His love for you. Hopefully, after habitual reading, you will gain a hunger and thirst for God's presence and Word, and you will be excited to meet with God.

We may find ourselves feeling superior to the crowd of people in John 6 who clamored for signs and wonders, but are we really that different from them? Is the posture of our heart so unlike their own? I wonder how many of us read the Bible only for content, for knowledge, or out of a sense of duty without believing in our hearts that the words of Christ are spirit, just as we are spirit beings also. If we understood that the Word of God is the bread of our spirit, the very food our spirit craves, how would it change our understanding of the Word itself and of the Holy Spirit? *Selah*. (Really think about that for a moment.)

We must get to know His Word, His truth. It is active and alive. It is not just words penned to paper. Let the Word be life to you. It is hope when you need hope, joy when you need joy, answers to life struggles, and comfort when you are distressed. Let the Word be bread to you: food for your soul and medicine for your body. It renews your way of thinking, bringing every thought captive to the obedience of Christ so that you may find rest for your soul. Let the Word be Spirit and truth to you. With the knowledge of Scripture rooted in our hearts, we can actively interact with the Spirit of God and enjoy conversations with Him. We can approach God anytime, anywhere, for anything because God speaks through His Word!

I encourage you to pray that God empowers you with an appetite and a thirst to drink His Word. Pray that you will hunger for it. Without it, you leave yourself vulnerable to demonic spirits and doctrines of demons. The Bible is the foundation of all other methods of hearing God for yourself and judging when others speak to you on behalf of God. Trust me, once you have tasted and seen that the Lord is good (Ps. 34:8) you will move from seeing the study of the Word as merely a discipline to developing a hunger for the Bread of Life.

Reflect

1. Why do you think Jesus performed the miracles recorded in John 6, even though He knew—in His omniscience—that it would not change the hearts of the people? What does this reveal about His character?

_____
_____
_____
_____

2. Restate the following sentence in your own words and explain what it means to your life personally: "Before we can hear God we must know Him as Bread, Life, Spirit, and Truth through His Word, the Bible."

_____
_____
_____
_____

3. Take a moment to examine your heart honestly. Do you really believe that the Word of God is the bread of our spirit, the very food our spirit craves? Do you live your life as if you would perish if you were separated from the Word, in the same way that your body would die if you went without food and water? How would grasping this revelation change your life and walk with God?

_____
_____
_____
_____

Pray

Father, I ask You to help me grow spiritually. Help me be diligent and disciplined concerning spiritual matters. Let me not be like a child, tossed to and fro from every wind of doctrine, but let me be like those who by reason of use have their senses exercised to discern both good and evil. And when I have no desire to pray or read Your Word, I ask You to give me a desire. Produce in me a spirit of discipline. Help me not to be sluggish in my spiritual disciplines, like prayer, reading Your Word, going to church, and communing with Your Holy Spirit. Revive and refresh me anew today. Let me taste and see that the Lord is good. I pray this in Jesus's name. Amen.

Exercise

Quiet your mind. Read and meditate on these scriptures: Ephesians 1:5–6, 11; 1 Peter 2:9; and Isaiah 49:15–16. Ask the Lord what He wants you to know about these passages by praying, "Lord enlighten my heart to what You want to tell me about these scriptures." Then journal your thoughts. Judge the words by taking what was written and comparing it to the Word of God. Begin to ask yourself if what you heard was biblical. Did it line up with Scripture? Does it match God's character? Was it pure? Peaceable? Full of good fruit? Did it draw you closer to God or draw you away from Him? Was it a full word/statement, or did your brain have to stop, process, and formulate words? Specifically, did what you hear just drop in your spirit and flow without help from you?

For those of you who have studied the Scriptures or who know the Greek and Hebrew words or Hebrew words and the context of these passages, I challenge you to ask the Lord to show you what you don't know and tune in to what you hear as opposed to writing down what you already know. Let Him speak these words to you.

My Story
The Word Brings Growth

It was the early spring, beginning of summer when I planted my first garden out here in Teulon. I happened to be reading about the parable of the sower and his seed. (See Luke 8:5–18.) As I read this passage of Scripture, though in context it speaks of salvation from babes to maturity, God spoke to me about the realities of His teachings and how in that season of my life it related to my garden. He often will use the physical to explain the spiritual. In this instance, He instructed me to speak life every day over my newly planted garden. I was to speak the "Word seed," and then I was to daily "water" my garden by declaring the Word over it. In obedience, I would go out each day and speak life-giving scriptures over my garden. Honestly, if people could see the acts I do out of obedience, let's just say I can't imagine what they would be thinking.

Anyway, when the time came to harvest, I had never seen such an abundant crop, nor anything so large! In fact, I was so overjoyed that I took samples of my vegetables to my prayer group to encourage them about the truth of God's Word. They were so amazed that a friend of mine asked if she could keep one of the potatoes! God's Word is indeed life, spirit, bread, and truth!

Lesson Three

God Speaks Through the Holy Spirit

Day 11

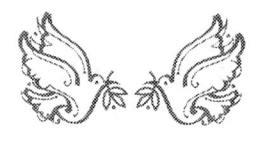

The Inner Witness

> It is the [Holy] Spirit who testifies, because the Spirit is the truth. [He is the essence and origin of truth itself.] … The one who believes in the Son of God [who adheres to, trusts in, and relies confidently on Him as Savior] has the testimony *within himself.*
>
> —1 John 5:6, 10, AMP, emphasis added

As we discovered earlier, we can be assured that it has always been the plan of our Father to communicate with man. It is vital to know that our heavenly Father has the heart for love, intimacy, communication, and fellowship with mankind. We were made for relationship with Him. All that He says or asks us to do is with the intention of doing us good, not harm. He is a good God, and we do not have to fear His voice or commands.

The Word of God tells us that when we believe in Christ as the Son of God who was raised from the dead and confess with our mouths that He is Lord, we are eternally saved and promised a more abundant life on Earth. (See Romans 10:9–10; John 10:10.) We have been redeemed and forgiven of all our sins: past, present, and future. That means the sin that once separated us from right standing with God no longer separates us. Through Christ we have been made righteous. Nothing we do will make us righteous other than believing in Christ and the message of the cross.

With that salvation, the Holy Spirit of promise comes to dwell within.

> And because we are his children, God has sent the Spirit of his Son into our hearts, prompting us to call out, "Abba, Father."
>
> —Galatians 4:6

Furthermore, because we are united with Christ, we have received an inheritance from God, for he chose us in advance, and he makes everything work out according to his plan. God's purpose was that we Jews who were the first to trust in Christ would bring praise and glory to God. And now you Gentiles have also heard the truth, the Good News that God saves you. And when you believed in Christ, he identified you as his own by giving you the Holy Spirit, whom he promised long ago. The Spirit is God's guarantee that he will give us the inheritance he promised and that he has purchased us to be his own people. He did this so we would praise and glorify him.

—Ephesians 1:11–14

He is the Holy Spirit, who leads into all truth. The world cannot receive him, because it isn't looking for him and doesn't recognize him. But you know him, because he lives with you now and later will be in you.

—John 14:17

The Bible says we are joined to the Lord and therefore "one spirit with Him" (1 Cor. 6:17), whereby we have relationship with the Father through Christ by the the power of the Holy Spirit:

Now all of us can come to the Father through the same Holy Spirit because of what Christ has done for us. … You are members of God's family.

—Ephesians 2:18–19

The Holy Spirit is the inner witness who testifies to us that we are now born of God, that we are now children of the Most High! He is the guarantee of our inheritance, but it is also through Him that we are able to hear from God. After all, what does it mean that the Holy Spirit "prompts" us to call out to God as Father (Gal. 4:6) if not that He is speaking to us through the voice of this inner witness?

Reflect

1. First Corinthians 2:12 says that God has "freely given us" "wonderful things." What are some of the wonderful things God has given you?

_____
_____
_____
_____

2. Is it easy for you to picture yourself as a part of the family of God and that God is your Father? Why or why not? What needs to happen in order for you to be able to freely accept Him as your loving, gracious Father?

_____
_____
_____
_____
_____

3. Think back on the moment you chose to make Jesus the Lord of your life. How did you feel when you invited Him to be your Savior and automatically received the Holy Spirit as an inner witness? Did you feel different on the inside? Could this feeling have been the Holy Spirit prompting you that you had been adopted into the family of God?

_____
_____
_____
_____
_____

Pray

Heavenly Father, thank You that I am united with Christ and that I have received an inheritance from You, for You chose me in advance and You make everything work out according to Your plan. Thank You that when I believed in Christ You identified me as Your own by giving me the Holy Spirit, whom You promised long ago. I belong to You. I am chosen. Thank you that the Spirit is Your guarantee that You will give me the inheritance You promised. Father, I praise and glorify You. Thank You for the Holy Spirit, who leads me into all truth. The world cannot receive Him, because it isn't looking for Him and doesn't recognize Him. I pray that as I grow in understanding the inner witness and become sensitive to His leading many will be blessed because of Christ in me. I pray this in Jesus's name. Amen.

Listen

Ask the Lord to show you what it means for Him to be your heavenly Father. Spend a few minutes silently and expectantly awaiting a response.

Day 12

The Sound of the Inner Witness

> "No eye has seen, no ear has heard, and no mind has imagined what God has prepared for those who love him." But it was to us that God revealed these things by his Spirit. For his Spirit searches out everything and shows us God's deep secrets.
>
> —1 Corinthians 2:9–10

It is the Holy Spirit who enables us to know the mind of Christ, to understand what He is speaking to us and what has been freely given to us by God. So what does the inner witness sound like? How will we perceive His word to us?

For most believers this sense of the Holy Spirit speaking is like a sudden nudge or prompting, enlightenment or quickening. It could even be described as a check in our spirit that may or may not be accompanied by a thought. It is not so much a voice, but an impression. It can also be like an instant "knowing that you just know," like a green light when something sounds or feels real or perhaps even a red light when something looks or just feels wrong and is often accompanied by a sense of peace. (I use the word *feel* cautiously here since this sensation is not an emotion, which comes from our soul, but a perception coming from our spirit.)

First John 2:20 in the Amplified Bible describes the inner witness this way:

> But you have an anointing from the Holy One [you have been set apart, specially gifted and prepared by the Holy Spirit], and all of you know [the truth because *He teaches us, illuminates our minds, and guards us from error*].
>
> —emphasis added

It is as though God stirs our hearts Spirit to spirit, that we might be *moved to action* and bear witness to His unction or nudging. (God can stir up our spirits to motivate and fulfill His destiny.

Read Haggai 1:13–15 as an example of this.) We cannot explain it, other than we sense in our spirit (again, not our souls) that it is right or wrong for that matter.

The Old Testament sometimes described this experience as a stirring in one's heart. In Ezra 1:1, 5 we read that God *"stirred the heart* of Cyrus to put this proclamation in writing and send it throughout his kingdom. ... Then *God stirred the hearts* of the priests and Levites and the leaders of the tribes of Judah and Benjamin to go to Jerusalem to rebuild the Temple of the Lord" (emphasis added). In both passages, the Hebrew word for "heart" here is *ruwach,* which is also translated "mind" and "spirit,"[16] and the word *stirred* is the Hebrew word *uwr,* meaning "to rouse," "awaken," and "to stir up."[17] It is a supernatural stirring, impression, or anointing manifested by a supernatural peace that comes from the Spirit within (and not from our minds) speaking to our spirit through this inward revelation or inspiration.

The inner witness prompts us with this stirring to deepen our intimacy with God and move us to obedience to Him and His instruction. It moves us to act, as it did in Haggai and Ezra. You may experience this stirring in your heart as a desire to suddenly read the Word, pray, and/or have worship time with God. But let's say you are busy or you are amid your daily routine like cleaning, watching TV, exercising, or shoveling snow. Whatever it is you are in the middle of, the question is, What are you going to do with that stirring to read the Word and pray? Will you obey it or ignore it?

The inner witness is also often at work when we perceive something we could not have knowledge of in the natural realm. According to Merriam-Webster's dictionary, to perceive is "to attain awareness ... to become aware of through the senses ... to realize."[18] Their English thesaurus uses similar words, like "behold, discern, and discover," to name a few, to describe the meaning of the word *perceive.* As Scripture reveals, the ability to perceive and "see" comes only from the Lord. (See Deuteronomy 29:4.) It is He who stirs one's heart or makes one aware through one's spiritual senses. He is the inner witness that enables us to perceive (or not perceive) in the spiritual realm by opening our heart so that we may have eyes to see and ears to hear. (See Matthew 16:13–17; Deuteronomy 29:4; Isaiah 6:9; Mark 4:12.)[19]

When Jesus asked the disciples, "Who do you say that I am?" Simon Peter replied, "You are the Christ ... the Son of the living God" (Matt. 16:15–16, NKJV). Jesus then explained that flesh and blood had not revealed this to Peter, but God had. The New Living Translation says, "My Father in heaven has revealed this to you. You did not learn this from any human being" (v. 17). In other words, Peter did not know this on his own, nor was he taught by any person. In fact, the word *revealed* in this passage is the Greek word *apokalyptō,* which means "to uncover, lay open what has been veiled or covered up; to disclose, make bare or to make known, make manifest, disclose what before was unknown."[20] This is a perfect example of the Holy Spirit allowing us to perceive spiritual truth we could not otherwise understand.

Finally, the inner witness speaks through a sense of conviction. In these instances, He bears witness to our spirit, letting us know when we sin and impressing us with a sense of guilt. Just as the stirring witness of the Spirit is designed to prompt us to action, this bearing witness to the conviction of sin is to move us to repentance, that we might confess and then turn from sin, because He is faithful and just to forgive us. There is no punishment. Repentance keeps our hearts sensitive to His impressions and voice, and it keeps us humble and dependent upon God.

Reflect

1. Have you ever felt a stirring to pray, read the Word, or worship the Lord? What did you do? If you obeyed this prompting from the Holy Spirit, what was the result? Did He give you a *rhema* word? Perhaps you found yourself surprised to receive another, similar prompting soon thereafter. If you did not obey, what would you do differently now that you know it was likely the Holy Spirit speaking to you?

_____

_____

_____

2. Think back for a moment over your walk with the Lord. Has there ever been a time when you perceived something that could only have been revealed to you through spiritual means? Did you know that this was the work of the Holy Spirit at the time, or is it only now, in looking back, that you are able to recognize it as the inner witness? (If the latter, do not feel condemned. Looking back is often how we learn.)

_____

_____

_____

3. Consider your experience with the inner witness testifying to your spirit through a sense of conviction. When you are convicted of sin, are you able to sense the Holy Spirit drawing you to Himself, or do you find yourself easily mired in shame and condemnation? If the latter, ask the Lord to open the eyes and ears of your heart so that His voice drawing you to repentance will become stronger than the voice of the enemy. Learn to change the word *problem* to *opportunity* and *weakness* or *sin* to *areas of growth for your development in Christ*. Do not accept condemnation or shame. Instead, see that God has great plans for you!

_____

_____

_____

Pray

Heavenly Father, I ask Your Holy Spirit to search out everything and show me God's deep secrets. I desire to know, understand, and be led by the inner witness. Help me to be sensitive to this perception. Help me to be obedient to the stirring of my heart and to the peace of God that may accompany it. Increase my perception and stir my heart to action. I pray this in Jesus's name. Amen.

Listen

Ask the Lord what you can do to serve Him today. Spend a few minutes silently and expectantly awaiting a response.

Day 13

The Testimony of the Inner Witness

No one can know a person's thoughts except that person's own spirit, and no one can know God's thoughts except God's own Spirit. And we have received God's Spirit (not the world's spirit), so we can know the wonderful things God has freely given us.

—1 Corinthians 2:11–12

We have seen that the inner witness always attests to the truth, and since we are born-again believers, we have this Spirit of truth in us. In addition to helping us to hear directly from the Holy Spirit and receive that quickening, or leading, as it applies to our own life the inner witness also enables us to bear witness to prophetic words that have been given to us by someone else. In fact, the Bible specifically directs us to hold any and every prophecy up to the Lord to "test the spirits" and determine if it is, indeed, from God:

Dear friends, do not believe everyone who claims to speak by the Spirit. You must test them to see if the spirit they have comes from God.

—1 John 4:1–3

Do not stifle the Holy Spirit. Do not scoff at prophecies, but test everything that is said. Hold on to what is good.

—1 Thessalonians 5:19–21

Upon hearing the word, the inner witness bears witness to our spirit that it is either a word from God or not. This inner witness sends a signal to our spirit that, yes, it is bearing witness within or that the word shared is like a red flag; it does not witness to our spirit. This function of the inner witness bears witness to the things that are really of God so that we are not led into error.

First Thessalonians 5:19–20 (above) implies that prophetic words are meant to be a regular part of our walk with God. They are a healthy sign of the free operation of the Holy Spirit in our fellowship with other believers and in our life. Because humans are not infallible, however, God has provided a safeguard in the form of His Holy Spirit that enables us to evaluate these prophetic words in order to know or to test the spirits whether they are of God or of our flesh or the enemy, whether they are of the Spirit of truth or the spirit of error. First John 4:6 says:

> We are of God. He who knows God hears us; he who is not of God does not hear us. By this, we know the spirit of truth and the spirit of error.

The word *know* in this passage is once again the Greek word *ginōskō,* "to perceive." So again, we are aware because of the inner witness bearing witness or providing understanding through our spiritual eyes and ears to alert us to the operation of the Spirit of truth and the spirit of error. (As stated earlier, when it bears witness, it is accompanied by an inner peace.)

Because this mode of the Holy Spirit's communication is not a voice, we may not understand at first what we are sensing. However, practice will help teach us to be attuned to the prompting of the inner witness so that we can learn to judge and discern prophetic words when they come to us to help keep us from being led astray.

It cannot be overstated that, as with everything we perceive the Spirit to be saying to us, this sense of stirring will always be in agreement with the Word, the Bible. Our ability to hear from the Holy Spirit in this way does not in any way trump or replace our need to be rooted and grounded in a strong knowledge of the Scriptures. Even seasoned believers who have been hearing from the Lord for many years must use their knowledge of the Word as an extra layer of checks and balances. This is not a sign of spiritual immaturity but one of maturity.

Reflect

1. How comfortable are you with the operation of the gift of prophecy? What can you do to stretch yourself and become more comfortable with it?

_____
_____
_____
_____

2. Have you ever had someone speak a prophetic word over you? As he or she was speaking, did you sense the Holy Spirit bearing witness to the word? Did you sense the opposite, that perhaps

the word was not for you or not on target? Perhaps you didn't sense anything. If the latter—and if you can remember the word now—hold it up to the Lord in prayer and ask Him to reveal to you if it was truth or error.

_____
_____
_____
_____

3. Many prophetic ministries record prophetic sessions so that those who receive words can take home an audio recording of the word spoken over them. How might this make it easier for believers to test the spirits and discern the accuracy of prophetic words?

_____
_____
_____
_____

Pray

Heavenly Father, thank You that You desire to communicate with me so earnestly that You will at times give others a word to share with me from Your heart. Help me to know how to test these words by listening to the inner witness. Confirm when it is indeed You speaking, and make it clear to me when a word is counterfeit and in error. I want to hear Your voice confidently in whatever form it may come and remain rooted and grounded in Your truth. In Jesus's name. Amen.

Listen

Ask the Lord for a word of encouragement that you can share with someone else today. Spend a few minutes silently and expectantly awaiting a response.

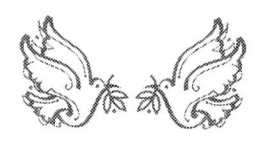

My Story
The Inner Witness Confirms Prophetic Words

Shortly after I was saved I attended a Foundations class at my church. After this class I decided to get baptized. A common practice during a baptism at our church is to be prophesied over. One by one, different people prophesied as the Spirit of God gave them utterance, and one by one my spirit bore witness to what they were saying. Some of it was confirmation of what I had already heard the Lord say to me, but most of it was God's heart toward me, both presently and in the future. I remember feeling incredibly awed by this sensing *that was happening on the inside of me. I knew that what they were saying was true and came directly from the Father's heart.*

One of the prophetic words given to me was a woman had seen a picture of a vine, and this vine was going straight up to heaven. The leaves of this vine were in the shape of hearts. She felt the Lord saying that I was abiding in the Vine. The hearts represented my love for Jesus and His love to me. She said she felt the Lord revealed that the vine reaching toward heaven was symbolic of me desiring intimacy with the Father. I had such a peace and felt comforted.

I was stunned yet captivated that God would speak through people to touch the deepest part of my being. Just that week I had been studying and praying John 15. My spirit within me leapt with joy as I bore witness to what they were speaking to me.

Day 14

The Power of the Inner Witness

"Go out and stand before me on the mountain," the Lord told him. And as Elijah stood there, the Lord passed by, and a mighty windstorm hit the mountain. It was such a terrible blast that the rocks were torn loose, but the Lord was not in the wind. After the wind there was an earthquake, but the Lord was not in the earthquake. And after the earthquake there was a fire, but the Lord was not in the fire. And after the fire there was the sound of a gentle whisper. When Elijah heard it, he wrapped his face in his cloak and went out and stood at the entrance of the cave. And a voice said, "What are you doing here, Elijah?"

—1 Kings 19:11–13

Just as the crowd Jesus taught in John 6 clamored for signs and wonders, it is easy to find ourselves wishing for a burning bush experience over the quickening, stirring, perception, or conviction of the inner witness. Especially as we are learning to hear the various ways of the Spirit relating to us, we may find ourselves frustrated by these gentle impressions of His Spirit upon our lives. But we must beware: Communication from God is within His will, and it will to come any way and in whatever form He chooses. Just as Elijah was surprised to hear the voice of God not in the strong wind that broke rocks from the mountain, the earthquake, or the fire but in a whisper, we must not look down upon the promptings of the inner witness as any less than what they are: God connecting with us, His Spirit to our spirit. (We will talk more about the still, small voice of God and Elijah's encounter with Him in 1 Kings 19 in Lesson Four.)

Since we have seen that Jesus taught that we would know Him through seeing Him first in Scripture, and since Jesus and the inner witness (Holy Spirit) are one, it may be beneficial to study some examples from the Word of God of the inner witness in action. Before you read over this list, I encourage you to stop and pray that the Lord would use it to strengthen your spiritual hearing and, if necessary, to help you see the work of the inner witness as no less important or impressive than any other means by which the Holy Spirit may speak to you.

- James, Peter, and John "perceived" God's grace upon Paul the first time they met him (Gal. 2:9, NKJV). This is evidence of the inner witness speaking to their spirits to confirm Paul's conversion. (Remember, this was especially important, as Paul had been a murderer of Christians. It was likely this unction of the Holy Spirit that gave James, Peter, and John the green light to release Paul into his ministry to the Gentiles.)

- After Peter's vision on the housestop, which changed not only the course of his ministry but also evangelism as a whole, he shared the *rhema* word he had received with the other disciples. He explained to them, "I *perceive* that God shows no partiality. But in every nation whoever fears Him and works righteousness is accepted by Him" (Acts 10:34–35, NKJV, emphasis added). In other words, it was the inner witness who revealed to Peter that the work of the Cross was available to all who would believe, not just the Jews.

- The Book of Nehemiah tells the story of the prophet Nehemiah, who received a word from the Lord to rebuild the walls of Jerusalem in order to provide protection for the city. While he had the enthusiastic help of many people, his efforts were met with great opposition from people in places of power, who tried repeatedly to thwart the building project and halt construction. In one instance Nehemiah visited a trusted peer, who warned Him, "Let us meet together inside the Temple of God and bolt the doors shut. Your enemies are coming to kill you tonight" (Neh. 6:10). Nehemiah considered the word but quickly determined it was not of God. In verse 12 we read, "Then I *perceived* that God had not sent him at all, but that he pronounced this prophecy against me because Tobiah and Sanballat had hired him" (NKJV, emphasis added).

- Even Jesus relied on the inner witness during His life and ministry. Matthew 22:18 tells us that he "*perceived* [the] wickedness" of the Pharisees as they questioned Him, though they attempted to play Him with compliments and words that seemed kind on the surface. (See v. 16.) We also read that He often perceived the thoughts of man within His Spirit, which allowed Him to speak specific words of life and truth. (See Mark 2:8; Luke 5:22.) In Luke 8:46 the Gospel writer tells us that Jesus "*perceived* power going out from" (NKJV, emphasis added) Him when the woman with the issue of blood touched His garment. This was a supernatural revelation about her need when she touched Him, since the press of the crowd would have made it impossible to distinguish her touch from others' through natural wisdom.

- Paul perceived that a certain man in Lystra had faith to be healed (Acts 14:8–10), and he perceived danger while preparing to embark on a voyage over the sea that ended up nearly costing the men their lives (Acts 27:9–10). Paul perceived these things, or was made aware of them, by the inner witness. He bore witness to the truth because his eyes were opened supernaturally.

- When Elizabeth heard the greeting of Mary, the babe John the Baptist leaped in her womb because he bore witness to the presence of the truth, Jesus Christ, in the womb of Mary. (See Luke 1:41–44.)

- As we have seen before, "the Spirit Himself *bears witness* with our spirit that we are children of God" (Rom. 8:16, NKJV, emphasis added). Our faith in our salvation alone is an evidence of the operation of the inner witness in our spirit.

Reflect

1. Be honest with yourself: Have you ever found yourself thinking that big, showy, unmistakeable messages from the Holy Spirit are better than the gentle unction of the inner witness? If so, ask the Lord to correct your thinking and help you to hear and receive His voice speaking to you through this means.

_____
_____
_____
_____

2. Which of the examples in this list resonates with you most strongly? Why do you think that is?

_____
_____
_____
_____

Pray

Heavenly Father, I am so grateful for Your Spirit in me, and I am so excited to be learning about You and how You lead and commune with me. Strengthen my perception. Open my spiritual eyes and enable me to hear Your Spirit within. Empower me to see the work of the inner witness as no less important or impressive than any other means by which the Holy Spirit may speak to me. Help me to get quiet before You so that I may know when He is bearing witness in me to something or someone whom You may be using to talk to me. When prophetic words come, tune my ears inward and teach me to recognize this method of communication. Help me to recognize Your purity, Your peace, and Your wisdom. I pray this in Jesus's name. Amen.

Listen

Ask the Lord to use the testimony of the inner witness to confirm for you how He wishes for you to respond to a circumstance or situation in your life that requires your action. Spend a few minutes silently and expectantly awaiting a response.

Day 15

The Inner Witness Is Our Encourager

> May God, who gives this patience and encouragement, help you live in complete harmony with each other, as is fitting for followers of Christ Jesus. Then all of you can join together with one voice, giving praise and glory to God, the Father of our Lord Jesus Christ.
>
> —1 Corinthians 2:11–12

In every one of its functions—quickening, stirring us to action, giving us supernatural perception often accompanied and motivated by an inner peace, convicting us of wrong, or bearing witness to the accuracy of a prophetic word—the inner witness will always do two things:

1. Support and confirm the truth of the Word of God
2. Encourage our hearts

Even when convicting us of sin, the mark of the Holy Spirit on our lives will be encouragement, support, and comfort. Luke wrote in the Book of Acts that "the church then had peace throughout Judea, Galilee, and Samaria, and it became stronger as the believers lived in the fear of the Lord. And with the *encouragement of the Holy Spirit* it also grew in numbers" (Acts 9:31, emphasis added). The word *encouragement* here is the Greek *paraklesis*, which means "exhortation, admonition, encouragement; consolation, comfort, solace; that which affords comfort or refreshment ... stirring address."[21] What a job description for the Holy Spirit!

A related word is used in this promise from Jesus to the disciples (and us):

> And I will pray the Father, and He will give you another *Helper*, that He may abide with you forever—the Spirit of truth, whom the world cannot receive, because it

neither sees Him nor knows Him; but you know Him, for He dwells with you and will be in you.

—John 14:16–17, NKJV, emphasis added

The word translated "Helper" here is the Greek word *parakletos*, which also means "an intercessor ... a helper, succourer ... called to one's aid."[22] It is from this Greek word *parakletos* that we get the English term *Paraclete,* which is often used to refer to the Holy Spirit. One author calls the inner witness "the Paraclete Encourager Spirit" because this function of encouraging and comforting is so intimately tied to His very nature.[23]

In whichever of His many roles, the Holy Spirit is still the Holy Spirit. His nature will not change with the message nor the mode with which He chooses to communicate with us. Any time He speaks—if it is truly His voice speaking to us—the message will be marked by a sense of this encouragement, comfort, or refreshment. In fact, on numerous accounts thus far I have stated that often this inner witness is accompanied by an inner peace. Peace gives us a sense of comfort. In Colossians 3:15 (AMPC) it states, "And let the peace (soul harmony which comes) from Christ rule (act as umpire continually) in your hearts [deciding and settling with finality all questions that arise in your minds, in that peaceful state] to which as [members of Christ's] one body you were also called [to live]. And be thankful (appreciative), [giving praise to God always]." The Word of God says that peace will be our umpire. When it is of the Spirit of God, peace will rule in our hearts. If you hear a word of prophecy that is not accompanied by this spirit of peace and encouragement, beware! If you are reading the Scriptures and find yourself filled with dread or fear, beware! If you are driving and you feel a sense of impending doom, beware! These situations may masquerade as the red flag of the Holy Spirit giving us a word or unction, but without the mark of encouragement or peace they are likely from the enemy tempting our soul. God will not warn without providing the promise of escape. He will not convict without the promise of hope and salvation. He will not speak without comforting our spirit. Why? Because providing comfort and encouragement is simply who He is.

Whenever you may find yourself unsure of whether or not you are hearing from the Lord, ask the Lord to show you the word of encouragement in the message and to give you a *rhema* word from Scripture that directly supports it. Also, do you have peace? Allow the perfect love of God to cast out any and all fear you may have about "missing it" or being led astray. (See 1 John 4:18.) Remember, with everything that God speaks to us, He has our freedom in mind, not slavery to fear (Rom. 8:15). The Word of God tells us that Christ came to preach the good news, to heal the broken-hearted, and to proclaim liberty to the captives and to those who are bound. He sent His Spirit to comfort those who mourn, to encourage, and to bring hope where there is despair. That is the heart of our Father, the purpose of our wonderful Counselor. He desires that we learn to hear His voice not so that we will cower from Him but so that we can be shown His heart for our lives, which is for our "good and not for disaster, to give ... [us] a future and a hope" (Jer. 29:11).

Reflect

1. We cannot have a healthy, intimate relationship with someone we do not trust or with someone we do not believe wants the best for us. Examine your heart: When you think of God the Father or the Holy Spirit, what characteristics mark His nature? Be honest with yourself. Do you think of Him as one who would send His Comforter and Encourager, or do you think of Him as a Judge, waiting to condemn or striking fear instead of awe? If the latter, ask the Lord to reveal His true nature to you so that you can experience the full freedom of communicating with Him—with who He really is.

_____
_____
_____
_____

2. If you are familiar with the voice of the inner witness, in which of His functions are you most accustomed to hearing Him speak: quickening, stirring you to action, giving you supernatural perception, that inner peace, convicting you of wrong, or bearing witness to the accuracy of a prophetic word spoken over you? Why do you think this is?

_____
_____
_____
_____

3. Can you think of a time when you were seeking God for direction or instruction and you had a sense of peace? Or perhaps someone prayed over you, and it was exactly what you needed to hear. Because of this, you instantly had a sense of peace and comfort. Describe the experience.

_____
_____
_____
_____

Pray

Heavenly Father, thank You that You give patience and encouragement. Help me to live in complete harmony with everyone I know, as this is fitting for followers of Christ Jesus. I desire to join together with one voice, giving praise and glory to You, God, the Father of our Lord Jesus Christ. I long to be intimate with You in all things. Teach me all there is to know in recognizing Your voice, promptings, and quickenings. I pray this in Jesus's name. Amen.

Exercise

Quiet yourself. Think of someone you know to pray for. Ask the Lord to give you a word for them. Pray, "Father, I pray and ask that by Your Spirit in me You would reveal something about this person. Father, You know this person well. I pray and desire to hear what You have to say about him/her, so I ask that You open my ears to listen to what the Spirit of the Lord would say about this person." Now rest and listen to what you hear or see. Write that word down and make a commitment to share it with him/her soon. Recognize how you feel on the inside. Ask questions. Press in. Be sure to ask your partner if what you said bore witness with them (if they sensed it was from God).

If you are going through this exercise in a group, you can pair up and practice prophesying with one another and see if what is being prophesied over you bears witness or not.

Lesson Four

God Speaks Through the Still, Small Voice

Day 16

What Is the Still, Small Voice?

> But you have received the Holy Spirit, and he lives within you, so you don't need anyone to teach you what is true. For the Spirit teaches you everything you need to know, and what he teaches is true—it is not a lie. So just as he has taught you, remain in fellowship with Christ.
>
> —1 John 2:27

In Scripture, we learn that the still, small voice is the voice of God. This is different from the inner witness. We learned that the inner witness is more like a supernatural knowing. It is a prompting, a quickening, bearing witness, or a discerning within our spirit, often accompanied by peace, whereas the still, small voice is exactly that: It is a *voice* within that is heard with the ears of our heart, spirit to Spirit.

Let's look again at 1 Kings 19:1–18, which is where the term *still, small voice* comes from. This passage reveals how the prophet Elijah fled quickly to Horeb because he feared what the queen, Jezebel, would do to him. His fears were justified. She opposed him because of his obedience to the word of the Lord and his faithfulness to obeying that word, and she sought to kill him. Elijah went a day's journey into the wilderness and, mired in despair, he prayed that he might die. To him, his circumstances looked grim. Twice the angel of the Lord came to provide food for him. The second time those provisions sustained him for forty days and forty nights until he reached his destination of Horeb, the mountain of God. There God spoke to Him and said:

> "What are you doing here, Elijah?" So he [Elijah] said, "I have been very zealous for the LORD God of hosts; for the children of Israel have forsaken Your covenant, torn down Your altars, and killed Your prophets with the sword. I alone am left; and they seek to take my life." Then He [God] said, "Go out, and stand on the mountain before the LORD." And behold, the LORD passed by, and a great and

strong wind tore into the mountains and broke the rocks in pieces before the LORD, but the LORD was not in the wind; and after the wind an earthquake, but the LORD was not in the earthquake; and after the earthquake a fire, but the LORD was not in the fire; and after the fire a *still small voice.*

—1 Kings 19:9–12, NKJV, emphasis added

What do we learn from this passage? First, on the surface we learn that we cannot judge the voice of God by external manifestations. God could have used the roaring wind, the earthquake, or the raging fire as the backdrop for His message to Elijah, but He did not. Instead, He was the "gentle whisper" (v. 12, NLT) that spoke softly and openly and communicated instruction with purpose. Did Elijah have to guess what to do or guess what God meant? No, it was a full, clear statement, not fragmented thoughts. Even though God speaks through different means at times—including some ways He chose not to use in this instance—it is significant that when the voice of God came, it was unmistakeable, if not showy. We must not judge the voice of God by what we see.

Second, we cannot make assumptions about how the Holy Spirit will speak based on past moves or even personal experience. In the Old Testament, the Lord appeared in a burning bush to Moses and was a pillar of fire by night as a sign for His people to know where to go and that His presence was with them. (See Exodus 3:2; 13:22; Numbers 9:15.) He had even answered by fire for Elijah once before. (See 1 Kings 18:24.) In the New Testament, fire is represented as or is symbolic of the Holy Spirit's attributes, and He is often compared to the wind that brings new life, refreshment, repentance, and cleansing. During this interaction with Elijah, however, He was the "still small voice" (v. 12, NKJV). Just because the Holy Spirit has and does move like the wind, earthquakes, or fire at times, that does not mean that we should always assume these shows themselves to be indicators of the voice of God.

Failure to test the spirits in this way could be detrimental to us. That's because, third, signs and wonders themselves, though impressive, do not necessarily point to a definitive move of God. Even though we may feel the manifestation of the wind when being ministered to or ministering to others, God was not in the wind when Elijah encountered Him at Horeb. (See Acts 2:2–4; Jeremiah 4:10–13; John 3:8; Job 38:1.) During His time on Earth, Jesus Himself rebuked the wind in order to quiet it. He did not make the mistake of thinking that strong winds meant the Father was speaking to Him; He rightly discerned the situation and used His voice to silence the storm. Though the soundings of an earthquake may be the result of the presence of God or angels or the end of things to come, we should not affirm that an earthquake itself is the voice of God. (See Matthew 28:2–4; Acts 16:26; Revelation 6:12; 16:18.). We must walk by faith, not by sight, and be discerning of the spirits (2 Cor. 5:7, NKJV). This means recognizing that these signs should not be the basis of our affirmations that something must be the voice of God.

The Scriptures are clear that we must be cautious against false signs and lying wonders, even and especially when they are accompanied by showy miracles or come through a false prophet. (See Mark 4:39; 2 Thessalonians 2:9–12.) Deuteronomy 13:1–3 warns, "If there rises among you a prophet or a dreamer of dreams, and he gives you a sign or a wonder, and the sign or the wonder comes to pass, of which he spoke to you, saying, 'Let us go after other god'—which you have not known—'and let us serve them,' you shall not listen to the words of that prophet or that dreamer of dreams, for the Lord your God is testing you to know whether you love the Lord your God with all your heart and with all your soul" (NKJV). By this passage we see that even though a sign or wonder may take place, and even though a prophecy pronounced may come to pass, that alone must not be how we determine or discern who is speaking. Instead, we must know God's ways, and it is imperative that we read, know, and understand the Word of God, especially in these days. The Word of God also declares that in the End Times lawlessness will run rampant, and false Christs and false prophets will arise, again with false signs and lying wonders. We are to watch out and not be deceived.

It is important not to cross over from caution in these matters into fear. Because the Spirit of God indwells us and we are *one* with Him, we are equipped to hear that still, small voice with the ears of our heart, spirit to Spirit. We should be confident that the Holy Spirit will speak to us, He will tell us of things to come, He will glorify Jesus to us, and He will declare what is of Jesus to us.

> But the Helper, the Holy Spirit, whom the Father will send in My name, He will teach you all things, and bring to your remembrance all things that I said to you.
>
> —John 14:26, NKJV

> However, when He, the Spirit of truth, has come, He will guide you into all truth; for He will not speak on His authority, but whatever He hears *He will speak*; and *He will tell you* things to come. He will glorify Me, for He will take of what is Mine and *declare* it to you.
>
> —John 16:13–14, NKJV, emphasis added

The still, small voice is not often audible (though God does speak audibly in rare instances to people today), but it is a voice that we can and will hear on the inside of us. As with the inner witness, it may be accompanied by a sudden, quick thought from our own mind. It often just sounds like we are talking, even in first person. Yet, to know the difference, realize that the Spirit of God will always exalt Jesus Christ. He will not exalt you (the person speaking). The Spirit of God will not exaggerate or focus on the experience you may be having, and neither will He concentrate on a single attribute of God (like love) as the only focus. (God is also just, and He is also truth, etc.)

When the Spirit of God speaks, He always points to Jesus Christ, the Son of the living God, who came in the flesh, died for our sins, rose again the third day, and is seated at the right hand of the Father.

Beloved, I care that you hear God correctly and not be led by experiences only. Although I want you to become a firm believer in encounters with God, I am equally concerned that you learn not to exalt signs and wonders and big, showy experiences over the gentle whisper of that still, small voice speaking directly to your heart.

Reflect

1. Have you had an experience hearing the still, small voice of God? If so, describe it.

_____
_____
_____
_____

2. Have you ever personally seen God speak through a showy miracle or demonstration of His power? What was that like? How did you know that it was God?

_____
_____
_____
_____

3. Has there ever been a time when you witnessed a significant show of the power of nature or even what appeared to be a miracle, and yet you knew in your spirit that it wasn't the Lord? Describe how you knew it was not a move of His Spirit.

_____
_____
_____
_____

Pray

Heavenly Father, thank You for Your Holy Spirit, who will teach me all things and bring to my remembrance all things that Jesus said. Equip me with ears to hear the still, small voice. Help me to be sensitive to You, Holy Spirit. Awaken me to the sound of Your voice. Increase in me the ability to absorb, remember, and understand all that is taught in this workbook. I desire to be a learned student in the school of Holy Spirit. Create in me such a thirst for You. Let me drink from the well of Your Spirit. Here I am, Lord. Your child is listening. I pray this in Jesus's name. Amen.

Listen

Ask the Lord to reveal to you any teacher, teaching, or belief to which you have ascribed that is not of Him. Spend a few minutes silently and expectantly awaiting a response. If you hear the still, small voice of the Lord revealing some doctrine or purported leader to be in error, thank Him for showing you, repent for listening to it—however unknowingly—and then stay away from the source of that information.

Day 17

The Voice of Authority

> For God speaks again and again, though people do not recognize it. … He protects them from the grave, from crossing over the river of death.
>
> —Job 33:14, 18

The still small voice within is clear, precise, gentle, and spoken with authority. Though it is like a whisper, it carries with it a sense of confidence and boldness. He will make us "turn from doing wrong" and "protects us from the grave," and He does it with authority in His voice (Job 33:17–18).

We see the authoritative nature of the still, small voice of the Holy Spirit through the life of Jesus. We learn from Scripture that Jesus had all authority and spoke with that authority.

> And so, it was, when Jesus had ended these sayings, that the people were astonished at His teaching, for He taught them as one having authority, and not as the scribes.
>
> —Matthew 7:28–29, NKJV

> Amazed, the people exclaimed, "What authority and power this man's words possess! Even evil spirits obey him, and they flee at his command!"
>
> —Luke 4:36

Since He is the same yesterday, today, and forever, we know the way He speaks does not change. Jesus Himself knew that His authority was supplied by God. He submitted Himself to the Holy Spirit as the Holy Spirit revealed God's will to Jesus.

Then Jesus answered and said to them, "Most assuredly, I say to you, the Son can do nothing of Himself, but what He sees the Father do; for whatever He does, the Son also does in like manner. … I can of Myself do nothing. As I hear, I judge; and My judgment is righteous because I do not seek My own will but the will of the Father who sent Me."

—John 5:19, 30, NKJV

For I have not spoken on My own authority; but the Father who sent Me gave Me a command, what I should say and what I should speak.

—John 12:49, NKJV

Don't you believe that I am in the Father and the Father is in me? The words I speak are not my own, but my Father who lives in me does his work through me.

—John 14:10

Remember, even though Jesus is the Son of God, He came to the earth as fully man. In coming to earth as fully human, He had to live His life the way we must learn: as people dependent on God and filled with the Spirit of God. Jesus is our model as we seek to be yielded, obedient vessels of His love and power. We, as children of God, have the same Spirit of God in us that spoke with authority to Christ. And we too can hear and see what the Father is saying and doing through that still, small voice that is like a gentle whisper, though authoritative and purposeful.

Reflect

1. Can you think of an example of a metaphor from Scripture in which God is portrayed as authoritative and powerful, as well as gentle and meek?[24]

_____
_____
_____
_____

2. Why is it significant for the Holy Spirit to speak with authority? What does it mean for you as a believer that the still, small voice carries such authority?

___

3. If Christ spoke authoritatively because of the Holy Spirit within Him, and if we have that same Holy Spirit speaking to us in His still, small voice, what does that imply about the power of the words you will speak when you declare the promises and plans He lays on your heart?

___

Pray

Thank You, Father, that Your voice is the voice of authority. As I learn to hear Your voice, empower me to submit to it, especially because if I don't, it leaves me spiritually vulnerable and I miss out on what You have for me. I confess in times past—perhaps even now—I have not always submitted to authority. I repent for any and all rebellion against You, as well as against anyone else who is in authority over me. I know I have not always been submissive, but instead I have rebelled in my heart. I ask that You create in me a soft, pliable, and teachable heart. Let me not rebel against correction or rebuke. Instead, empower me with a submissive spirit and a servant's heart, for this is what I desire, Lord. Quicken me by Your Spirit to recognize when I am yielding to pride, rebellion, or and when I am not recognizing Your voice of authority. I pray this in Jesus's name. Amen.

Listen

Ask the Lord to give you direction regarding a decision you must make. Spend a few minutes silently and expectantly awaiting a response.

My Story
A Literal Move of God

It was 2004, and both my husband, Brian, and I knew we had wanted to move—again. We felt that God was leading us. But where? In our own reasonings and musings we thought that perhaps living right beside his dad on his dad's property was a gift or blessing from God. We immediately put our house up for sale, and immediately, everything went wrong. Strange occurrences began to happen. The foundation suddenly cracked, a huge and intimidating crack. Then our tree in the back yard got struck by lightning, splitting it in half. Next, our tap in the kitchen exploded, and water burst through the pipes. Expense after expense began to consume us, and with all these odd happenings, no one wanted to purchase our house.

Finally, I heard an authoritative and yet gentle voice say, "I want you to fast. Go get the oil, and pour it on your head." At this point in my journey, I did not know that anointing one's head was biblical. However, I knew I was hearing from God because His words were impeccably clear and boasted with authority, so I immediately obeyed. So there I was, kneeling before the Lord with a bottle of olive oil in hand, worship music playing, committing to obedience before God to a time of fasting and prayer. As I bowed before Him, I poured this oil all over my head, and tears were streaming down my face as I felt the weight of His holiness.

On the third day of the fast I heard His still, small voice say, "Read Genesis 12." Again, it was very matter-of-fact and with great authority. I was not sure what Genesis 12 was, so I quickly opened my Bible and began searching for this Scripture. I found it at the front of my Bible.

> *Now the LORD had said to Abram: Get out of your country, from your family, and from your father's house, to a land that I will show you.*
>
> *—Genesis 12:1, NKJV*

Wow! I was in shock at God's uncanny ability to get through to me so precisely. "Get out of your country" was confirmation we were still to move, and "from your family, and from your father's house" was a clear indication we were going in the wrong direction. "To a land that I will show you" was a vivid instruction that He was going to lead us elsewhere. This was a beautiful example of God's logos word becoming a rhema *just for me.*

I remember telling God that He would have to tell my husband that living on his dad's property was not God's plan for us. I felt that God had to be the one to tell Brian and not me. Therefore, I held this instruction in my heart and chose to pray daily for Brian instead.

God is faithful. Week after week, Brian would come home from work only to inform me of yet another reason he felt we shouldn't be moving onto his dad's property until finally I could not contain myself any longer and boasted about my time in fasting and prayer with God. Both of us had a good laugh. Of course, by then we had already taken our house off the market because our six-month time with our realtor was up with no—and I mean zero—offers.

I kid you not, not even a week later Brian and I were finishing up the dishes when we heard the doorbell ring. As I opened the door, tea towel in hand, a very conservative, professional-looking lady in a long, tan trench coat proceeded to say, "Hi there. This may sound strange, but I noticed that you're for-sale sign has been taken down for quite some time. I was wondering if you were still thinking of moving. Would it be OK if I came in to see your home?"

I was stunned. "Sure," I replied.

After she finished the tour, she turned to look at both Brian and I and said, "This is my home. I don't know what you think of this, but I believe that God is giving me this home, and I am to buy it. Does that sound strange? I knew it the moment I saw your plaque that says, 'Faith, hope, and love, but the greatest of these is love.'"

All we could do is smile. Because I had listened to and obeyed the authoritative and gentle voice of the Holy Spirit, God sold our house without a realtor and for more than asking price!

Day 18

God Speaks Spontaneously, Unmistakeably, and with Purpose

So shall My word be that goes forth from My mouth; It shall not return to Me void, But it shall accomplish what I please, And it shall prosper in the thing for which I sent it.

—Isaiah 55:11, NKJV

Unless you are actively pursuing God in prayer or reading the Word with the expectation of His leading, the still, small voice of God will often come spontaneously and may seem out of the blue. These messages usually come as an interrupted thought or idea, something that you were not thinking about.

All throughout Scripture we find the phrase "the word of God came, saying …" or "the word of God came to me." In most instances in which this reference is used, the people were not thinking about God or even communicating with God at the time of the message. Instead, God came and immediately said something. He appeared or showed up suddenly and immediately began speaking His heart.

We see an example of this in 1 Chronicles 17. The chapter begins with David sharing his concerns to Nathan, the prophet. Nathan settled David by telling him to do all that was in his heart, for God was with him. Presumably, then, they parted ways. In the following verse it says, "But that night the word of God came to Nathan, saying …" (v.3, NIV). It doesn't tell us that Nathan was seeking God or that he was already conversing with God. Instead, it says it happened "that night the word of God came … saying." This implies that it was suddenly or spontaneously. Nathan wasn't expecting it or seeking it. Instead, God appeared to Nathan and immediately began correcting him. Remember, Nathan's logical counsel to David was for him to do all that was in his heart. God, on the other hand, showed up and instructed Nathan to set the record straight. David was not to do what was in heart, which was to build God a house to dwell in. Even though David's purposes were good, it was not the will of God. God interjected His thoughts and heart to Nathan concerning David; thus, Nathan acknowledged it was indeed God speaking.

Remember the story of Samuel? The boy was lying in bed, when "*suddenly* the LORD called out to him" (1 Sam. 3:4, emphasis added). Samuel ran to Eli, thinking it was the voice of his mentor, but Eli confessed that it was not him, nor had he heard the voice calling to Samuel. (This is another proof that Samuel was hearing the still, small voice of the Holy Spirit.) Then a second time the Lord spoke to Samuel, and again he went running into Eli's room, saying, "Here I am, for you called me" (v. 5, NKJV). Three times God called on Samuel until finally Eli perceived that it was the Lord and instructed Samuel to respond, "Speak, your servant is listening" (v. 10). Now Samuel, even though he was dedicated to God and was ministering unto the Lord, he did not yet know the Lord intimately. Samuel had not heard His voice, which is why the message was not only sudden but also unfamiliar. (On one hand, he was a young boy who was still growing in the things of God. On the other hand, the voice of the Lord was not yet revealed to him because the word of the Lord was rare in his time; there was no widespread revelation.)

Let's not forget Paul. "As he journeyed he came near Damascus, *and suddenly* a light shone around him from heaven. Then he fell to the ground and heard a voice saying to him, 'Saul, Saul, why are you persecuting Me?'" (Acts 9:3–4, NKJV, emphasis added). And Paul replied, "Who are you, lord?" (v. 5). Here was this man who was busy persecuting Christians and on his way to Damascus when suddenly—out of the blue—the Lord spoke to him and called Paul to go into the city, and he would be told what he must do.

In the cases of both Samuel and Paul, neither was expecting or waiting on a word from the Lord. His voice interrupted their actions suddenly, and yet is significant that each message was unmistakeable. Even though God's initial message to Samuel came only as his name—"Suddenly the LORD called out, 'Samuel!'" (1 Sam. 3:4)—God persisted in His message until Samuel understood that it was God and then responded. In the conversation that followed, there was no guessing what was being said. When God spoke to Paul, His voice might have come out of the blue, but the message was immediately clear and purposeful. If we were to scan the pages of the Bible from beginning to end and stop to read every time we see, "And God said," or, "And God did," we would see that God is understandable. God never left anyone confused or having to guess at His purpose when He spoke a word to them, and neither did He perform signs without purpose. There is an important lesson here for us: If you must guess whether or not you are hearing the Lord, it's probably not God. His voice is authoritative and spontaneous and abundantly clear.

However, we must not mistake the spontaneous nature of the voice of God as meaning His words to us lack planning and intent. Whenever God speaks, He has a purpose in mind. In the stories of both Samuel and Paul, we must not overlook the fact that the Lord's message in each case came with a clearly stated purpose. In Isaiah 55:11 God says that His spoken words will always "accomplish all I want ... [them] to, and ... prosper everywhere I send it." This implies that every message from the Lord carries a distinct purpose, which is certain to be fulfilled.

A perfect example of the purposeful and effective nature of God's spoken word is the story of Creation. God's voice echoed in the heavens when He said, "'Let there be light,' and there was light. ... God called the light 'day' and the darkness 'night.' And evening passed and morning came, marking the first day" (Gen. 1:3, 5). God spoke specific commands, and matter formed into the Earth and space from nothing. When He speaks, His word "always produces fruit" (Isa. 55:11). God had a purpose, specific reasons, for creating the world. In the Book of Psalms it testifies, "The heavens *declare* the glory of God; the skies *proclaim* the work of his hands" (Ps. 19:1, NIV, emphasis added). Apparently God created the heavens and our world as a visible expression of His handiwork.

Regardless of how God chooses to speak, His intentions remain the same: to draw us into deeper fellowship and intimacy with Himself and give us abundant life. We may rest assured that if we have a heart to know Him more deeply, He will not only reach out to our spirit with His voice, but He will do it in such a way that we cannot miss His call.

Reflect

1. In your own words, what does it mean that the voice of God is often spontaneous, always purposeful, and unmistakeable? What does this mean for your life specifically?

_____
_____
_____
_____

2. Which of the three biblical events shared in this chapter—Samuel's encounter with God, Paul's conversion encounter on the road to Damascus, or the Creation story—resonates with you most strongly? What is it about the way in which God speaks in that particular account that strikes a chord in your spirit?

_____
_____
_____
_____

3. Have you ever found yourself surprised by the voice of God speaking into your life at a particular moment? If so, describe the experience. Were you able immediately to identify the way in which the message was purposeful and clear, or did it take some follow-up prayers to understand it fully?

_____
_____
_____
_____

Pray

Heavenly Father, I invite You to speak to me anytime You desire. Break through the noise in my day and visit me. I long to walk in Your purposes for my life. I desire to follow You. Guide my steps and enlighten me to Your path. When I read stories in the Bible of how You came to others, Lord, this excites me. I want that too! Give me ears to hear, eyes to see, and a heart that is receptive to the moving of Your Spirit in my life. I pray this in Jesus's name. Amen.

Listen

Ask the Lord to direct you regarding whom to pray for. Spend a few minutes silently and expectantly awaiting a response and then pray for him or her as led.

Day 19

The Wisdom of God

But the wisdom from above is first of all pure. It is also peace loving, gentle at all times, and willing to yield to others. It is full of mercy and the fruit of good deeds. It shows no favoritism and is always sincere.

—James 3:17

When God speaks, it is wise, insightful, and carries powerful boldness with it. And as the above scripture reveals, it is also pure, peace-loving, gentle at all times, and willing to yield to others. God's wisdom is full of mercy and carries the fruit of good deeds. It shows no favoritism and is always sincere. When you hear it, either within yourself or through someone else, you know that it wasn't something that came from the human mind but instead from the Spirit of wisdom above.

Peter and John are great examples of the wisdom of God in operation. We read in the Book of Acts that when they preached people perceived that they had been with Jesus because both Peter and John spoke with incredible wisdom, though they were uneducated and untrained men. (See Acts 4:13.) The wisdom that had come from their mouths made it undeniable that they had been with Wisdom Himself.

Paul's life and ministry bore witness to the same. He wrote in 1 Corinthians 2:6–7, 10–13:

> We do, however, speak a message of wisdom among the mature, but not the wisdom of this age or of the rulers of this age, who are coming to nothing. No, we declare God's wisdom, a mystery that has been hidden and that God destined for our glory before time began. ... These are the things God has revealed to us by his Spirit. The Spirit searches all things, even the deep things of God. For who knows a person's thoughts except their own spirit within them? In the same way no one knows the thoughts of God except the Spirit of God. What we have received is not the spirit of the world, but the Spirit who is from God, so that we may understand

what God has freely given us. This is what we speak, not in words taught us by human wisdom but in words taught by the Spirit, explaining spiritual realities with Spirit-taught words.

—NIV

Each of these men of God also carried an authority that revealed their encounter with Jesus.

You and I are filled with the same Spirit of wisdom that ignited the words of Peter, John, Paul, and Jesus during their ministries. We should expect that He will share with us the same powerful insight and knowledge that He gave them. We should also expect, however, that wisdom to come to us in a variety of forms. Sometimes it is an impartation of wisdom in the things of God so that we can grow in our knowledge of Him and share it with others. At other times it may be wisdom about a circumstance or situation we are facing and about which we need guidance. It can also come as a discerning of spirits during prayer. When this happens, God will reveal what spirit(s) is coming at an individual so that they can take authority over the spirit and repent of sin if necessary in order for the warfare or attack to cease.

One way in which we receive an impartation of the Holy Spirit's wisdom is when during a ministry time or when praying with someone and the Holy Spirit gives us a word of knowledge, which offers us supernatural insight into a person or circumstance that we couldn't have known without the leading of the Lord. Then we receive a word of wisdom with respect to what that individual needs to do in that situation. Words of knowledge offer supernatural knowledge that informs, but a word of wisdom is the supernatural knowing of how to apply what was revealed. Then it is up to the recipient to receive and act on that word.

Sometimes this insight may come through a word or phrase spoken by the still, small voice. At other times it may come to you as a picture or visual representation as you pray for someone. As a means of showing rather than telling you what the process of receiving a word of knowledge and/or a word of wisdom and then sharing it with someone looks like, I've included a number of examples from my own life and ministry. As you read them, I urge you to consider a few factors:

1. In what form did the word of knowledge and/or word of wisdom come? Was it through the still, small voice, through a picture or vision, or a combination of the two?

2. What did the interaction between my thought process and the Holy Spirit look like? Was it a one-sided impartation of information from God, or was it a back-and-forth conversation?

3. What was the "tone" of the message or word? Was it marked by the comforting and encouraging presence of the Paraclete Encourager Spirit?

4. Was there confirmation of the word spoken to each person? If so, what did it look like?

5. What might have been the scriptural support for the word of knowledge and/or word of wisdom the Holy Spirit laid on my heart in each case? How would each of these individuals have gone about testing the spirits?

Chopping Wood

As I was praying in the Spirit for a specific individual, I began to see the person chopping wood. I could see someone else with them, and I could identify that the relationship was estranged, as the two individuals were not side by side but had great distance between them. (Seeing the chopping of the wood, the two individuals, and the estrangement were all words of knowledge.)

In my mind, I kept asking God what the interpretation was, but all I heard Him say was to reveal the vision literally, without interpretation. The still, small voice kept repeating that I was to tell this individual precisely what I saw and then to encourage them. I obeyed and immediately related what I saw. Then, upon my obedience, I received a word of wisdom. The Lord revealed that as they kept coming together with this other individual, there would be a breakthrough in the relationship.

When I finished relating what I had seen, the person commented with absolute shock that they were going to chop wood together that weekend, though the relationship between both parties had been a difficult one. This individual was thinking about canceling chopping wood together in despair that the attempts to repair the relationship weren't making any difference. This fresh word of knowledge and the word of wisdom that came from the Lord were the encouragement this person needed to keep trying.

The Fragrant, Dried-Up Daisy

Another time, as I was seeking the Lord as to what He wanted to say to a specific individual, I saw a picture of a dried-up daisy. It was all alone and shriveled up. The stem and leaves of this daisy were brown and brittle. In fact, this flower was so dry that if you were to pick it, it would break. I perceived that the flower was symbolic of this individual. It was an instant supernatural knowing, a wordless impression. Yet, coming from this flower was this fantastic and sweet smelling-aroma. The fragrance was so aromatic that people all around it were attracted to the smell. As I continued to pray through this vision, I saw the Lord drizzling little raindrops from the heavens upon the flower, and immediately I was made aware of the interpretation. The still, small voice began to speak to me.

The interpretation was as follows: These drops of rain were symbolic of God restoring the person for whom I was praying. It represented a slow process of healing—God being intimate with her little by little and giving to her precisely what she needed. If He were to pour His rain upon her, it would just break her. He revealed that tiny drops of rain would allow her to drink it up, giving nourishment right down to the root, then up the stem and into the flower.

When I was finished, she confirmed that she was, in fact, all dried up. She had felt all alone in her walk with God and with others. She shared that she was quite depressed. She also confessed that the daisy was her favorite flower. Now, several years later, this prophetic word has come to pass, and this individual has grown leaps and bounds.

Striking Out

Once again, while I was praying for one particular individual I began to see her playing baseball, except she kept striking out. (This was a word of knowledge.) I thought, "Lord, this doesn't look very encouraging," but I kept pressing in. In other words, I kept asking God, "What else?" And, "What are You saying, Lord?" I sensed the Lord say she was feeling like there were many things in her life lately where she felt she was just striking out and getting nowhere. This sensing was supernatural in that I was not linking my thoughts together or thinking this vision through. Instead, I supernaturally perceived it. It was an instantaneous knowing what the interpretation was. It was like God dropped the entire meaning of the vision into my consciousness word for word. However, He *told* me (I heard Him say this very clearly and precisely) that she was about to hit the ball, so she should not lose heart but keep trying. I felt the Lord wanted me to relate to her the picture I saw and compare it to how He told me she was feeling recently. (This was a word of wisdom.)

When I was finished, she turned and looked at me with a grin on her face and said, "Yep, I love baseball, and in reality, I usually strike out!" Isn't it neat how God will bring natural things in our lives to relate to us spiritually?

The Wheel Within a Wheel

I had been praying for a friend of mine around the time I was first learning to hear God. As I was interceding for her, suddenly I saw a wheel inside of a wheel. The Lord quickened me to Ezekiel 1, John 4, and Isaiah 11:2. I immediately grabbed my Bible, and the Scriptures confirmed that God was showing me the seven spirits of God, or the seven attributes of the Holy Spirit (since there are not seven of the Holy Spirit Himself but rather just one). He also revealed to me that she was going to need the Spirit of wisdom for an upcoming decision. I had to tell her what I saw, so as soon as I spotted her at church I immediately went over to share.

When I had finished telling her, she said, "If I didn't know any better, I'd think you have been in my prayer closet with me. I am studying the seven spirits right now, and I am on the Spirit of wisdom. Yes, I do need wisdom for a specific decision." I was so encouraged by her response. I really felt that that word was just as much for me as it was for her in that it encouraged me to know that I had been hearing God correctly and accurately. It was very much a learning experience in hearing God.

Reflect

1. By now you have been listening for the voice of the Lord for four weeks as we have journeyed through this study together. In that time, what have you heard from the Lord? Has it been a word or message for you specifically, or have you also received a word for someone else, as in the examples above? Choose one instance in which the Lord spoke to you and examine the experience using the five questions at the start of this chapter.

_____
_____
_____
_____

2. It is important to check in regularly with the Lord to ensure we are growing and following the path He would have us on. As you reflect on the words or messages you have received from the Lord, and after reading the testimonies in this chapter, is there anything you feel the Holy Spirit prompting you to change or adjust with respect to how you seek His voice?

_____
_____
_____
_____

Pray

Heavenly Father, thank You for Your wisdom. I covet Your wisdom in every area of my life, as well as when ministering to others. You said in Your Word that we are to earnestly desire the best gifts and to desire earnestly to prophesy (1 Cor. 12:31; 14:39). Therefore, Father, I desire to prophesy and to receive words of knowledge and words of wisdom. I also ask that You train my ears to know when wisdom is speaking to me. Help me to remember Your Word, which reveals that Your wisdom is pure, peace-loving, gentle at all times, and willing to yield to others. God's wisdom is full of mercy and carries the fruit of good deeds. It shows no favoritism and is always sincere. (See James 3:17.) I pray this in Jesus's name. Amen.

Listen

Share with the Lord something that has been weighing on your mind. Ask the Lord to replace your concern or worry with His peace and give you a word of wisdom about how to proceed. Spend a few minutes silently and expectantly awaiting a response.

Day 20

God's Wisdom Is Greater

For My thoughts are not your thoughts, nor are your ways My ways, says the Lord. For as the heavens are higher than the earth, so are My ways higher than your ways, and My thoughts than your thoughts.

—Isaiah 55:8–9

God's wisdom often defies the logic of the human mind. It supersedes human reasoning and therefore requires faith in God's Word. Remember:

- David killed the giant Goliath with a stone and a slingshot. Man's wisdom said David needed armor, needed to be bigger and stronger, etc. (See 1 Samuel 17:45–50.)

- Gideon defeated one hundred thirty-five thousand Midianites with only three hundred men. Even at full size, Gideon's army of thirty-two thousand was outmatched by the Midianite horde, but God gradually pared down the number of the Israelite army until so small a number remained that logic would have seemed to dictate that victory would be impossible. But nothing is impossible with God. (See Judges 7.)

- The walls of Jericho fell after Joshua's men encircled them seven times at the command of the Lord. (See Joshua 6.) Logic would say, "Get behind me, Satan. How could circling a building bring the walls down?" Nonetheless, Joshua's obedience to the Lord's instructions brought them victory.

- The Shunammite widow cried out to the prophet Elisha asking for his help saving her sons from the creditors who were threatening to sell them into slavery. (See 2 Kings 4:1–7.) Under the inspiration of the Holy Spirit, Elisha instructed her to borrow as many empty jars as she could and then begin to pour olive oil from a flask—the only thing she had left in her house—into those jars. Inexplicably, the oil in the flask was multiplied so that every jar she had collected was full of oil to the brim. Had she not heeded Elisha's counsel, as odd as it may have been, she would not have received her miracle. Had she reasoned within herself, she may have talked herself out of seeing God's provision. Or, had she been lazy, she would have remained in poverty and lost her sons.

- Though she only had a handful of flour and a little oil in a jar to feed her family, the widow of Zarephath honored God by feeding the prophet Elijah first and was rewarded when God multiplied the flour and oil so that she was able to feed her household for many days. (See 1 Kings 17:8–16.) Logic would have reasoned that the handful of flour and the wee bit of oil would have disappeared after one use, but her obedience to the word of the Lord through the prophet saved her family.

- Jesus told the fisherman to let down their nets again for a catch after they had toiled all night and caught nothing. Upon His word, they extracted a significant number of fish, so many that their net was breaking! (See Luke 5:4–6.) What did logic say in this story?

Logic will often reason within oneself and question the operation of faith. After all, it was logic and reasoning that got Eve into trouble when the serpent whispered, "Did God really say?" (Gen. 3:1). Hebrews 11:1 tells us that "faith is the substance of things hoped for, the evidence of things not seen" (KJV). God operates in the realm of faith because His words are substance; they carry life, spirit, wisdom, power, and creative ability. Man, through human logic, cannot comprehend this. Often man wants to see, know, hear, first, and then believe, but faith requires one to accept first, obey second, and *then* it will manifest. It takes faith to hear and obey God, because God operates in the realm of faith—His spiritual law that is governed in the earth! His wisdom supersedes our human logic. Childlike faith requires obedience against what the mind wants to reason. The bottom line? One must learn to surrender his/her logic and will to God's wisdom and control.

> The message of the cross is foolishness to those who are perishing, but to us who are being saved, it is the power of God. For it is written: "I will destroy the wisdom of the wise; the intelligence of the intelligent I will frustrate."
>
> —1 Corinthians 1:18–19, NKJV

All throughout Scripture, we read how God gave instructions, directions, and purpose to both men and women upon their willingness to hear and obey. We often don't understand God's wisdom—His way of doing things—but our obedience to His voice carries benefits that far exceed our intelligence! I ask you, What would have happened if David had panicked because all he had were stones and a slingshot? Or if the fisherman had they obeyed their logic instead of the voice of Jesus? Imagine Noah and how he must have felt building an ark when it hadn't even rained yet or poor Abraham when God first told him he would have descendants as many as the stars in the sky, yet he was one hundred years old and had a barren wife? Logically speaking, these scenarios made no sense.

We must hear and obey. Learn to set aside logic and reasoning only when and if what you hear lines up with who God is, His ways, and His Word. Many people miss the move of God in their lives because they are not acquainted with the voice of God. Instead, they allow their voice of reason and logic to talk them out of God's move in their life. You will not be confident if you are not sure what the Bible says, so build up your confidence and dive into the Word. Only you are responsible for renewing your mind to the truth that God is a good God; if He is asking you to do something, believe it is because He loves you. He knows better than you do. He has your future in mind. He can see all things, and He knows what He has purposed for you to do in this lifetime. Guaranteed, it will be more incredible than you and I can do in our striving or logic.

I can certainly attest to that. I have lived a life of faith and obedience, and it has been nothing short of an adventure. It might seem scary at times, even stressful, but rest assured God will go with you. It may seem illogical, but God knows best!

Reflect

1. Has God ever prompted you or asked you to do something that seemed crazy or even impossible? What was it? Did you obey, or did human reasoning and fear get the better of you? If you obeyed, what was the outcome? If the latter, what would you do differently if you could go back and do it all over again?

_____
_____
_____
_____

2. Summarize Hebrews 11:1 in your own words. What does it look like in your life and walk with God when you walk in the full assurance that "faith is the substance of things hoped for, the evidence of things not seen" (KJV)?

_____
_____
_____
_____

3. Do you find that it is easy for you to accept even "illogical" instructions from the Lord, or is it hard for you to get past human reasoning in order to obey? If the latter, make a plan for how you will surrender your mind and will to the Lord so that you can walk in full obedience without doubt.

_____
_____
_____
_____

Pray

Heavenly Father, I come hungry for Your wisdom. I am tired of doing things in my own strength and with my own wisdom. Your wisdom supersedes anything I could ever think or imagine. You are the One who knows all things, sees all things, is before all things, and knows the beginning to the end. I choose to lay down my logic and ask that You align my mind, my will, my emotions, and my intellect with Your wisdom. I surrender my logic and will to Your wisdom and control, for Your thoughts are not my thoughts, nor are my ways Your ways. As the heavens are higher than the earth, so are Your ways higher than my ways, and Your thoughts than my thoughts. In any situation I face where I lack wisdom, I will ask for Your wisdom, believing and not doubting that You will give wisdom to me liberally and without reproach. I pray this in Jesus's name. Amen.

Exercise

Worship. Then ask the Lord, "God, will you speak to me with Your still, small voice? Tell me what Your vision is for my life (or health, family, ministry, finances, business, etc.)." Journal what you hear. Judge what you hear.

My Story
Trusting His Word for Me

December 8, 2008. I was having my quiet time with the Lord. I sat still before Him, waiting for His still, small voice. This is what I heard:

My daughter, oh, how you have grown and sprouted in Me. I fashioned you from the beginning and will complete you until the day of Jesus Christ. Abide in Me, and I in you. For it is no longer you who lives, but Christ in you. You have been crucified with Christ on the cross. Every nail I endured, every thorn that was driven in My skull, every lash that I was beaten with, I did for you that you could be free.

You have memories from the past that cause self-hatred. Today, I am washing that away. Remember the vision where I was with you, and you were nailed to the cross? It was symbolic of you dying, the old you as well as dying daily to Me. My blood washes you clean from all your past. All things are forgiven. Today, you will walk resurrected from the strings or cords that link you to past behaviors, for you are a new creation in Me. I have loved you with an everlasting love, and with lovingkindness I have drawn you.

Rest in Me, for rest belongs to My children. Be confident in this new season of favor. I have anointed you and given you a new level of authority. Do not hold back because of your youth. Be prepared to operate in every good gift that I have given you. Do not be concerned what others are thinking, for I have placed within their hearts a longing for Me through you. Be strong and of good courage, for I am with you.

This word proved to be true. On January 11, 2009, I had my first women's book exchange. God began revealing Himself so powerfully to these women through me that even I was surprised at times. He was faithful to His word. Those women longed for Him, and He responded with healings, plus accurate prophecy like I had never experienced. Words of knowledge and words of wisdom were spoken through my mouth with boldness and authority.

Many of these women had not experienced God in this way. In fact, many had doubts that this was even possible for today. But with God nothing is impossible, and He loved them with extravagant love. He drew them closer to Himself. He created a hunger for His love, for an intimate connection with His voice, and impartation began to explode. Women who had never experienced prophecy knew without a shadow of a doubt that God was speaking to them. They experienced visions that not only confirmed His intimate involvement within this group but revealed His affectionate involvement in their personal lives. Jesus was lifted high.

Had I reasoned against this word or let fear settle in my heart, I would have missed all that God did through me for these precious women. Don't miss what I am saying: Though fear was present, I did it anyway. Instead of yielding to my own wisdom or the fear that tried to cease God's plan, I obeyed God and moved passed the fear. Had I waited for some sign in heaven—or simply waited for God to move—it never would have happened. I heard the word and made the necessary arrangements to begin a simple book exchange in my home. Upon obedience, then God birthed it into what He wanted in the first place.

Lesson Five

God's Voice, Satan's Voice, and Your Voice

Day 21

Not Every Thought Is Your Own

We demolish arguments and every pretension that sets itself up against the knowledge of God, and we take captive every thought to make it obedient to Christ.

—2 Corinthians 10:5, NIV

As we saw in the last lesson, it is important for us to realize there is a difference between when God speaks and our intellectual, logical thinking, which comes from our soul. Man's thoughts tend to be sequential, which means we are built to logically think things through by joining thoughts together. When God speaks to our spirit, however, it is a sudden and complete thought that often interrupts our natural thought processes. You see, man analyzes. He reasons within himself and with others. He tries to figure things out to make sense of things. It's the story we tell ourselves. God created man this way, to think with the soul, but He also endowed us with a spirit that is built for hearing from and speaking to His Spirit. We must learn to tell the difference between thoughts coming from our soul, from His Holy Spirit, and from other, evil spirits.

Before we can discern the source of a thought or word that we think we have received, it is important for us to know how God made us. The Bible says we have a soul, which is made up of our mind, will, and emotions; a spirit; and a physical body. First Thessalonians 5:23 says, "May the God of peace Himself sanctify you completely; and may your whole spirit, soul, and body be preserved blameless at the coming of our Lord Jesus Christ" (NKJV). Thus, we are three-part beings—spirit, soul, and body—made in the image of God, who also is a triune being. (See Genesis 1:26.) Hebrews 4:12 verifies this as well: "For the word of God is living and powerful, and sharper than any two-edged sword, piercing even to the division of soul and spirit, and of joints and marrow" (NKJV). The phrase *joints and marrow* refers to the body. We need to know this to be able to differentiate between our soul—the way we think and our spirit—how God speaks to us.

Our spirits, which have been made new upon salvation and are now one with the Spirit of

God, already have the mind of Christ and know all things (1 Cor. 6:17; 2:10–12, 16). But our souls need to be renewed to those truths which can only be learned through God's Word. When we read God's Word we are receiving His wisdom with our physical eyes. As we meditate on it, pondering with our soul and then asking the Holy Spirit to speak to us and enlighten these truths to us, He then opens our spiritual eyes, and the light bulb goes on, so to speak. Suddenly we see it differently. Now we see it with the eyes of our hearts, which can also be seen with our spirit. (Remember the Greek word I mentioned earlier *ruwach*, which is translated "heart" or "spirit"?) That is when our spirit and our soul become one mind and we bear witness to God's truth. In other words, when God's Word takes root in our mind, that same knowledge which already exists in our spirit rises and bears witness, and now our soul and spirit are in harmony! It bears witness because we have the Holy Spirit within as our inner witness.

When our soul and spirit are not in harmony, then we are in double-mindedness. Double-mindedness is where doubt creeps in because our mind will reason against what God says, especially if we don't understand the message. This is often when Satan tempts our soul to reason against God's Word and instead induces us to believe in our feelings, circumstances, or what we see with our physical eyes or consider to be logical. So, let's begin to differentiate and discern between God's voice, Satan's voice, and our own so we can avoid this error.

Reflect

1. What does it mean that we are three-part beings, made in the image of a triune (three-part) God?
_____
_____
_____
_____

2. What is our soul made up of? How is it different from our spirit?
_____
_____
_____
_____

3. How does not having our soul and spirit in harmony make us susceptible to the temptation of Satan?
_____
_____
_____
_____

Pray

Heavenly Father, thank You that I am made in Your image and that because of Christ's work on the cross I am one with your Spirit and have the mind of Christ. Lord, I want my whole being—spirit, soul, and body—to be in total agreement with Your will and Word. Renew my mind to Your truth so that my soul and spirit may function in perfect harmony, as you created them to function. Protect me from any attempt of the enemy to confuse me or cause me to exalt my own reasoning over Your Word. Help me to learn how to distinguish between Your voice, my own thoughts, and the whispers of the enemy. In Jesus's name, amen.

Listen

Ask the Lord to bring to your memory or otherwise lead you to a Bible verse that communicates how He feels about you. Spend a few minutes silently and expectantly awaiting a response.

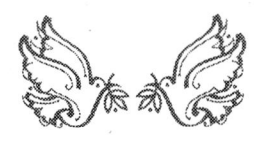

Day 22

The Characteristics of God's Voice

> To Him who rides on the heaven of heavens, which were of old! Indeed, He sends out His voice, a mighty voice.
>
> —Psalm 68:33, NKJV

Let's start our study on how to differentiate between our voice, God's voice, and Satan's voice by looking at the characteristics and qualities of God's voice or forms of communication. We know that when God speaks to our spirit, it is a spontaneous, purposeful, and complete thought, prompting, picture, or knowing that is just dropped in our spirits. To discern whether or not to trust it, we know that we must measure it against Scripture. While we are still growing in our familiarity with the Bible, James 3:17 is an excellent litmus test that allows us to judge a word based on our knowledge of the nature of God:

> The wisdom that is from above is first pure, then peaceable, gentle, willing to yield, full of mercy and good fruits, without partiality and without hypocrisy.
>
> —NKJV

First, ask yourself, is what you are sensing pure? God is, above all, pure. He will never ask you to do something that is impure, unholy, or immoral (according to His moral standards, not ours). Because He is holy, He will lead in holiness and purity. God will never tempt you to do wrong.

> Let no one say when he is tempted, "I am tempted by God"; for God cannot be tempted by evil, nor does He tempt anyone.
>
> —James 1:13, NKJV

Second, does it give you peace or pressure? God's voice is peaceable because He is peaceful, patient, gentle, and willing to yield. (See Isaiah 9:6; 26:3; 28:16; Galatians 5:22; Ephesians 2:14; Philippians 4:7; Romans 8:6–9, 12.) God gives us a sense of peace when He leads us and we obey because He always instructs according to His character and nature. As stated earlier, we are also instructed to "let the peace that comes from Christ rule in … [our] hearts" (Col. 3:15). Another version of that scripture says it this way: "And let the peace (soul harmony which comes) from Christ rule (act as umpire continually) in your hearts [deciding and settling with finality all questions that arise in your minds, in that peaceful state] to which as [members of Christ's] one body you were also called [to live]" (AMPC). Isaiah 48:18 tells us, "Oh, that you had listened to my commandments! Then you would have had peace flowing like a gentle river," and Isaiah 26:3 promises, "You will keep in perfect peace all who trust in you, all whose thoughts are fixed on you!" Peace is our umpire that will alert us to when we have our eyes, thoughts, and heart focused on the Lord.

Third, God is never in a hurry but is willing to yield. Why? Because He is peace, and the fruit of His Spirit is patience. He does not pressure but leads through His peace and patience. There are situations when we sense an urgency or bubbling forth from within and need to respond, like an urgency to pray, speak, or act in a way that can be time sensitive; yet we will still be at peace in the midst of the situation. The Word tells us, "Whoever believes will not act hastily" (Isa. 28:16, NKJV), so we know that God would not pressure us into acting "hastily" because it goes against His character and Word. God doesn't need us to rush ahead.

Further, we know that the opposite of peace is confusion, and "God is not the author of confusion but of peace" (1 Cor. 14:33, NKJV). If what you are sensing brings befuddlement or feels like a sense of pressure to act now, without the witness of peace, then know that it is not from God but of the devil through the flesh. (See James 3:14–16.) In this state of mind, do not act, but wait on the Lord for clarity of peace and pray. Learn to not act out of emotion. Instead, take all emotions to God, including worry and pressure. Philippians 4:6–7 admonishes us, "Don't worry about anything … You will experience God's peace, which exceeds anything we can understand." If a word is from God, you will experience His peace.

Fourth, God's Word is full of mercy and good fruit, and it is without favoritism (Rom. 2:11) and hypocrisy. When He speaks it is to produce good fruit and will never contradict His Word, the Bible. He will not act for someone else's good but not for yours. That would be favoritism. He will not say one thing in His Bible and then something opposite in prayer or in bearing witness to you. That would be hypocrisy.

This four-point litmus test from James 3:17 is helpful, but it does not do away with the need for us to be discerning of our heart. A very good friend of mine says this: "There can be times when we don't like what God may be asking, or we are not ready to obey God. Therefore, choosing the path of least resistance brings our soul into a false sense of peace because we have now removed the thing through disobedience that is causing us pressure." When this happens, our spirit may be at peace upon the unction, but our soul has not yet recognized it. This is a clue that the false sense of peace we are experiencing is soulish and not deep in our spirit. (It takes practice to understand the difference.) If we hear something over and over; if it keeps coming to our mind; and if it lines up with God's character, Word, and nature but you don't want to do it, *do it*! That is God trying to get your attention. We don't want to fall into a false peace and miss what God has for us.

Nonetheless, if you still find yourself confused or unsure about whether or not what you are hearing is God, there is hope. Even when we are struggling to understand the word of the Lord for us, God will persist in His desire to communicate what He needs to get across. If we are not sure that what we heard was from God, in His goodness He will repeat Himself. In Genesis 41:32 the Word tells us, "And the dream was *repeated* to Pharaoh *twice* because the thing is established by God, and God will shortly bring it to pass" (NKJV, emphasis added) Another example of God's persistence is found in 2 Corinthians 13:1, where it reads, "This will be the third time I am coming to you. 'By the mouth of two or three witnesses, every word shall be established'" (NKJV). Finally, as the last example, if we read the story of Abraham we will notice how often God spoke His word to Abraham about having descendants from Isaac. Not only was this to encourage Abraham because of the circumstances that looked opposed to the fulfillment of God's word, but it was also to establish in his heart that when God speaks, He will bring it to pass.

God will also offer gentle correction, opening and closing doors to steer us back into His will, when we miss His voice speaking to us. In Acts 16 we read that Paul wanted to go and preach the gospel in certain cities. Obviously his intentions were good, but it was, however, not what God had desired for him to do. The Book of Acts tells us he and Silas were "forbidden by the Holy Spirit to preach" and that "the Spirit did not permit them" (Acts 16:6–7, NKJV). Finally, God appeared to Paul in a vision to provide him with unmistakeable direction since Paul and Silas were having a hard time discerning the will of the Lord. Recognize what took place in this story: The apostles were not experiencing the peace of God in their ministry because they were out of sync with the Lord's direction, so the Holy Spirit came to Paul in another way, through a vision. He revealed to Paul where he was to go with unmistakeable clarity. Even if we think we have heard from God and step out by faith motivated by love to do what we believe, God is willing and able to close those doors and lovingly bring us back to where we need to be. So don't be afraid to step out, because if your heart is pure, God will redirect you peacefully and without undue pressure. God honors the purity of our hearts to serve Him.

Reflect

1. Why do you think James 3:17 tells us that the wisdom of God is "*first* pure," and then those other things? What is the significance of purity such that it would be first?

_____
_____
_____
_____

2. Sometimes when we are just learning to hear from the Lord the process of discernment can feel stressful and complicated, making it hard for us to sense His peace. Think back on a time when you felt the Lord gave you a word to share with someone else or an action item that made you nervous. How did you know it was the Lord in spite of your stress and confusion? Looking back, what hallmarks were there of His presence even in the midst of the whirlwind of emotions? Or, now that you look at the situation in retrospect, is it possible that it wasn't the Lord?

_____
_____
_____
_____

3. Paul is one of the great men of the Bible, and even he struggled on at least one occasion with hearing the direction of the Lord clearly. What does this mean for you as you learn to discern His voice? How should you feel about your growth in this area, knowing what you do about Paul and about God's willingness to make His message unmistakeable?

_____
_____
_____
_____

Pray

Father, it is so refreshing to know that You are speaking to me. It brings my heart joy to know that You desire to communicate with me. When I consider the lengths to which you will go to help me hear Your voice it fills me with hope and drives away my worry about missing the mark or failing to hear you well. God, give me a passion for Your written Word so that judging a message or word against it becomes like second nature. Give me confidence and practice recognizing the hallmarks of Your voice, and help me not to become frustrated or confused while I am still learning. In Jesus's name, amen.

Listen

Is there a word or answer you feel the Lord has given you either directly or through another person, but you still want confirmation that it is from Him? Ask the Lord to confirm that word for you clearly and unmistakeably. Spend a few minutes silently and expectantly awaiting a response.

My Story
Whispers of Love

I was out having a birthday lunch for a very good friend of mine, and in the midst of a deep, engaging conversation I heard the Lord speak to my spirit, saying, "I want you to give your waitress twenty dollars and tell her I love her." When she finally came back to check up on us, I pulled the money out of my wallet, smiled at my waitress, and said, "Hi. I'm a Christian, and I felt like God wanted me to give you this." Handing her the money, I explained, "He wants you to know He loves you."

At first there was only silence. Then her mouth dropped and a tear slid down her cheek. "Really?" she cried.

"Yes," I whispered.

Tears now streamed down her face as she replied, "You have no idea what this means to me. Thank you, I … thank you … you …" She became so choked up that she couldn't even finish her sentence, and she excused herself from our table.

My friend and I smiled at each other and waited in silence for our waitress to return. When she came back she cleared her voice and said, "I've been going through some stuff lately, and I've been searching for God. I just want to thank you so much." Tears caressed her face again, and then she bent over to hug me. I stood up to meet that hug.

After a brief but strong embrace I looked at her and said, "God heard you. He loves you very much, and He is listening."

"Wow, this is crazy." She stumbled, then excused herself again.

God is so amazing. His love is so awesome! I am sure that waitress has a lot to ponder. That day a seed was sown, and now I pray, "God, bring someone else to water it!"

Day 23

The Voice of Our Soul

> Fix your thoughts on what is true, and honorable, and right, and pure, and lovely, and admirable. Think about things that are excellent and worthy of praise.
>
> —Philippians 4:8

Our soul consists of our mind, our will, and emotions. It is the battlefield on which we hear God, our logical thoughts, and the enemy. Since we have already revealed how the soul thinks, we will focus more on the importance of learning to reprogram it. You see, our soul is the part of us that has not been made new. We must renew it through the Word of God. Paul instructs us—pleads with us, even—to do this in his letter to the Romans:

> And so, dear brothers and sisters, I plead with you to give your bodies to God because of all he has done for you. Let them be a living and holy sacrifice—the kind he will find acceptable. This is truly the way to worship him. Don't copy the behavior and customs of this world, but let God transform you into a new person *by changing the way you think.* Then you will learn to know God's will for you, which is good and pleasing and perfect.
>
> —Romans 12:1–2, emphasis added

Did you get that? We have the responsibility to renew our minds. Once born again, our spirits are joined with the Lord automatically. (See 1 Corinthians 6:17.) Our spirits are regenerated at salvation (that is our new nature), but our souls remain the same until we give our "bodies to God … a living and holy sacrifice." Only then will our minds be renewed by the Word of God, "changing the way … [we] think" and allowing us to "learn to know God's will for" us.

Because of our past, our upbringing, culture, or belief systems, our soul can hinder our ability to hear God accurately, especially while we are still unfamiliar with God's personality and His ways through His Word. In other words, we all have a mental filter through which we see ourselves, the things that affect our perception of God Himself, and His words to us. For example, if I grew up with a father who was harsh, demanding, and was never pleased with me, chances are I will view God as harsh, demanding, and believe I will never measure up. This could be the lens through which I read Scripture and approach God, especially if what I have been taught about God lined up with my experience with my father. In order to renew my mind to the truth of who God really is, I would either need to get healing in my heart because of my past and/or sit under a biblical teacher who preaches and abides in the Word of God. Freedom and healing come from knowing the truth, and the truth is and comes only from the Word of God. Scripture says, "If you abide in My word, you are My disciples indeed. And you shall know the truth, and the truth shall make you free" (John 8:31–32, NKJV).

Another example: Let's say my interpretation of Scripture or my misunderstanding of Scripture (because of wrong teachings or incorrect/false interpretations) teaches me that God is a taskmaster and I have to live up to His standards of holiness. I would live and act as if I were still under the Law, needing or feeling I had to measure up or that He would judge me every time I sinned. This wrong view of God would cause me to be afraid that when He spoke—if I even gave Him the chance—He might condemn me. Insead of approaching Him with a ready heart to receive from the Comforter and accept the encouragement of the Holy Spirit, I would expect to hear He doesn't love me or for Him to tell me I had blown it. I would likely even begin to think the condemning thoughts I felt toward myself were really God expressing His disappointment in me. But when you know Scripture and you know who God is, you can recognize those condemning thoughts as Satan or your own heart condemning you, not God. Then you can cast down that argument by refusing to accept it as truth and bring that thought into captivity to the obedience of Christ, who says, "There is no condemnation for those who belong to Christ Jesus" (Rom. 8:1). None!

I love what Neil T. Anderson writes in the introduction in his book *Who I Am in Christ*:

> Tragically, most Christians *never* come to appreciate who they are in Christ. From the time of birth we are programmed by our environment and the people in our lives. We interpret the meaning of life's experiences through the grid of our personal orientation and react accordingly. For the many who have experienced rejection, abandonment or abuse from earliest childhood, entrenched in their belief systems is an attitude that says, "I am of no value," "I don't measure up," "I am unlovable." Even those of us whose childhood seemed wholesome have been victimized in some way by the enemy's subtle deceptions. …
>
> We are no longer products of our past. We are primarily products of Christ's work on the cross. But remember, when we were dead in our trespasses and sins,

we had learned to live our life independent of God. Our identity and perception of ourselves were programmed into our minds through natural orders of this world. That's why Paul says in Romans 12:2, "Do not conform any longer to the pattern of this world, but be transformed by the renewing of your mind. Then you will be able to test and approve what God's will is—his good, pleasing and perfect will."[25]

Regardless of the experiences of our past, we all approach God at the moment of salvation with a flawed mental lens that needs to be restored through the renewing of our minds. This process of changing the way we think begins with accepting that we are righteous because of what Christ did on the cross. He took all punishment for sin upon Himself. Jesus Christ came in the flesh to reveal the heart of the Father, which was redemption for mankind. When you study the life, acts, and character of Christ, you will see the Father's heart because Jesus is the exact representation of God! When you know Christ, you experience God. And when you take your thoughts captive, you have just recognized a lie of your flesh or the enemy and replaced it with God's truth. See how important it is to know His truth?

The need for our minds to be renewed to the things of God does not mean that God made a mistake when He designed us as He did. It is a positive thing that our soul analyzes and sees things from a logical perspective. It thinks things through with linked thoughts that are often fragmented until we ponder longer and harder on information that we have stored up or sought out, and then we are able to join them together to make sense of it. God gave us minds like these for thinking things through for everyday life and solving problems. It is not a mistake. It just means it is our responsibility to know ourselves and learn to surrender our whole being—spirit, soul, and body—to Him daily so that our minds can be renewed and our thoughts can line up with who God is and what His Word says.

Reflect

1. In your own words, what does it mean to renew your mind? How do you do this—or how will you do this—in your life specifically?

_____
_____
_____
_____

2. What past experiences or misconceptions tainted your understanding of God and His Word before you got saved? Were they resolved immediately when you made Him the Lord of your life, or did it take time and healing to overcome them? Do you still need to seek healing for those wounds

or false teachings so that you can freely accept all that God has for you and approach Him with an unburdened mind?

_____
_____
_____
_____

3. Why do you think we need to renew our minds daily? Why isn't it sufficient for us to do it once a week, month, year, or just at salvation?

_____
_____
_____
_____

Pray

Heavenly Father, quicken me daily to renew my mind to the word of Your truth. Help my mind to remain pure and untainted by my past. Cleanse my mind from all untruths, deceptions, lies, false beliefs, and false doctrines. Remind me, Lord, to be aware of my thoughts and take every thought captive. Help me stop all ungodly thinking, fearful thinking, and distorted thinking, and instead help me to think on thoughts that are true and honorable and right and pure and lovely and admirable. Equip me to think about things that are excellent and worthy of praise. I pray this in Jesus's name. Amen.

Listen

Ask the Lord to reveal to you if there is any mentality from your past, upbringing, culture, or experience that is hindering your ability to hear God accurately. Spend a few minutes silently and expectantly awaiting a response.

Day 24

The Voice of the Enemy

Stay alert! Watch out for your great enemy, the devil. He prowls around like a roaring lion, looking for someone to devour.

—1 Peter 5:8

God wants us to hear His voice. He wants to speak unmistakeably to our spirit so that we know His thoughts toward us and for us. Satan, on the other hand, is a deceiver. He wants us to think his thoughts are our thoughts or that his thoughts are really the voice of the Lord— "And no wonder! For Satan himself transforms himself into an angel of light" (2 Cor. 11:14, NKJV). We can learn to recognize his voice or the ideas that he implants in our minds when we find out who he is, as well as his nature and his character.

Matthew 7:17–18 gives us a simple test for determining the nature and purpose of Satan: "A good tree produces good fruit, and a bad tree produces bad fruit. A good tree can't produce bad fruit, and a bad tree can't produce good fruit." So, let us look at the fruit he has born in the lives of people throughout the Bible. First Chronicles 21:1 says, "Now Satan stood up against Israel, and moved David to number Israel" (NKJV). How did he move David to number Israel (take a census)? Through David's thoughts. Remember what happened to Ananias and Sapphira? They sold their property in order to have money to give the disciples but then turned over only part of the proceeds, though they lied and said that was the full amount. Peter received a word of knowledge about what had really happened, and he asked Ananias, "Why have you let Satan fill your heart? You lied to the Holy Spirit" (Acts 5:3). Satan filled his mind with that thought to withhold money. Let's not forget about Judas. The Bible tells us that by the time of the Last Supper, the devil had "already put it into the heart of Judas Iscariot, Simon's son, to betray" Jesus (John 13:2). Satan's promptings, suggestions, and whispers only ever produce bad fruit in the lives of those who listen to his voice.

Guarding Our Heart

After all our talk about our souls and mind, don't get confused just because it talks about Satan moving on the hearts of these men. *Heart* in the Bible is often used to refer to the soul. (Remember our mind, our will, and our emotions make up our soul.) For example, the Bible describes people knowing (Deut. 8:5, NKJV), praying (1 Sam. 1:12–13, NKJV), and meditating in their hearts. They devise plans (Ps. 140:2), doubt (Mark 11:23), and believe in their hearts too. All these abilities of the heart involve the mind.

We also see that the heart is used in the Bible to mean the center of our emotions. It often refers to the glad heart (Exod. 4:14), the fearful heart (Josh. 5:1), and the courageous heart (Ps. 27:14, NKJV) to name just a few.

Last, the Bible reveals that the heart is the center of the human will, which could be defined as one's desires or ability to choose. A hardened heart that rebels against God is a mind choosing to disobey. (See Exodus 4:21.) A heart that is yielded or submitted to God is a heart that wants to obey Him and walk in His ways. (See Joshua 24:23.)

The Bible says in some passages that God gives us a new spirit and changes our heart when we become born again.

> And I will give them singleness of heart and put a new spirit within them. I will take away their stony, stubborn heart and give them a tender, responsive heart, so they will obey my decrees and regulations. Then they will truly be my people, and I will be their God.
>
> —Ezekiel 11:19–20

With this new heart, God creates in us a desire to love and to obey Him. We no longer *want* to do evil, and our heart is no longer evil—though it can yield to evil. Andrew Wommack says it this way: "If you're truly born again, you have a desire to live for God. 'And every man that hath this hope in him purifieth himself, even as he is pure' (1 John 3:3, KJV). There will be varying degrees of this purity manifest in your actions and thoughts, but every born-again person seeks to purify themselves."[26]

In no way does this deny the continuous struggle with temptation and sin. In fact, Christians, as much as nonbelievers, choose to sin, and many are dominated by the flesh and deceived by the devil. (See 2 Corinthians 5:16–21). If one is truly born again, Romans 7:15–20 reveals that it is not our heart that is evil anymore, but our flesh is weak and can be tempted by Satan to do evil. Why? Because man has God-given needs in every area of his/her spirit, soul, and body. If man gets all his needs met conducive to Scripture, and in ways God has provided, he will be walking in the Spirit. But, if man neglects his needs, is ignorant of his needs, and/or focuses more on one need than the other, then Satan will come to pervert God's moral standards of getting our needs met and begin tempting us to do evil, thereby getting those needs met in ungodly ways. Because the flesh is weak (it continually desires pleasure and to have those pleasures met) we may yield to those temptations and thus commit sin or do evil. Upon immediate gratification and acting on that temptation, the redeemed heart is sorrowful, guilty, and feels awful. Why? Because upon conversion, we've been given a new heart; thus, our heart is no longer evil. Both our heart and our spirit desires to do good and please God. Therefore, Jeremiah 17:9, "The heart is deceitful above all *things*, And desperately wicked; Who can know it?" (NKJV), no longer applies to us as new covenant believers. This is what Jesus meant when He told us to watch and pray because "the spirit is willing, but the flesh is weak" (Matt. 26:41).

Satan knows that if he can get us to choose and believe in his lies and deceptions, then he can control us and get us to act independently of God. But he cannot force us. We have a choice! Christ defeated him at the cross. This is the victory we have. It is also why we must be cautious not to blame Satan and say, "Satan made me do it." That is a lie. The truth is, the Bible says, "Sin shall not have dominion over you, for you are not under law but under grace" (Rom. 6:14, NKJV). This implies we can have victory over sin by appropriating the grace of Christ through His defeat of Satan.

This also reveals that we have a responsibility to get our bodily needs, our soul's needs, and our spiritual needs met conducive to Scripture and in ways that are pleasing to God. Just so you are informed about what I am talking about, I will give you a quick synopsis of what I mean. Our physical body has four basic needs: water, food, oxygen, and rest. Without these needs getting met, we will begin to experience physical breakdown, and if not met at all, we will die. No one can meet those needs for us; we must do it ourselves. In normal situations, it is up to each of us as individuals—not God, nor others—to provide our bodies with nutrients, water, sleep, and oxygen. (Though God has provided the air, we have to breathe in and exhale.) It is not that God can't, but rather He has given each of us that responsibility. He has laid out in Scripture the kinds of food we can eat to have full health and well-being. He even talks about getting a good night's sleep. It is up to us to choose and abide by His guidance in order to experience strong physical health.

Next, our soul (mind, will, and emotions) also has needs. As a temperament therapist, I teach that every individual has three basic, God-given temperamental needs in their soul, though the specific expression of those needs is very unique to each person. (You may discover your specific needs through a temperament test.) God has designed each of us for relationships, and it is in these relationships and work situations that our needs for inclusion (of the mind), control (of the will), and affection (of emotions) are met. Inclusion is our need for socialization and association. It is our need to love and receive love, to encourage, to associate, and have human conversation and companionship. This meets the need of feeling significant or worthy. (See Genesis 2:18.) Control is our need for carrying out responsibilities, making decisions, and to rule and to reign in life. This meets the needs of feeling competent and secure. (See Genesis 1:26–27.) Affection is our need for deeper love and sexual pleasures. This meets the need of deep love, intimacy, and acceptance. (See Genesis 1:28.) Without these needs getting met by and through others, mental and emotional breakdown begins to set in.

As you can see, most of the soul's needs are met by and through other people. We don't meet these needs ourselves—though many try and suffer with mental and emotional issues because of it—and neither does God meet these needs. Again, it is not that He can't, but He made it clear (when He said to Adam while Adam had God all to himself and God had Adam all to Himself) that it was not good for man to be alone. Once He brought Adam and Eve together, He then told them to go and multiply and fill the earth, to create families. Man needs relationships to thrive and succeed. He is not an island in himself. In God's infinite wisdom, He designed each of us to need each other. It takes humility to invite another human being into our lives, into our weaknesses and vulnerabilities, as well as to use our strengths to serve others. To thrive mentally and emotionally, our need for inclusion, control, and affection must be met. Sadly, most people are not aware of their temperament, thus they are unaware of their specific needs. I highly recommend you take a temperament test to discover the details of how God uniquely created you.

Finally, our spirit has needs. First, our one, basic need is to be born again and be reconciled to God, the one, true God, through Jesus Christ by the power of the Holy Spirit. Once the spirit is born again, then other needs must be met for continual growth and spiritual contentment (e.g., prayer, intimacy with God, fellowship with other believers, attending church, etc.). When our spiritual needs are not met, we begin to dry up spiritually.

We can choose to walk in the Spirit (be led and empowered by Him getting these needs according to God's plan and purposes), or we can decide to be led by Satan, who seduces us to yield to the weaknesses of the flesh and get our needs met in ungodly ways. If we yield to the flesh, we must take responsibility for choosing to sin.

To avoid this pitfall, we simply have to reject his whispers. So how do we discern if the voice we are hearing in our spirit is his? Just as James 3:17 gave us an easy test for determining when we are hearing the voice of the Lord, James 3:14–15 tells us this about the enemy's voice:

> But if you are bitterly jealous and there is selfish ambition in your heart, don't cover up the truth with boasting and lying. For jealousy and selfishness are not God's kind of wisdom. Such things are earthly, unspiritual, and demonic. For wherever there is jealousy and selfish ambition, there you will find disorder and evil of every kind.

Satan speaks lies and deceives. His thoughts will seek to tempt you to be selfish and jealous. His thoughts are disorderly and demonic and result in disharmony and confusion. The fruit is strife and competition—precisely the opposite of God. Why are these the hallmarks of his voice? Because "what you say flows from what is in your heart" (Luke 6:45). Satan can only speak condemnation, lies, and temptation because it is who he is.

What Is Satan's Nature?

Revelation 12:10 (NKJV) says he is an accuser of the brethren. If what you are hearing sounds accusatory— "you're a failure," "you can't understand God," "you're not spiritual enough," "you will never hear Him accurately," or even, "I'm stupid" (he can speak to you in the first person to make you think of yourself negatively)—this is not God but the accuser of the brethren. Satan can also tempt you to be the accuser of the brethren by tempting you to focus on the faults of others. He can tempt you to judge their weaknesses. The enemy will seduce you to criticize, condemn, or judge them. Know that these temptations are not from God, and neither is it from you. Remember, you have a new nature. But if you believe those thoughts and act on them, you have just yielded your members (your mouth, in this case) to Satan to tear down others. It takes time and energy to renew your mind to the truth of your new identity.

Satan is also a liar and the father of lies. (See John 8:44.) He is a deceiver. Satan will try to twist God's Word and to deceive you any way that he can. The only way to detect a lie is to know the truth or go to someone who does. This is also why we need the body of Christ. Others can see in us what we cannot. They can see our blind spots. It is good and beneficial to be teachable, open, and willing to receive correction. Deception blinds us. Still, if we allow others to speak the truth in love, we can be set free! Proverbs 11:14 advocates the scrutiny of others: "Where there is no counsel, the people fall; But in the multitude of counselors there is safety" (NKJV).

Sometimes we are not even aware of the lies we believe and accept them as a part of our character, which is why it is so imperative that we learn to hear God and His truth and to recognize our feelings. What you are feeling can be a barometer to what you are thinking and believing. If you are feeling fear, ask yourself, Where does fear come from? And what is the root of that fear?

Of course, not all fear comes from Satan. There is a healthy fear that God has empowered the body with. It is our natural fight, flight, and freeze response to impending danger. When it is real, our bodies respond, giving us the added ability, or adrenaline, to escape. However, if the fear is imagined, then that is when we can know it is Satan playing on our weaknesses and vulnerabilities. But again, that is not to say that we have to accept it. We have the ability to take our thoughts captive and deactivate our bodies from this imagined fear.

Satan is also a tempter, tempting us to say, act, or do what is evil using the weaknesses of our flesh. (See James 1:13–16; Matthew 4:1; Ephesians 4:27–29, NKJV.) We must keep in mind that our flesh and soul have not been made new; only our spirit has. Our flesh and our soul are the areas of vulnerability in our being that Satan uses to tempt us to sin and give in to the works of the flesh. (See Galatians 5:19–24; 1 Corinthians 5:1–13; Ephesians 4:17–32.) We must guard these!

Satan Versus the Flesh

We perceive the flesh as our body. It is the physical part of us. Our soul is our emotional being. The soul is a part of our flesh. (However, be aware that our soul is sometimes related to and used interchangeably with the term *the heart*, which we talked about earlier.) This flesh, including our soul, is weak, so anything that stirs up evil desires within you and tempts or entices you to go opposite of God's ways can be rooted in the flesh.

Nonetheless, Satan only has the power to influence us if we cooperate with his lies or temptations. Temptation itself—whether from Satan or from fleshly thoughts or promptings—isn't sin. It is how we respond to it that determines whether we step into sin or continue to walk in holiness. First John 2:15–16 reminds us not to "love the world or anything in the world … For everything in the world—the lust of the flesh, the lust of the eyes, and the pride of life—comes not from the Father but from the world" (NIV).

As Christians, our once-sinful nature has been crucified with Christ. We no longer have a sinful nature because we have been made new. We have a new nature. We are created in righteousness and true holiness. But we must learn our new identity in Christ. We are not sinners trying to become saints, but rather we are saints trying to become more Christlike. It is a matter of our focus and putting off our former conduct and putting on the new man. When we were born again, we were born of the Spirit. Because of Jesus, the Bible tells us that "the sharing of our faith may become effective by the acknowledgement of every *good thing which is in you* in Christ Jesus" (Philem. 1:6, emphasis added; see also Romans 6 and Ephesians 4:20–24.) We are no longer evil with evil hearts. Sin is evil, and sin is only sin when it is acted upon. Therefore, the sin we commit is evil. Sin is not who we are. It does not have to have dominion over us, and the fact that we will be tempted does not mean that we are doomed to commit wrongdoing. We are not doomed to sin because our flesh is vulnerable. It is not the flesh itself that is evil but the works of the flesh, the act of giving in to the temptation of sin:

> Temptation comes from our own desires, which entice us and drag us away. These desires give birth to sinful actions. And when sin is allowed to grow, it gives birth to death.
>
> —James 1:15

That is why in Galatians 5:24 we are reminded that those who are in Christ have crucified the flesh. This process of "nailing the passions and desires of our sinful nature to the cross" happens once upon salvation, but then it becomes a moment-by-moment decision as we grow in Christ and live each day. Our flesh is weak and always will be vulnerable because it can be influenced by the evil one. However, we can renew our minds to God's truth, recognize our God-given needs and meet them morally, and learn to recognize Satan and his schemes. (See Ephesians 4:23.) Being diligent to this practice will make it easier for us to say no to Satan and stay holy.

Ephesians 6:10–13 reminds us that our struggle isn't against flesh and blood. We are not fighting against our flesh, as though one part of us is bad; no, this scripture reveals that we war against Satan and his demons. As new creations, our focus and struggle aren't against our own flesh (or against others, for that matter) but against demons, who could be lying, accusing, tempting, and deceiving us, either directly or indirectly (through others). As we grow and believe these truths, learning to recognize the spirit of error when he speaks, Satan loses his power toward our flesh. We must know the Spirit of truth from the spirit of error, as he will try to lead us astray. As soon as we recognize his temptations, we can immediately submit to God at that moment and cry out to Him to deliver us from that temptation by declaring, "Father, make a way of escape. Right now I submit to God and resist this temptation." The devil must flee when we recognize we are being tempted, decide that we no longer want to sin, and call on the Lord for help. This belief is key to our freedom. If we see ourselves as evil with a sinful nature, we will constantly be in conflict with ourselves and striving to overcome all evil. We will be sin-conscious, and we will not accept our weaknesses as part of our humanity.

Let me give you an example of the way in which Satan whispers to our flesh to tempt us to sin to get our needs met in ungodly ways. Sex is God's idea. It was part of His plan for marriage between one man and one woman. Sex is a God-given need and desire for both males and females. It fulfills our need for love and affection. He designed it for procreation, intimacy, and pleasure between husband and wife. However, if a husband's or wife's needs and desires of love, affection, and sex are not being met in the marital bed, the enemy can come and pervert God's plan for sex by his temptations, lies, and deceptions. (This is why Paul reminds us in 1 Corinthians 7:5, "Do not deprive one another except with consent for a time, that you may give yourselves to fasting and prayer; and come together again so that Satan does not tempt you because of your lack of self-control" [NKJV].)

Satan knows we have these needs. If these needs go unmet, the body rages (if you know what I mean). All it takes is a "dirty" thought or a pornographic picture, and the seed to sin, or the path to destruction, is sown. Satan is relentless. He will water that seed, fertilize it, and continue cultivating it until you give in to the sin and act upon it or until you take that thought captive, submit to God, and flee from the temptation. How is he relentless? He will whisper temptations to the flesh to look at pornography to arouse you, engage in masturbation, or even to commit adultery.

This vulnerability doesn't mean there is something wrong with us. After all, God knows the way He created our bodies and the arousal and pleasure we get from sex. James 1:12–17 explains this beautifully:

> Blessed is the man who endures temptation; for when he has been approved, he will receive the crown of life which the Lord has promised to those who love Him. Let no one say when he is tempted, "I am tempted by God"; for God cannot be

tempted by evil, nor does He Himself tempt anyone. But each one is tempted when he is drawn away by his own desires and enticed. Then, when desire has conceived, it gives birth to sin; and sin, when it is full-grown, brings forth death. Do not be deceived, my beloved brethren. Every good gift and every perfect gift is from above, and comes down from the Father of lights, with whom there is no variation or shadow of turning.

—NKJV

This verse explains first that it is not God who tempts us with anything. But each of us is tempted when we are "drawn away" by our "own desires and enticed." We have God-given desires, but if they are not met in godly ways, Satan will come to entice us. Then, the scripture says, "when desire is conceived, it gives birth to sin." This means that when we yield to that enticement, which is perverted, we sin.

This is why we must be vigilant and get the God-given needs of our spirit, soul, and body met if possible, conducive to God's moral standards. Otherwise, when the temptation comes, we need to crucify our flesh, renew our minds, and guard our hearts so that we can avoid sin and walk in holiness. As soon as we recognize the whisper of the enemy, it is a good idea to call out to the Lord for help resisting Satan's temptations. In the example of sexual temptation, this means that when sex is not possible in the moment, then we will need to refrain from ungodly sexual acts in spite of the reality that one may be aroused. We must remind ourselves that sex outside of marriage is ungodly, that we are right with God, holy, and a saint. (Sinners sin, but saints don't! If the belief is that you are still a sinner, you will have an excuse to succumb.)

The good news is that as we grow in Christ sin will be less and less enticing because our spirit desires the things of God. (See Ephesians 4:17–24.) We need to grow in our new nature, and we need to learn to recognize the enemy's voice when it speaks to our heart and flesh so that we can resist him. If Satan is tempting us, it is a good indication that either a spirit, soul, or bodily need is not being met.

Reflect

1. What does it mean to guard your heart, renew your mind, and crucify your flesh? What do these processes look like in your life?

_____
_____
_____
_____

2. If the flesh is vulnerable to the temptation of Satan, why do you think God designed us with it?

_____
_____
_____
_____

3. Based on James 3:14–15 and what you know about Satan's nature, what are the red flags that would indicate if a thought or temptation is coming from the enemy instead of our own mind or God?

_____
_____
_____
_____

Pray

Heavenly Father, thank You that as a born-again child of God I have a new nature that desires to please You. Thank You that upon conviction of sin I am sorrowful, knowing that I have sinned against You and desire to be holy, as You are holy. I ask that You keep my heart soft and pliable, willing to be corrected, ready to be obedient. Cause me to be humble before You and others. Train my ears to discern the difference between Your voice, Satan's voice, and my own voice of reason. Help me to know and understand my God-given needs so that I can get them met conducive to Scripture and in ways that are pleasing to You so I won't be tempted to get them met in perverted ways. I pray this in Jesus's name. Amen.

Listen

Ask the Lord to reveal to you if there is any lie from the enemy that you have believed and accepted, not realizing it is part of Satan's plan to interrupt your effectiveness for the kingdom of God. Spend a few minutes silently and expectantly awaiting a response.

Day 25

Practicing Discernment

> Keep watch and pray, so that you will not give in to temptation. For the spirit is willing, but the body is weak!
>
> —Matthew 26:41

The Bible teaches that we are to prove or test *all things* according to the Word of God and to test the spirits. (See 1 Thessalonians 5:21; Hebrews 4:12; 1 Timothy 6:3-4; 1 Corinthians 2:15; 1 John 4:1.) To do this we must understand:

- Our soul affects how we think. We analyze, we reason, and our thoughts are often fragmented. We link them to make sense of things and perceive the world around us—as well as the Word of God and God Himself—through the lens of our experiences and what we have been taught. We must renew our mind to the Word of God in order to bring our soul into alignment with our spirit so that we can hear clearly from God.

- When God speaks it is first pure, then peaceable, good, fruitful, wise, complete, and spontaneous. It can come as an urge, prompt, quickening or unction, or even a word or picture, but again, it will be pure. It will always cause us to draw closer to Him. Whatever you hear the Spirit of God saying, whether as a witness within or still, small voice, know that it will line up with His Word. (See 1 John 5:6–7.)

- When Satan speaks it is evil, tempting, and accusing. He lies, deceives, and pressures us. He wants to stir up our flesh, so he preys upon our vulnerability, whispering to our flesh in order to tempt us into acting in sin. Satan desires to lead us away from God and convince us that we are powerless to resist temptation.

Here is a scenario to demonstrate the differences between God's voice, Satan's voice, and our thoughts. Imagine I am driving to a family gathering, and suddenly I get an unction or urge (prompting, quickening, or knowing) on the inside of me to make a sharp left turn instead of going straight like I normally would do. The unction is clear enough for me to recognize it easily, yet rationally the direction doesn't make any sense at all because it is the long way around. I then begin to question the unction. A mini conversation ensues in my head as my thoughts are trying to join themselves together in succession in order to either understand the unction or prove it wrong (reasoning against it). I might reason to myself, "That doesn't make any sense. It's way longer to go that way, and I don't want to because I am going to be late. Hmmm, I wonder where this thought came from." And so forth.

I might feel this pressure to go straight because I know I would get there faster, yet the unction to make that sharp left turn instead of going straight is still strong. With that pressure, not only am I now confused, but fear has begun to grip my heart. As these feelings and thoughts bombard me, I stop and consider the initial prompting and realize the unction to turn was peaceful, sudden, clear, and direct. It was a full statement that I witnessed in my spirit. Logically, it makes no sense because it is going to make me late, but the pressure to continue going straight makes me question everything and infuses unbelievable fear. Do I obey the unction or my reasoning and the pressure behind it?

I decide to follow the unction and make the sharp left turn, taking an extra half hour to get to my destination. Perhaps I later learn that there was a massive accident on the road I would have taken had I not listened and obeyed the unction. Let's look at this scenario for evidence of the different voices acting in concert.

The unction came suddenly. It was a sensing or witness in my spirit that was out of the blue and lined up with the nature and character of God in that it was an awareness, without fear, to go another direction. It was a complete, whole thought or statement that made absolutely no sense at all but manifested with a supernatural peace that surpassed my understanding. It was sudden, clear, and purposeful. It came without me even thinking about it. Because of obedience, it produced good fruit.

Satan came to tempt me by appealing to my flesh. He whispered, "If you go this way it makes more sense." The sense of pressure I felt also came from the enemy, who appealed to what could have been the weaknesses of my flesh (pride and impatience) by prompting me to continue going straight and ignore the unction, thereby disobeying God. Had I acted on Satan's prompting and disobeyed God and instead agreed with my own reasoning, then I would have sinned. (This is characteristic of Satan, whose goal is to get us to act independently of God.) It was clearly the enemy, because all thoughts in my soul became clouded with confusion, and I felt fearful. My doubt was of my soul, as my mind tried to make sense of the situation with analytical processing and hastily link my disjointed thoughts.

In situations like this scenario, the outcome could be negative if we fail to recognize that fear is not of God but of Satan. He comes to steal, kill, and destroy. He tried to tempt me through pride and impatience, but I did not follow through. When we are careful to recognize his schemes and refuse to yield our weaknesses to him, submitting to God instead, we remain protected and in "the secret place" of His will (Ps. 91:1, NKJV).

It's important also to stress that not all unctions will be strong. Sometimes it's very gentle and will lift if disobeyed or not recognized. Usually, the strong promptings are easy to identify. Most people have a hard time with the gentle promptings, and this takes time to develop and discern. Hebrews 5:14 says, "But solid food is for full-grown men, for those whose senses and mental faculties are trained *by practice* to discriminate and distinguish between what is morally good and noble and what is evil and contrary either to divine or human law" (AMPC, emphasis added). Be patient; we have a lifetime to practice hearing God and growing in our relationship with Him.

The Holy Spirit within us is constantly speaking to us, bearing witness that we are children of the Most High God and wanting to draw us near to the Father. He desires to glorify and testify of Jesus and to empower us to grow in our new nature as Christians through the renewing of our minds. Our spirits are new, but our souls are the battleground. We must learn to believe God's Word and His word to our hearts over what the world says, over what our circumstances appear like, over what seems logical and reasonable, and even over what we feel. This is what Hebrews 10:38 means when it says, "The just shall live by faith" (NKJV).

This expectancy to hear from the Holy Spirit is our portion as new creations in Christ. Therefore, when we have promptings or our thoughts show the pattern characteristic of an unction of the Lord, we must learn to recognize that it is the Spirit of God within us speaking to us. If we ignore, put off, delay our response, or just deny His promptings, then eventually we can grieve or quench Him to the point we no longer hear Him. (We will address this in Lesson 10.) While you are learning to distinguish between God's voice, your voice, and the enemy's, use this chart to help you judge and test each word to determine the source.

God's Nature, His Character, and His Ways	Satan's Nature, His Character, and His Ways	Our Soul
God is peace, He gives peace, and He leads with peace. (See Isaiah 9:6; 26:3; Galatians 5:22; Ephesians 2:14; Philippians 4:7; James 3:17.)	Satan is a liar. He lies and fills a person's thoughts and heart with lies. (See John 8:44; Acts 5:3.)	Our souls need to be renewed to who we are in Christ as new creations and what belongs to us. (See 2 Corinthians 5:16–17; 10:3–6; Romans 8:6–9; 12:1–2.)
God is love, He gives love, and He leads with love. (See 1 John 4:7–8, 19; Galatians 5:22; John 15:7–10.)	Satan is an accuser. He condemns and accuses. He pressures us to act hastily and torments us with fear. (See Revelation 12:10.)	Our soul reasons and is the filter through which all things must go. However, we are prone to overanalyzing, as our mind attempts to make sense of circumstances and situations logically by linking up what we know and casting aside what we cannot verify with our senses. (See Mark 2:6–8)
God is just. He loves justice, and He leads in righteousness. (See Deuteronomy 32:4; Job 37:23; Psalm 33:5; John 16:7–11; Revelation 19:2.)	Satan is a tempter. He tempts, and He tempts us through our flesh. (See James 1:13–16, 3:14–15; Matthew 4:1; 6:13; 26:41; 1 Corinthians 7:5.)	God speaks to our soul and our spirit, for we are one spirit with Him, but Satan can only talk to our soul. (See 1 Corinthians 6:17.)
God is truth. He loves truth, and He leads us into all truth. (See Titus 1:2; Ephesians 5:9; John 14:16–17, 26.)	Satan is a deceiver. He deceives. (See Acts 13:9–10; 2 Corinthians 11:3–4, 14; Revelation 20:7–8.)	
God's thoughts will produce emotions of His character, nature, and ways. His thoughts are life and give life. Love produces love; joy produces joy; peace produces peace, etc. (See Philippians 4:6–9; John 6:63; 10:10; Isaiah 55:8–9.)	Satan's thoughts will produce emotions of his character, nature, and ways. His thoughts produce death. Fear produces fear; condemnation produces condemnation; pressure produces pressure, etc. (See John 10:10; Romans 8:1–2.)	When your soul lines up with God's Word, your spirit will bear witness to this, and you will be single-minded. When your soul is ignorant to or opposes God's Word or disbelieves it, you will be double-minded. (See James 1:5–8.)

Reflect

1. In your own words, what is the difference between God's voice, Satan's voice, and your voice?

_____
_____
_____
_____

2. How can you trust if God is speaking? How will you know if it is your soul? The enemy?

_____
_____
_____
_____

3. Try to think of a time in your own life in which the Holy Spirit gave you a word or direction that seemed to make little to no logical sense. Write out what you remember about the experience, and then look for evidence of God's voice, the enemy's voice, and your own thoughts in the scenario. How did you determine that it was the Holy Spirit speaking to you? How did you silence the whispers of the enemy and quiet your mind? What, looking back, could you do differently next time?

_____
_____
_____
_____

Pray

Heavenly Father, You are so good. I am in awe that You sent Your Spirit to dwell inside of me and draw me closer to Your heart. Lord, I submit my mind, will, and emotions—all of my soul—to You, along with every other part of me. I choose today to trust You over what I feel and what I think, and I expectantly wait for each new step in my journey with You. Renew my mind, just as you gave me a new spirit. Help me always to respond right away to Your promptings so that communication between us remains open and free, and protect me from the enemy's attempts to confuse or frustrate me. Thank You for leading me. In Jesus's name, amen.

Exercise

Find someone to pray with this week. Before praying, seek the Lord and ask Him to speak through you. Ask Him what His heart is for the other person. Listen quietly and speak what you hear. Then ask your partner if it bore witness with them. Switch.

If you are not able to find someone to pray with face-to-face or over the phone, select a person to pray for and seek God about. Write down what you hear for that person from the Holy Spirit and share that message with him or her promptly.

Lesson Six

God Speaks Through People and Circumstances

Day 26

God Speaks Through People

How then shall they call on Him in whom they have not believed? And how shall they believe in Him of whom they have not heard? And how shall they hear without a preacher? And how shall they preach unless they are sent? … So then faith comes by hearing, hearing by the word of God.

—Romans 10:14–15, 17, NKJV

God created us for Christian community. In Genesis 2:18, God said, "It is not good for the man to be alone." First He made animals to keep Adam company, but soon He realized that "still there was no helper just right for him" (v. 20), so He made Eve. Centuries later, Jesus spoke to the importance of healthy, thriving Christian fellowship when He said, "I am giving you a new commandment: Love each other. Just as I have loved you, you should love each other" (John 13:34). It should be no surprise, then, that God often chooses to use these relationships to speak to us.

One of the primary ways God speaks to us through others is at church through our pastors, evangelists, or speakers. When the Word of God is preached to the body at church, we can apply that message to our everyday lives, whether it is for content, history, growth, correction, encouragement, edification, or anything else. However, the Spirit of God can also illuminate God's Word when it is preached so that it goes a little deeper, like a *rhema* word, which touches us to the core of our hearts. When this happens we know it was God speaking His word directly to our hearts, and we know the message was just for us.

Other interactions at church can impact our lives as well. God can also use the gifts and talents of the worship team as they select and play worship music that sings to the beat of your heart. Perhaps someone you met in the foyer mentions a story or scripture that fits your life, or during the altar call someone prayed exactly what you needed to hear. God uses willing vessels to relate His heart to mankind.

Of course, God is not limited to using a preacher/pastor or even our church family to speak to us. He also speaks through teachers of the Word, like those individuals leading our adult Bible study, home groups, small groups, or even TV teacher-preachers. He may even speak through everyday people who may or may not be teachers. The Spirit of God can make alive the words that are spoken through various people to get our attention.

In truth, God can speak through anyone who speaks: the people on the radio, through worship music, friends, family, in prayer, during a phone call, or while you are reading a book. You name it. God can use even donkeys! (See Numbers 22:21–29.) And yes, God speaks through unbelievers as well. In 2 Chronicles 35:21–24 we read about Josiah, who heard this message, "What do you want with me, king of Judah? I have no quarrel with you today! I am on my way to fight another nation, and God has told me to hurry! Do not interfere with God, who is with me, or he will destroy you" (v. 21). This was sent by King Neco of Egypt, who was the king of a pagan nation. Verse 22 says, "But Josiah refused to listen to Neco, *to whom God had indeed spoken*, and he would not turn back" (emphasis added). We should never assume either by prejudgement of someone's beliefs or past sins that God couldn't use them to speak to us. Whenever someone says something to you, and suddenly it is like a light bulb went on, take note, because it is probably the Lord trying to get your attention. Proverbs 11:14 encourages us, "Without wise leadership, a nation falls; there is safety in having many advisers." Why? Because God speaks through the mouths of witnesses.

We often hear that we must not limit God or box Him in, but are we listening when He uses the voices of others to get our attention? Or do we hear a voice in our head that dismissively says, "I've heard this before," or, "This couldn't be God"? We must not harden our hearts but instead be humble enough to consider that God could be using these people as vessels to show or teach us something important.

Reflect

1. Through whom does God most often seem to speak to you? Is it your pastor, a Bible study leader, an author, a worship singer, or someone else? What is it about this person's style of delivery or message content that resonates with your spirit?

_____

_____

_____

_____

2. The Bible instructs us to test the spirits and be discerning regardless of the source of the word we think we have received from Him. However, what are the unique challenges associated with discerning whether a word spoken through another person is from God or not?

_____
_____
_____
_____

3. Has God even spoken to you through an unlikely source? If so, how did you confirm that it was, indeed, God?

_____
_____
_____
_____

4. Take a moment to consider your heart honestly. Are you receptive to receiving from the Lord from others, even those without ministry credentials? If not, take a few moments to find out what might be at the root of that mistrust and then ask the Lord to open your heart to hear from Him through whatever means or person He may choose.

_____
_____
_____
_____

Pray

What word do you have for me today, Father? Thank You, Lord, for the healthy, godly relationships you have put in my life. I recognize that they are a gift from You to me to build me up, encourage me, and even to help me grow in You. I ask that You would help me to view these relationships not merely as fellowship but as another avenue through which You might speak through me and to me.

Give me opportunities to hear you through those around me, and give me the sensitivity to hear a word You may give me for someone else and the boldness to share it with them. In Jesus's name, amen.

Listen

Ask the Lord to bring to your memory a message from a sermon, lesson, or Bible study that you need to apply to your life today. Spend a few minutes silently and expectantly awaiting a response.

My Story

The Voice of God Through the Writings of Another

On November 22, 2006, I felt a strong impression to fast and pray for forty days. During the first day of this fast, as I was in prayer, the Lord revealed to me that I had been wearing fear like a blanket, and it needed to come off. He explained that this blanket kept me comfortable, and it kept me cozy. Being fearful had become a benefit for me. It kept me from taking risks of all kinds.

This sounded strange to me and almost offensive. I remember questioning what I had heard. I had never thought of fear being a benefit, nor did I understand what the Lord meant when He said that I was comfortable holding on to it. I believed that fear bound me, that I was powerless to its grip. To think that I was the one holding on to it was foreign to my logic. I never imagined that it was me clinging to fear. Could I have power over it by only letting it go?

To understand how to have victory over this fear I grabbed the book Fasting for Spiritual Breakthrough *by Elmer Towns. As I scanned the table of contents my eyes were fixed on the chapter about the Elijah fast, which read, "Fasting to break crippling fears and other mental problems (1 Kings 19:2–18). Through fasting, God will show us how to overcome negative, emotional and personal habits."[27]*

"Good!" I thought. "Exactly what I need." At that moment I needed all the help I could get. So I quickly turned to page eighty-one and began reading its contents. I was fascinated to learn about this Elijah fast. As I continued to read I came across a paragraph that sent chills down my spine. It was confirmation to me that I was hearing from God. This is what the paragraph said:

> *A habit is a behavior pattern acquired by frequent repetition that is reflected in regular or increased performance. The word "habit" comes from a root meaning "clothing that is usually worn."[28]*

In my mind, the image of myself wrapped in that fear blanket, my chosen clothing, flashed like lightning. I immediately jumped up from the couch and started screaming praises to God. Suddenly, in my joy, I ripped off my housecoat and threw it to the ground. Before I knew it I was stomping on my housecoat, shouting out loud, "I choose to let go of this blanket and clothing of fear. I refuse to be bound by my behaviors. I will not wear fear like a blanket. Fear does not comfort me. Fear has no benefit for me. Fear is under my feet."

In that testimony, God spoke directly to my heart through His still, small voice and then confirmed it through that book. That book became the second witness of God to affirm what I had been hearing.

Day 27

The Nature of Prophecy

> Pursue love, and desire spiritual *gifts*, but especially that you may prophesy … But he who prophesies speaks edification and exhortation and comfort to men.
>
> —1 Corinthians 14:1, 3 NKJV

Prophecy is to speak publicly as a messenger of God under the inspiration, anointing, and grace of the Holy Spirit. It is basically sharing God's heart for His people. Prophecy can come through those appointed to the office of prophet or through pastors, teachers, or lay believers who hear from the Holy Spirit. (We will talk more about the office of prophet and when God uses laypeople to prophesy more in this lesson). It can take a variety of forms depending on the word and the speaker.

The Word of God, who is Jesus Christ, is the spirit of prophecy. (See Revelation 19:10, NKJV). Whenever anyone speaks or teaches God's Word, he/she is prophesying if they are preaching and teaching it under the inspiration of the Holy Spirit according to God's truth, God's character, and His nature (see 2 Pet. 1:20). Why? Because God's Word is filled with hope, edification, encouragement, comfort, advice, etc.

Prophecy is also God speaking through His people things that only God could know. This type of prophecy is often called a word of knowledge. It is directly speaking forth God's heart under the inspiration of the Holy Spirit to bring edification, exhortation, and comfort. (See 1 Corinthians 14:3.) To edify is to build up. *To exhort* means "to urge, advise, or caution earnestly; admonish urgently; to give urgent advice, recommendations, or warnings."[29] Of course, to comfort is to cheer up. This is the nature of life-giving prophecy. These prophetic words should either reveal or confirm what God has already been dealing with or telling someone, which is why these prophecies are one way that God trains believers to hear Him.

Finally, there is prophecy that foretells of a future event, which is usually a role of the prophet. Graham Cooke explains, "Another aspect of the prophetic role is in predictive prophecy, called *foretelling*—communicating the future as it is perceived in the mind and heart of God. This is used to shape the direction of the church; to cause a desire for godliness; to empower and release people."[30]

Second Peter 1:20–21 has much to teach us about prophecy:

No prophecy of Scripture is of any private interpretation, for prophecy never came by the will of man, but holy men of God spoke as they were *moved by the Holy Spirit.*

—NKJV, emphasis added

The King James Version expresses verse 20 this way: "No prophecy in Scripture ever came from the prophet's own understanding." As with any word from the Lord, prophetic words should reflect the character and nature of God, who spoke the word, and will always line up with Scripture. If someone claims to have received a prophetic word about or through the Bible, but that word does not line up with the rest of the Word, it is not of God. The Holy Spirit and the Word of God work in harmony at all times, but especially as it relates to prophecy. They will never contradict one another. (See 2 Timothy 3:16–17; 1 John 5:6–7.)

Further, if God's Word is preached as a tool to control or dominate through fear, legalism, or condemnation, then this is not the spirit of prophecy. If a prophetic word—of any kind, whether a word of knowledge or revelation about the Bible—does not build up, stir up, comfort, encourage, or move us to godly action, it is likely not of the Holy Spirit. Any prophecy that speaks condemnation, judgment, accusation, or brings death to a person's spirit is not from the Spirit of God, for we are under a new covenant.

It is also imperative to remember that the one prophesying the message is an imperfect vessel. We must be careful not to expect perfection and to always test the spirits and ask the Holy Spirit to confirm whether or not He is the source of a word. We all need grace for one another. Even though the gift is perfect, man is not. As Paul wrote, "We know in part and we prophesy in part" (1 Cor. 13:9).

In spite of the potential for error, the Scriptures communicate to us that we are not to quench the Spirit of God, which means we are not to suppress or subdue or put out His natural flow through prophecy. In the same passage Paul instructs us, "Do not scoff at prophecies," or, as the New King James Version puts it, "despise" them (1 Thess. 5:20). Why is this? Because God still speaks through prophecy and prophets.

Reflect

1. Have you had firsthand experience with the operation of the gift of prophecy? If so, through whom are you accustomed to hearing prophetic words: prophets, pastors, or laypeople? If not, why

not? Has your church background and religious upbringing not exposed you to this move of the Spirit, or have you avoided it because of discomfort?

_____
_____
_____
_____

2. How has your perception of the gift of prophecy and the operation of the prophetic changed since you began this study?

_____
_____
_____
_____

3. How should we posture our heart both to be open to receive prophetic words and also to be cautious and discerning, knowing that even practiced, mature human vessels can hear incorrectly?

_____
_____
_____
_____

Pray

Heavenly Father, I thank You for the gift of prophecy. Thank You that You speak through people and You desire to speak through me to benefit others. You said in Your Word that we are to desire to prophesy. Lord, I desire to prophesy. Use me as Your messenger to bring glory to Your name. Speak life through me, speak hope through me, and empower me to be a vessel of Your love and intimacy for others. Well up in me living water that will refresh, revive, and restore. I pray this in Jesus's name. Amen.

Listen

Ask the Lord to lay on your heart a word of knowledge about someone you know. Spend a few minutes silently and expectantly awaiting a response and then pray for that person in accordance with the word of knowledge you received.

Day 28

God Speaks Through Prophets

Surely the Sovereign LORD does nothing without revealing His plan to His servants the prophets.

—Amos 3:7, NIV

As noted in an earlier chapter, prophets of today differ from their Old Testament-era counterparts. I love how Graham Cooke differentiates between Old Testament prophets and New Testament/contemporary prophets in his book *Developing Your Prophetic Gifting*. He writes:

> In the Old Testament, prophets were very forthright in rebuking, warning and chastising people, and were often used to denounce people and their sins. In the Church, prophets minister the word by exhortation, teaching, example and confirmation. The Gospel is redemptive, and we are serving a God of grace and mercy; therefore, our prophetic utterances are tempered by the Kingdom message.
>
> Christian prophets should not have the function or personality of their Old Testament counterparts. Prophets were feared before the time of Jesus. They were eccentric, intimidating, authoritarian individuals who gave messages of great portent, often with a foreboding or a sense of impending doom that seemed to hang around them. They were strangely independent, not easy to receive and at times deeply unpopular. Whether their lack of acceptance was due to their presentation, personality or their message (or a combination of all) is perhaps open to question.
>
> By contrast, the Christian prophet must be exhibiting the fruit of the Spirit with all grace and humility. They must be accountable members of the Body of Christ and living under authority while acting as team members, not an individual ministry."[31]

In spite of these differences in delivery and message, the point is that God still speaks through prophecy and prophets of today.

Today, under the new covenant, the prophet can be part of the eldership of the church to equip the saints for the work of the ministry. In addition to Ephesians 4:11–12, from which we obtain the fivefold offices of the ministry (apostles, prophets, evangelists, pastors, and teachers), prophets are listed in 1 Corinthians 12:28 along with "apostles … teachers, then those who do miracles, those who have the gift of healing, those who can help others, those who have the gift of leadership, [and] those who speak in unknown languages."

Prophets serve three primary functions:

1. They bring words of edification, comfort, and exhortation. (See 1 Corinthians 14:3; Acts 15:32.)
2. They build and establish the church through discipleship. They train people how to hear God for themselves so people can know the will of God for their lives. (See Ephesians 2:19–20; 1 Timothy 4:12–14).
3. They also bring direction and confirmation through God's Word, as well as foretell as the Lord leads. As Cooke explains, they "bring the Word of the Lord either in inspired preaching or by supernatural prophetic utterance."[32] (See Acts 21:10–11.)

Regarding the first function, we have already examined the way in which all prophesy. Regardless of the speaker, it must be edifying, comforting, and encouraging in nature, for the gospel of Christ is redemptive. Words from the Lord should turn one away from evil and give one hope, exalting Jesus Christ. (See Jeremiah 23:16–32.) Prophecy is never given to condemn. Correct, yes; condemn, no.

Second, God needs prophets to help build and establish the church. They often have a strong teaching gift because they have the heart to teach God's people how to hear Him and to come into a place of purity and maturity. After naming the fivefold ministry offices in Ephesians 4:11, Paul continues, explaining the function of those offices:

> And He Himself gave some to be apostles, some prophets, some evangelists, and some pastors and teachers, for the equipping of the saints for the work of the ministry, for the edifying of the body of Christ, till we all come to the unity of the faith and of the knowledge of the Son of God, to a perfect man, to the measure of the stature of the fullness of Christ; that we should no longer be children, tossed to and fro and carried about by every wind of doctrine.
>
> —Ephesians 4:11–14, NKJV

Have we come to the point yet where we are all living in "the unity of the faith" as "perfect" men and women, of "the measure of the stature of the fullness of Christ"? No. Therefore, prophets are still for today, and they are still God's spokesmen/women.

Finally, prophets of today are like watchmen. They watch to see what is coming up ahead. They are like God's mouthpiece with messages of what is or what is to come in order to reveal His plans in the lives of His people. Sometimes God does this simply because He is God and knows all things. He sees what's going to happen—the changes in people's lives or in the life of the church that are about to take place—and so He wants to prepare us and assure us of His love. Amos 3:7 declares, "Surely the Sovereign LORD does nothing without revealing His plan to His servants the prophets" (NIV).

Prophets flow in prophecy all the time and will flow in words of wisdom, words of knowledge, and discerning of spirits. They carry with them the presence of God, and often it is felt or witnessed by others. They also carry an authority that is often witnessed by others as well. Prophets hear God more keenly and with deeper accuracy and consistency than those who are not anointed to this office. In the next section we will look at the gift of prophecy and the call of all believers to prophesy.

Reflect

1. How does Ephesians 4:11–14 demonstrate that prophecy and the office of prophet are still for today?

_____
_____
_____
_____

2. In your own words, what are the three primary functions of the work of the prophet and what qualities or characteristics mark their ministry as different from those who prophesy without this particular position?

_____
_____
_____
_____

3. Sometimes God sets aside people for offices or positions, but they are never officially anointed to that role because they do not attend a church in which their calling is recognized or validated. Spend some time reflecting on your areas of gifting, and ask God what your calling is (if you do not already know). Are you plugged into a church in which your gifting is supported? Would the leadership of your church be likely to help you mature in a gifting related to one of the fivefold

ministries and anoint you to that role, or would they be unlikely to promote this sort of growth and development?

_____
_____
_____
_____

Pray

Heavenly Father, I thank You that You do not change. Thank You that You are speaking today through prophets, just as you did in the Old Testament era. Lord, open my heart fully to receive any message you may have for me, whether it comes to me directly or through one of your anointed prophets. Remove any skepticism from my heart about whether or not prophecy is for today, and settle it in my spirit that You have anointed men and women with the gift of prophecy. I don't want to miss any word from You because of unbelief. Give me an open heart and open ears to hear and respond to Your voice. I pray this in Jesus's name. Amen

Listen

Ask the Lord for the name of someone you need to invite to church or share His love with today. Spend a few minutes silently and expectantly awaiting a response and then follow up with that person.

Day 29

God Wants Us to Prophesy

And it shall come to pass afterward That I will pour out My Spirit on all flesh; Your sons and your daughters shall prophesy, Your old men shall dream dreams, Your young men shall see visions. And also on My menservants and on My maidservants I will pour out My Spirit in those days.

—Joel 2:28–29, NKJV

As we saw in the last section, some individuals are appointed to the office or position of prophet in the church, while others operate in the gift of prophecy. However, the ability to prophesy is not exclusive to these two groups of people. The Bible says that all can prophesy:

For you can all prophesy one by one, that all may learn and all may be encouraged.

—1 Corinthians 14:31, NKJV

In fact, the Bible exhorts us to desire to prophesy. Paul told the Corinthians to "pursue love, and desire spiritual gifts, but especially that you may prophesy" (1 Cor. 14:1). Why?

If all prophesy, and an unbeliever or an uninformed person comes in, he is convinced by all, he is convicted by all. And thus, the secrets of his heart are revealed; and so, falling on his face, he will worship God and report that God is truly among you.

—1 Corinthians 14:24–25, NKJV

Why does he fall and worship God? Because God's love through prophecy causes a love and acknowledgment of God. The Word of God comes alive when men and women of God speak it under the inspiration of the Holy Spirit. When we yield to what the Spirit of God is saying in our spirits—whether God speaks to us in a church service or elsewhere—people are touched, changed, renewed, restored, and God is made real. When the secrets of one's heart are revealed to and through another person, the person receiving the prophetic word knows that God is alive and well, for who could have known what was in their hearts but God? They realize that God loves them and has chosen to speak to them. This is the power of the Spirit moving through God's people to prophesy.

So how do we distinguish between those appointed to this position, those anointed with this specific gifting, and those who simply hear from the Lord as a part of their regular walk with the Holy Spirit? The office of prophet differs from the gift of prophecy, which is spoken of in 1 Corinthians 12:10:

> He gives one person the power to perform miracles, and another the ability to prophecy. He gives someone else the ability to discern whether a message is from the Spirit of God or from another spirit. Still another person is given the ability to speak in unknown languages, while another is given the ability to interpret what is being said.

A person with the gift of prophecy flows in the prophetic more often than someone who occasionally prophecies, but the operation of their gift still does not happen with the same ability or position as those appointed to the office of prophet. Nevertheless, God's heart through prophecy—whether spoken through the prophet, one operating under the gift of prophecy, or simply a layperson who prophesies—is always to speak God's heart, God's nature, and God's will. He desires that His people hear Him and know He is speaking to them.

Of course, it goes without saying prophecy must be done in order and under the guidance of the pastoral leadership when done in a church setting by someone not appointed to the office of prophet. We must also be cognizant of the reality that people are broken and struggle with various issues, beliefs, and hurts. If God speaks a word through us, we must take care to share it in the spirit of "edification and exhortation and comfort to men" (1 Cor. 14:3) in order to avoid offending others or making them feel condemned. Sometimes people will simply be offended by the truth, but we have a responsibility to grow in delivering the message so that we can ensure no harm will come to the recipients. If you receive a word from the Lord that seems like a word of correction or even direction, it is often best to share it with a trusted mentor in order to get their confirmation that it is, indeed, from the Lord and that it is appropriately couched in a message that will build the recipient up and not leave them feeling condemned or fearful.

Reflect

1. Have you ever received a word of prophecy for another person? Did you share it with him or her? What steps did you follow to ensure that you were hearing from the Lord? After going through this study, is there anything you will do differently in the future when God gives you words to share with others?

_____
_____
_____
_____

2. Read the account of Jesus's encounter with the woman at the well in John 4. In this story, Jesus spoke to a woman who had been divorced five times and was living with a man to whom she was not married. At the end of their conversation the woman was encouraged and recognized Him as the Messiah. Study Jesus's words to her in this passage. What was it about the way that He spoke to her that made it possible for her to receive such a difficult word and come away uplifted and knowing the love of God for her?

_____
_____
_____
_____

3. If you find that the Holy Spirit often gives you prophetic words for others, it may be wise to approach trusted leadership in your church to ask for mentoring and help identifying if you are operating in the gift of prophecy or if God is preparing you to assume the office of prophet. Identify one or two individuals in your church leadership who you could approach about this.

_____
_____
_____
_____

Pray

Heavenly Father, I thank You that You not only want to speak to me, but You also want to speak through me. Lord, how I desire to be Your mouthpiece! I earnestly long to speak words that draw people to You and cause them to acknowledge You. Like David, I pray the words that I speak, as well as the meditation of my heart, would be pleasing to You, O God. May everything I say and do point others to You and allow them to know Your heart and will for them more fully. I pray this in Jesus's name. Amen.

Listen

Ask the Lord to lead you to a class or person who could teach and mentor you in the operation and function of the prophetic. Spend a few minutes silently and expectantly awaiting a response. Follow up on the class or connection the Holy Spirit shares.

Day 30

God Speaks Through Circumstances and Object Lessons

This is why I speak to them in parables: "Though seeing, they do not see; though hearing, they do not hear or understand."

—Matthew 13:13, NIV

God made us visual learners. We imagine in our minds words that are spoken to us, and we look at and learn from our surroundings. God knows these things. He created us that way. This is why many times in Scripture we see how God used circumstances and object lessons to reach, teach, and speak to His people.[33] We will look at a few examples in this section.

I think the most obvious story in Scripture of God using events to communicate His will and word to man is the story of Jonah. In the Book of Jonah we read that the word of the Lord came to Jonah, telling him that God required him to go to Nineveh and cry out against it. Jonah responded by running away from the presence of God. He got on a boat and decided he would flee from that assignment. Not long after they set out to sea, God sent out a great wind over the water, causing fear among the other men on the ship. Jonah lay fast asleep in the lowest part of the ship while every other man called to his god. Yet nothing changed. They even began throwing cargo overboard in hopes of lightening the load.

Then the captain of the ship came to Jonah and woke him up. He instructed him to call on his God so that perhaps God would consider them and keep them from perishing. Jonah revealed that he was a Hebrew and that he feared the Lord, the God of heaven, who made the sea and the dry land. Jonah confessed his disobedience to God and instructed the men to throw him overboard. After first attempting to row against the tempestuous wind and pleading to the Lord, the God of Jonah, they picked Jonah up and threw him overboard. Almost immediately the sea ceased from its raging. We read next that God sent a great fish to swallow Jonah. This got Jonah's attention.

When Jonah prayed from the belly of the fish seeking God's forgiveness for his disobedience, we see that not only did God speak to the fish to vomit Jonah onto dry land, but God spoke to Jonah a second time. This time, Jonah obeyed.

What can we learn from this story? When speaking to Jonah's spirit didn't work, God used the circumstances of Jonah's surroundings to communicate His will unmistakeably and get him back on course so that he could complete God's will for his life. Sometimes adverse circumstances can be God's way of revealing we are going in the wrong direction. Whenever this happens, it is a good idea to stop and pray. Ask Him, "God, is this situation happening because I am going the wrong way? If so, then please, Lord, redirect me and tell me which way to go." Just as God was merciful and just to reach out to Jonah through whatever means it took to draw him back to Himself, God will honor your prayer for clarification about the details of challenging circumstances in your life. God is a redemptive God, redeeming us from destruction.

At other times in the Bible we see how God may use us and our testimony as an object lesson through which He can draw others to Himself. Two of the most extreme examples of this in Scripture are the prophets Hosea and Ezekiel. God used Hosea's life as an object lesson for the entire people of Israel. Israel was unfaithful to God. They kept turning to other gods. So God chose Hosea to perform a difficult and at first humiliating object lesson to reveal God's heart to His people. God told Hosea to marry Gomer to paint a picture of God's betrothal to Israel. (See Hosea 1:2, 7; 2:19.) Hosea was a faithful husband, but Gomer was unfaithful to Hosea, just as Israel was unfaithful to God. Her adultery vividly illustrated Israel's disloyalty to God, just as Hosea's unwavering love for Gomer demonstrated God's staunch devotion.

Even after Gomer's adulteries had destroyed their marriage and she became the slave, or concubine, of another man, Hosea was instructed to buy her back. Hosea's act of mercy toward his wife was a striking picture of the Lord's great love for His people. Through him, God told His people, "I will make you my wife forever, showing you righteousness and justice, unfailing love and compassion" (Hosea 2:19). This sounds extreme, yet it paints a beautiful picture of the Bridegroom's heart.

Ezekiel was another chosen vessel whom God used to portray some strange object lessons. On one occasion God asked Ezekiel to lie on his side to demonstrate that the length of Babylon's siege would correspond to the number of years that Israel sinned against God. He spent three hundred and ninety days on his left side and forty days on his right! (See Ezekiel 4:4–8.) In another instance, Ezekiel had to bake bread over dung to illustrate that their impending captivity would force them to eat polluted food that would reflect the "stink" of their sins. (See vv. 9–17.)

From Acts 21:10–11 we learn that God sent the prophet Agabus to bind Paul's hands and feet with his belt to demonstrate the danger that was waiting for Paul in Jerusalem. This was not a new word but was instead confirmation to Paul of something God had already told him about the "chains and tribulations [that] await[ed]" him there (Acts 20:22). When there is much at stake, or when we are seeking confirmation that a word is from the Lord, God may use prophecy in the form of an object lesson to illustrate His message.

Perhaps the best examples of God using object lessons or scenarios to communicate with us are the parables Jesus used during His earthly ministry. Jesus often spoke in parables using pictures of everyday life to instill in the minds of His listeners what He was trying to say. He knew that the audience listening to Him was diverse and that many lacked education in the Scriptures, so He spoke using relatable imagery and circumstances to ensure that everyone to whom He preached would understand His message. Those parables are still relevant for us today and serve to offer deep insight into the nature and love of God.

Reflect

1. How and why does God speak through circumstances? Has God ever spoken to you through a situation or object lesson? If so, how? Was it to speak a new message, confirm a word you already heard, or to get your attention?

___

2. Take some time today to read some of the parables of Jesus. Which one resonates with you most strongly? Why?

___

3. The same principle behind God's decision to use circumstances, object lessons, and parables to speak to us is part of what makes fictional books, movies, and television so powerful. Try to think of a book, movie, or TV show you have seen that reflected some biblical principle or precept. It doesn't have to be a Christian book or film; there are many secular books and other media that unknowingly or unintentionally teach a godly lesson.

___

Pray

Thank You, Father, for the many different ways You speak. Thank You that You can use the circumstances I experience and observe to get my attention and teach me lessons. You are a loving Shepherd, always leading me toward what is best and good for me. Open my spiritual eyes to perceive You speaking to me this way and open my heart to receive the message. I pray this in Jesus's name. Amen.

Exercise

Ask the Lord to lead you to a scriptural principle, message, or word of instruction from the Bible. Then write your own parable to illustrate the concept by imagining a modern-day situation that could be used to convey that message. Write out the story or scenario and share it with a friend or your study group.

Lesson Seven

God Speaks Through Visions and Dreams

Day 31

God Speaks Through Visions

There is a God in heaven who reveals secrets.

—Daniel 2:28

Visions from God are pictures, images, and visualized flashes of thoughts. They are usually given while awake and are seen or perceived within a person's mind. In many cases throughout Scripture we read about visions that were given, yet there is no mention of anything tangible that was seen. Likewise, it is clear that none of the visions came from the thoughts of the person receiving the vision. Any images you must imagine or think up are not from God; they are from your own mind (or possibly the enemy). Visions are from the Holy Spirit to our spirit. Though they are perceived with our mind, they do not originate there.

When we study Scripture, we see that all visions either came suddenly or appeared in prayer as God initiated them or as one looked to God in prayer. When we pray to the Lord we can ask that God speak to us and wait with expectation, knowing and believing that God desires to reveal His heart to us, but I am always cautious when I hear people teach that we can "activate" an experience with God or that man can summon a holy God to speak to us at our beck and call. To me, that is not biblical, and neither is it reverential to a holy God. I would caution against it. I do realize, however, that some use activation simply to mean being proactive in our pursuit of God while waiting on Him expectantly with anticipation of Him speaking to us. Also, we can "activate" ourselves or stir up the gifts within. In this sense, I agree 100 percent with the word *activation*.

When God is the direct source of our visions and dreams, He will provide an interpretation for us. There are times that we may receive a vision or a dream and not have full understanding or interpretation. A word of caution: Don't stop receiving the vision or interrupt it to guess or try to figure it out. Instead, take in the whole vision and then pray, ask God for the interpretation, listen. God wants to be understood. That is the whole purpose of the vision, after all! He will either provide an interpretation or send someone who can hear Him to provide understanding. God is not a God who keeps us guessing, nor does He want us to be confused about His word for us.

The Book of Daniel gives us great examples of how we can learn to consider visions, especially those that are not immediately clear, and ask for understanding. It also demonstrates the faithfulness of God to reveal the message or the purpose of any vision He gives us. Daniel 7:1–2 informs us that Daniel saw visions (as well as dreams), wrote them down, but then continued to consider the vision. The Scriptures tell us he continued to look actively at the visions and pondered what was happening (v. 6). After many visions that troubled him, Daniel wrote, "I, Daniel, was grieved in my spirit within my body, and the visions of my head troubled me" (v. 15, NKJV). Why was he troubled and grieved? Partly because at this point he had no understanding of the meaning of the visions. He did not yet know the interpretations.

In the next verse we read that Daniel pressed into God and asked Him questions, specifically, what the vision meant: "So he told me and made known to me the interpretation of these things" (v. 16, NKJV). God made the interpretation known to Daniel after he asked questions. Daniel did not have to guess, feel confused for days, or try to reason it out. Neither did he use dream books to understand symbols.

We learn from Daniel that we can ask for the explanation if we do not immediately understand. By communicating with the Lord and asking questions, God responds. As with any time God shares a word with us, when we seek the Lord and inquire of Him, He will answer. If He doesn't, perhaps the vision or message wasn't God, it's not for now, or we may be too distracted and need to continue to press in and be patient.[34]

Peter's experience receiving the vision of the clean and unclean animals in Acts 10 also reinforces God's willingness to provide the interpretation of visions He gives us. It also teaches us an important lesson about the posture of our heart while we are waiting for the interpretation when there is a delay. With this vision, God desired to show Peter the state of his heart, a wrong mind-set, and also instruct him in what was to be a primary message of his ministry.

As we learned earlier, Peter was steeped in Jewish tradition. Certain foods were forbidden to be eaten, Jews and Gentiles should not eat together for risk of defilement, and salvation was thought to be for the Jews only. When God gave him the vision on the roof, Peter did not fully understand at first, even though God repeated it three times. Acts 10:17 says, "Peter was very perplexed. What could the vision mean?" A few verses later we read that "as Peter was puzzling over the vision, the Holy Spirit" told Peter He had sent three men to him (v. 19). The Spirit reassured him not to worry, and Peter chose to step out in faith, believing that God would provide the interpretation. Peter had to act on the vision and step out in obedience, and then understanding came. God strategically used the men He sent that day to help provide the interpretation to the vision. The notes of the Life Application Bible explain, "It took a three-part heavenly vision for God to change Peter's mind. One of the most basic and practical lessons from this encounter is that when God speaks, we must not challenge what he says. Doubting God is the rebellion of Eden. When God says something is so, we must not debate with Him. The right response is humble submission to his revealed truth."[35] God is persistent to reveal Himself to us when we are obedient to His instructions and patient to hear His voice.

This principle is true for us today. In Joel 2:28 we read a prophecy that promised, "It shall come to pass afterward that I will pour out My Spirit on all flesh; your sons and your daughters shall prophesy, your old men shall dream dreams, your young men shall see visions" (NKJV). Jesus confirmed this prophecy in Luke, and it was fulfilled on the Day of Pentecost. (See Acts 2.) The same Spirit that was poured out then is living in and speaking to us today. There is no reason to believe that these gifts ceased after the New Testament era. The testimonies of believers who are still receiving biblical, life-giving visions speaks to the operation of this mode of Spirit communication today. If you want to receive visions from the Holy Spirit, you need only ask for them, seek God, and maintain a posture of obedience toward the Bible and His specific words for you.

Reflect

1. What is your experience with God speaking through visions? Has it been positive or negative?

_____
_____
_____
_____

2. Have you ever received a vision from the Holy Spirit? If so, what was it, and how did you know it was Him? If you have only observed/heard as others received visions, how did you go about testing the spirits to see if your spirit bore witness to the interpretation?

_____
_____
_____
_____

Pray

Heavenly Father, how great are You that You would visit me with visions! Lord, I desire to receive and understand when You are trying to speak to me through visions. Help me to press in to You and ask You for interpretation. Keep me from adding to Your vision. Prevent me from speaking from my own interpretations. I pray this in Jesus's name. Amen.

Listen

Is there a Scripture verse or passage you have struggled to understand or a question you have for God? Ask the Lord to give you clarity and an answer through a vision or some other mode of His voice. Spend a few minutes silently and expectantly awaiting a response.

Day 32

What Do Visions Look Like?

Thus says the Lord ... "Call to Me, and I will answer you, and show you great and mighty things, which you do now know."

—Jeremiah 33:3, NKJV

Visions are nothing more than visual communication from God's Spirit to your mind. Simply put, when you receive a vision it will look like images or pictures. The images may last for several seconds or even minutes, or they may simply appear as quick flashes of pictures in your mind's eye. They will likely be spontaneous, interrupting your thoughts, unless you are purposefully seeking the Lord and beholding Him in prayer at the time of a vision.

When we study Scripture, we learn that God initiates visions as He chooses. He communicated then and communicates today with people through images of many kinds. God is the one in control of His visitations and ways of communication. He may choose to respond to our prayers through a vision, or He may give us a vision as a piece of revelation, a word of knowledge, or another message of prophecy. Depending on the message and interpretation, our visions might be as simple as seeing an image of a friend or someone that we know of with the thought to pray or phone them, or He may reveal a vision that is far more detailed and precise.

Below is a list of some of the visions God gave to different men in the Scriptures. They provide an excellent overview of the different forms and purposes visions may take.

- Genesis 15:1 says, "After these things the word of the Lord came to Abram *in a vision*, saying, 'Do not be afraid, Abram. I am your shield, your exceedingly great reward'" (NKJV, emphasis added). God used this vision to encourage Abram and gave him a picture of who God was to him: a shield and a reward.

- Isaiah tells us that he "*saw* the Lord" in a very descriptive vision that revealed the holiness of God (v. 6, emphasis added). As he was in the vision, God spoke a word of instruction and direction to him.
- While still blinded from his encounter with the risen Christ on the road to Damascus, Paul (then still known as Saul) saw a vision of a man aiding him in receiving his sight once again. (See Acts 9:12.) This encouraged Paul to know that he was going to regain his sight and gave him confidence that God was going to be faithful to continue to provide the answers and direction He promised.
- In another story, both Cornelius and Peter received visions from the Lord to fulfill the purposes of God. (See Acts 10.) Cornelius was a devout, God-fearing man who gave alms and prayed, yet he did not know Jesus, for he was an Italian gentile. So in a vision an angel of the Lord gave him instructions to send men to Joppa to find Peter, and he immediately obeyed. While these men journeyed to Joppa Peter was in prayer and received his now-famous vision of a great sheet bound at the four corners being let down to the earth and descending to him. In it were all kinds of animals, both clean and unclean. He was instructed in this vision to kill and eat them, which for Jews was against the commandments of the Law. The Lord spoke in this vision saying, "What God has cleansed you must not call common" (v. 14, NKJV). As we saw in the last section, God's close pursuit of man broke through the letter of the Law for the sake of God's ultimate plan of salvation. Cornelius' faithfulness to obey the vision he received resulted in his salvation and provided Peter with the confirmation he needed in order to fully understand and step out in obedience to the vision God had given him. Because of this encounter, Peter was able to reach thousands with the message that the gospel was for all people and not just the Jews.

Throughout the book I have shared portions of my testimony or journal that demonstrate and reinforce some of the lessons we are learning about how to hear the Holy Spirit speak. There are many stories I could share to show how God has used visions to guide, direct, and encourage me. However, the one below is one of my favorites.

> My husband called, and there was panic in his voice. He proceeded to tell me to pray. Our son had fallen from about three feet onto a forklift, just missing the prongs that were pointed upward. It could have been catastrophic. Nevertheless, our son was still in lots of pain. There was a concern of broken ribs or other bones as our son traveled to the hospital for observation.
>
> I immediately went into my prayer room, closed the door, and entered the presence of God. At first I only shared the fear and apprehension I was feeling. Getting emotions off my chest has always been routine in prayer. I knew if I wanted to pray effectively, fear had to go, and perfect love from My Father is the greatest antidote! Peace is my portion,

and God knew I needed it. But first, I had to unload my burdens by confessing to God the fear that was trying to grip my heart. "Be anxious for nothing," declare the Scriptures, "but in everything by prayer and supplication, with thanksgiving, let your requests be made known to God; and the peace of God, which surpasses all understanding, will guard your hearts and minds through Christ Jesus" (Phil. 4:6–7, NKJV).

Once I experienced peace I prayed and pressed in to God for His heart concerning my son. After several minutes I saw a huge hand cupping my son as he fell from the truck onto the forklift. It was God who not only protected his fall but guided his path strategically so he wouldn't be punctured by the prongs. In this vision, I heard the Lord say, "And he will have no broken bones."

Immediately I felt prompted to text my son and tell him what the Lord had shown me and what He was promising. My son responded, "I don't know, Mom. I am in a lot of pain, and it does feel like something is broken." I encouraged him to trust in what God had shown me.

A few hours passed when I heard the beep of an incoming text. It was my son. "NO BROKEN BONES" was typed in bold, capital letters.

As we see in these examples, the visions God gives are purposeful and reveal God's character. When we pray and ask, God is diligent to provide an interpretation Himself or to send someone with a message that makes the interpretation clear.

Reflect

1. Why or under what circumstances might God choose to provide a vision spontaneously, outside of our time of prayer and study of the Word?

___

2. In the last two sections we have looked carefully at Peter's vision on the rooftop that changed the course of his entire ministry. Read Acts 10 and consider why God chose to reveal that message to Peter in the way that He did. Why did He choose to speak to him in a vision? What is significant about the way in which He confirmed that vision for Peter?

___

Pray

Heavenly Father, thank You for giving Your followers Your Word to use as a tool and a guide. It truly is a lamp before my feet and a light on my path. Even as I am learning how I might hear from You in visions, Your Word contains many, many examples of others who saw and heard You speak to them this way. These examples encourage and instruct me. Please continue to teach me, Lord, how to be open to visions, and help me not to be discouraged if You choose not to speak to me this way at first. I trust in Your sovereignty and long to hear You in whatever form You choose. In Jesus's name, I pray. Amen.

Listen

Ask the Lord to give you an inner picture or vision that communicates His love for you. Spend a few minutes silently and expectantly awaiting a response.

My Story

A Vision of Trouble

On February 3, 2011, while praying in the Spirit, the Lord gave me a vision. I saw myself in a room walking toward a bed. On this bed lay a sleeping newborn. She was sleeping on her tummy, her bum up in the air and her tiny, little legs curled under her. She looked so pure, innocent, and precious as she lay there sleeping, completely naked and unashamed.

Then I saw myself lay down beside her, watching this precious child. Suddenly she rolled on her side with her little bum now facing me. To my surprise, she began pooping, and instantly I stuck my hand out to catch it. It was messy, and I found myself covered in it. That then ended the vision.

I pressed into God and asked Him for the interpretation. I felt the Lord impress upon me that someone whom I thought of as being as innocent as this precious newborn baby was not so innocent and was in deep trouble. Finding out the truth was going to feel like I was being "pooped on," and it was going to be messy. I continued to pray in the Spirit.

The very next day I found out that a young lady I had known since her birth was in deep trouble. I immediately remembered the vision the Lord gave me the day before. God had sent this vision to warn me and prepare my heart. Immediately I wanted to pray fervently for her, but I didn't know exactly how to pray because fear immediately gripped my heart. God is a God of justice, and she had committed wrongdoing; in light of that, how was I to pray? Thus, I prayed in the Spirit every moment I could. I also prayed that God would be a Father to her.

At that moment, Hebrews 12:5–11 came to mind. I was unaware of exactly what that scripture was about. I eagerly reached for my Bible and scanned the pages for its location. The Holy Spirit was using that scripture to tell me He was chastening her to ultimately draw her closer to Him. For weeks on end I watched the Lord's hand upon her. No matter what that young lady did, even as she continued to make wrong choices and hang around negative and ungodly influences, the police force was everywhere she was. She was not getting away with anything!

It was so hard to watch and go through, but my heart was settled in the reality that whom the Lord loves, He chastens. It is often in suffering the consequences of our actions that we change. I agreed with the Word of God. In fact, I continued to pray that she would get caught every time she made the wrong decision but that God's grace would go before her. I held on to the promise that afterward the discipline she was receiving would yield the peaceable fruit of right living to those who have been trained by it. This young lady slowly began suffering emotional distress that brought her toward making better choices.

Then the Lord gave me another vision. In this vision God revealed that He was going before my friend to give her grace and favor. He revealed that she would be free of her trouble, but neither would God be mocked. In other words, I was to warn her that God was giving her mercy. She was to repent for her wrongdoing and turn from the way she was going. I was to tell her that God was a Father to her and that He was the one who was going to help her.

Though all odds were against her—and circumstantially it looked bleak—God is faithful, and He broke through for her. Today, I can say that this young lady has turned her life around. Though my human, motherly heart would have eased my friend's trials, God, in His infinite, loving wisdom, fathered her—His child—in ways that He knew would actually benefit her.

Day 33

God Speaks Through Dreams

If there is a prophet among you, I, the Lord, make Myself known to him in a vision; I speak to him in a dream.

—Numbers 12:6, NKJV

Throughout history and today, God has appeared in dreams or gives dreams to His followers as a means of communicating with them. A dream is described as several images and series of events during sleep. I once heard dreams explained as "night parables."

As with visions, when God gives dreams, He interprets them or sends someone who can. There are many examples in the Word where God used dreams in the following ways:

- To encourage (Judges 7:15)

- To instruct or counsel (Abimelech's dream in Genesis 20:3–7 and Jacob's in Genesis 31:11–13)

- To reveal, guide, or prophesy of the future (Jacob's dream in Genesis 28:12–17, Joseph's in Genesis 37:5–11, Solomon's in 1 Kings 3:5–15, as well as those of Ezekiel and Daniel)

As in all God-given dreams (and with visions and prophecies) one needs to have a sound basis in the Bible and a solid understanding of who God is and what His nature and character are to be sure that it is God giving the pictures or images. People have imaginations and can easily see what their mind or flesh desires. We can make false presumptions, or the enemy can plant pictures as well.

This is why we must continue to test the spirits. God is direct, purposeful, clear, and when it's from God, it will come to pass. (See Deuteronomy 18:20–22.) If you or someone else dreams something that tempt you to move away from God and follow other gods, even though it may come to pass, it is not of God. I caution you, before you go around telling people you had a dream or vision, especially if it is of the future, be careful that you don't automatically assume that it was from God. Test it, because your character and integrity is at stake as well as God's. I highly recommend that one gets accountability and practice in the safety of one's church body or small groups.

On another note, often in modern-day praying, like Theophostic, Immanuel, listening, or healing restorative prayer, we seek the Lord to reveal His heart for particular sorrows, grief, or blockages and ask Him to show us lies that we may be believing, knowing that by His Spirit He desires to reveal His truth. When He does speak in prayer in these settings, God, in His love for us, may reveal images, pictures, or memories of our past where the lies were first implanted. These visual messages may come in the form of visions upon immediate ministry. However, if nothing occurs during ministry time, God may speak to the individual in a dream. Once these lies are exposed, we must ask the Lord to replace them with the truth.

As with any move of God, there is no reason to be afraid of prophetic dreams, even if they offer reminders of past experiences that caused us hurt. Even and especially in those instances God will often show us a picture or images of the truth of His love for us, such as of Himself lovingly alongside us. He does so to bring healing to our hearts and minds. (See Psalm 107:19–20.) Our God is a God of comfort. He cares about the broken-hearted.

That is the purpose for which God speaks to us through dreams. He desires that we be free from the lies and deceptions of the evil one. Even more, God desires that we know His truth. God wants for us to prosper in all things and be in health even as our soul prospers (3 John 2). For that to happen, our minds need to be renewed to His truths, for we will only prosper and be in health as our hearts are restored to the truths of His Word. He is ever willing to walk us through, in our wakeful and sleeping states, to comfort all who mourn, to console us, to give us beauty for ashes and the oil of joy for mourning! (See Luke 4:17–20.) But we must recognize the one speaking.

I have found it to be a helpful practice to keep a written record of any prophetic dreams (or even particularly vivid dreams) I have. In fact, I keep a separate journal specifically for any dreams I dream. I date them as well. The minute I wake up I write my dreams down and then ask the Lord to provide the interpretation, if He has not done so already. Because it is not uncommon not to remember everything from a dream, don't be afraid to write and talk to God as you are journaling. God is able to bring to your remembrance key pictures or interpretations where you have forgotten them. Reading and rereading these journals are a wonderful and edifying way of encouraging yourself in the Lord and reminding yourself of the messages He has spoken to you. I have years' worth of journals—everything from dream journals to vision journals to fasting and prayer journals—and rereading them is one way I reflect on the Lord's goodness and get stirred in the Spirit.

Reflect

1. Why might it especially be important to test the spirits regarding prophetic dreams (as opposed to visions or other messages from the Holy Spirit)?

_____
_____
_____
_____

2. In your own words, what is the purpose of prophetic dreams?

_____
_____
_____
_____

3. Have you ever experienced a prophetic dream? Write about it. How did you know the interpretation? How did you discern that it was from the Holy Spirit?

_____
_____
_____
_____

Pray

Heavenly Father, help me to pay attention to my dreams. Help me to seek You for interpretation if the dream is from You. Make me sensitive to all the ways You speak, Lord, especially in visions and dreams. I pray this in Jesus's name. Amen.

Listen

Think of a dream you had recently or in the past that was particularly memorable. Ask the Lord to reveal the interpretation, if any. Spend a few minutes silently and expectantly awaiting a response.

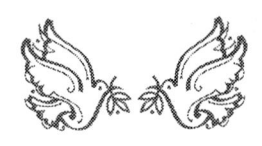

Day 34

What Do Prophetic Dreams Look Like?

For God speaks again and again, though people do not recognize it. He speaks in dreams, in visions of the night, when deep sleep falls on people as they lie in their beds. He whispers in their ears and terrifies them with warnings. He makes them turn from doing wrong; he keeps them from pride.

—Job 33:14–17

In the next session we will discuss how to recognize when a vision or dream is not of the Lord, that is, either from our own mind or from the enemy. In this section we will focus instead on how prophetic dreams are portrayed in Scripture and some of the different lessons we can learn from these accounts.

The stories of Joseph's dreams and his gift for interpreting them stand out in the Bible as some of the most striking examples of God speaking about the future through prophetic dreams. Joseph was a shepherd who spent much of his days out in the field. When he had a dream as a young man it consisted of "binding sheaves in the field" alongside his brothers (Gen. 37:7, NKJV). His sheaf, or bundle, arose and stood upright. His brothers' bundles stood tall and bowed down to Joseph's sheaf. When Joseph shared his dream with his brothers, even they perceived the interpretation of the dream, for they declared, "Shall you indeed reign over us? Or shall you indeed, have dominion over us?" (v. 8, NKJV).

Then Joseph had yet another dream, and this time, the sun, the moon, and the eleven stars bowed down to him. (See Genesis 37:5–11.) The sun and moon represented his father and mother, and the eleven stars stood for his eleven brothers. He revealed this dream to his father and brothers, and his father rebuked him. Once again, they immediately perceived the interpretation of the dream because God gave them understanding and the symbolism was clear. Both of these dreams were fulfilled decades later after Joseph rose to a position of prominence in Egypt. His father and brothers did, indeed, bow down to him and seek his help in order to save their lives and families.

Before Joseph was promoted in Egypt, however, he was falsely imprisoned because of a lie his master's wife told about him. Genesis 40 tells us that while Joseph was there in prison Pharaoh's butler and baker had offended Pharaoh, so he placed them in the same jail where Joseph was confined. Both the butler and baker each had a dream. The butler dreamed of grapes, vine branches, Pharaoh's cup, and him serving Pharaoh. When the baker dreamed, he saw baskets and baked goods for Pharaoh. Joseph heard the men's dreams and gave them the interpretation: the butler's dream represented his life, and the baker's dream represented the baker's life.

Notice how these dreams were both symbolic and literal. When Joseph dreamed of eleven stars, the stars were symbolic of his brothers, while the number eleven was literal. Likewise, the baker's three baskets meant three days. So we see that dreams can be symbolic, literal, or a combination of both.

These accounts also tell us that dreams can hold unique significance for the dreamer. The baker's and butler's dreams both represented the trajectory of their lives specifically. Joseph's dreams foretold his future rise to power in Egypt, even to the point of ruling over his family. While those dreams involved his family, the interpretation angered them because it wasn't meant for them; they struggled to understand why Joseph would so openly share dreams that seemed to glorify him over them. They didn't receive the message because the dream wasn't meant for them, though they were part of it.

Genesis 41 tells the story of a particularly confusing dream Pharaoh had while Joseph was still in prison. Pharaoh saw seven cows come up out of the river—nice, fat-looking cows—and begin feeding by the meadow. Then he saw seven other cows that came up out of the river, but these cows were ugly and gaunt. Suddenly the seven thin cows ate the seven fat cows. The Bible reveals that he woke up, fell back asleep, and had a second dream. It was the same principle as the first dream but used different symbols. This time he saw grain instead of cows.

When he awoke his spirit was troubled, so he called for all the magicians of Egypt and all the wise men to provide an interpretation. Interestingly, they could not interpret these dreams, which came from the Lord. Then the Scriptures tell us that Pharaoh's butler remembered that while he was imprisoned Joseph had interpreted a dream that he had, and everything that Joseph had interpreted had been genuine and came to pass. The butler confessed that up until that moment he had forgotten all about Joseph.

So Pharaoh called for Joseph and explained his dream to him, saying, "I have heard that when you hear about a dream you can interpret it" (v. 15). Joseph responded, "It is beyond my power to do this ... But God can tell you what it means and set you at ease" (v. 16). When Pharaoh was finished relating his two dreams to Joseph, Joseph replied, "The dreams of Pharaoh are one; God has shown Pharaoh what He is about to do" (v. 25, NKJV), and proceeded to tell Pharaoh the interpretation about seven years of plenty and seven years of famine. Then Joseph said, "The dream was repeated to Pharaoh twice because the thing is established by God, and God will shortly bring it to pass" (v. 32, NKJV). At that point Pharaoh recognized that Joseph was filled with the Spirit of God, placed him charge over the land of Egypt, and renamed him Zaphnath-Paaneah, which means "God speaks and lives." (See vv. 38, 45.)

This account perfectly demonstrates the way in which the appropriate move of the prophetic draws unbelievers to the Lord. We must notice also that Joseph did not take credit as a dream interpreter; instead, he made sure to let them know who would interpret the dream—God. He gave credit where it was due and reaped a reward for his humility.

As an interesting comparison, I looked up the meaning of these same dreams from a few secular Internet sites on dream interpretation. I thought it would be fascinating to see if they would be able to rightly interpret Pharaoh's dreams or if they would fail, as Pharaoh's wise men and magicians did. Here is what I found:

- A fat cow means longevity and prosperity.
- A thin cow represents drought.
- Thin cows eating fat cows means coming into prosperity.
- Meadows represent happy reunions and future prosperity.
- The number seven is an outer expression of an inner spiritual principle and initiation. In another dream book it said the number seven is the number of God's completion and perfection.

Based on these meanings, many interpretations could be arrived at. I might even conclude that the dream meant God was giving me longevity and prosperity. However, this would be way off and nothing like the interpretation that God gave to Joseph. The bottom line is this: Like the wise men and magicians Pharaoh consulted, modern dream books are a poor source of interpretation for prophetic dreams.

If God gives a dream, why would we turn to a book instead of turning to the One who gave the dream? If we don't turn to the Lord for His interpretation, we could totally miss what God is saying. How could we expect to know exactly what a prophetic dream means unless we ask God, the one who gave the dream to us?

Also, I am hesitant to believe that certain symbols or numbers all mean the same thing to all people in all dreams. God is a personal God. It seems most likely that if God uses any symbols, numbers, or animals in a dream, the meaning would be unique to the one He is speaking to. Only seeking God for the interpretation will be fruitful in understanding what He is revealing to you through a dream.

Daniel 2:1–49 provides us with another excellent example of God being the only one able to reveal "secret things" (v. 22, NKJV) through prophetic visions and dreams. In this passage we read that King Nebuchadnezzar had dreams, and his spirit was so troubled by these dreams that he wasn't sleeping. He called on the wise men in his kingdom (e.g., the magicians, sorcerers, astrologers, and the Chaldeans) to interpret the dream. They could not, and this angered the king, who ordered all the wise men to be killed, including Daniel and his friends (even though they had not provided any interpretation).

Daniel sought the Lord, asking Him to reveal the secret of this dream. Verse 19 tells us that "the secret was revealed to Daniel in a night vision" (NKJV). So Daniel blessed the Lord, saying, "For wisdom and might are His. ... He reveals deep and secret things; He knows what is in the darkness, and light dwells with Him" (vv. 20, 22, NKJV).

When Daniel approached the king, he said, "The secret which the king has demanded, the wise men, the astrologers, the magicians, and the soothsayers cannot declare to the king. But there is a God in heaven who reveals secrets, and He has made known to King Nebuchadnezzar what will be in the latter days" (v. 27–28, NKJV). He then proceeded to tell the king not only what the dream was but also the interpretation, to which the king replied, "Truly your God is the God of gods, the Lord of kings, and a revealer of secrets since you could reveal this secret" (v. 47, NKJV).

Notice how the interpretation of the dream was given in its entirety in order to fulfill God's purpose and to reveal who is the revealer of secrets. Also, yet once again we see that Daniel did not take credit for interpreting dreams but explained to the king that the God of heaven is the one who "is the God of gods, the Lord of kings, and a revealer of secrets." Instead, in humility and gratitude Daniel blessed God.

We also see examples in the New Testament of God speaking through dreams. In the Book of Matthew we read that the angel of the Lord appeared to Mary's husband, Joseph, in a dream instructing him to take Mary and Jesus to Israel because there were those who sought to kill Jesus. (See Matthew 2:19–20.) It was given to Joseph to warn him of impending danger. No interpretation was necessary because the angel's message was clear and literal. Likewise, Pilot's wife was given a dream to warn Pilot not to pass judgment on Jesus because he was "innocent" and was a "just Man" (Matt. 27:19, NKJV). By the time the dream ended, Pilot's wife was sure of the message God had spoken to her.

All of these examples make it clear that when God gives us prophetic dreams, He will provide an interpretation. (Remember, the same is true of visions.) Sometimes the dream is clear enough or literal enough that we can understand the message ourselves, sometimes He may send another person to help provide the interpretation, and other times yet we may need to continue to press into God and ask Him questions to help us to understand, just as Daniel did.

We also see from Scripture that when God speaks or gives visions and dreams He gives them for a purpose. They are another way He lets us know He desires to speak into our lives and demonstrate His power, His love, and His desire for intimacy with us.

Reflect

1. When Joseph shared his dreams with his brothers and father, they did not respond well to the message. What can we learn from these accounts about how or with whom we should share prophetic dreams (and visions) the Lord gives us?

_____
_____
_____
_____

2. Why do you think God would choose to share prophetic dreams with unbelievers, as in the case of Pharaoh and King Nebuchadnezzar? What does this tell us about the Father's heart for relationship?

_____
_____
_____
_____

3. Think of the trusted, believing friends in your circle of influence. Which one or ones could you approach confidently with a prophetic dream about which you need interpretation?

_____
_____
_____
_____

Pray

Dear God, thank You that when You give me dreams and visions You won't leave me to consult secular books about the interpretation of dreams or leave me to wonder at their meaning; instead, I can be confident that the dreams and visions from You will be accompanied by a clear interpretation. As I reflect on the examples in the Scriptures of the ways in which You spoke to Your people through dreams and visions, it builds my faith in You and Your desire to communicate with me clearly. Speak to me, Lord, however You desire; I am listening faithfully. In Jesus's name, I pray. Amen.

Listen

Ask the Lord to give you a message for someone else in the form of a vision. Spend a few minutes silently and expectantly awaiting a response.

My Story
Warning, Instruction, and Freedom

September 4, 2009. A couple of nights ago, Brian and I were deep in discussion. He had been sharing with me how exhausted he was because he hadn't slept much the night before. I asked him why he hadn't slept, and he confessed it was because of a "stupid" dream that woke him up and kept him up for most of the night.

I questioned if he understood what the dream meant and if he was willing to share it. Unbeknownst to him, it had significant meaning, which we were about to discover.

He dreamt that he was a beekeeper. As he was attending to the bees, one flew up his nose. He saw himself in this dream trying to blow this bee out of his nose, but to no avail. It irritated and annoyed him, as it would anyone. While he was dreaming this, he suddenly woke up because his nose felt like it had a real bee in it. Instantly he sat up, reached for a Kleenex, and proceeded to blow his nose. All night long he said it felt like something was tickling his nose, and he just couldn't break free from its annoyance.

I asked him what a bee meant to him. He replied, "Honey." I immediately received partial interpretation, accompanied by a word of knowledge. I asked him, "Did someone hit on you yesterday?"

He instantly had this bewildered look. "Yes," he replied.

"Tell me what happened," I said.

While Brian was driving his semi, a woman pulled up beside him and began flirting with him. He sped up, but then so would she. This continued for a few minutes. To his surprise, she began performing indecent acts, and he confessed that momentarily he couldn't look away. Some time later, he broke from his gaze, ignored her seduction, and sped away as quickly as he could, refusing to look at her any further. "I felt so guilty. In fact, I still feel guilty," he moaned.

I then asked him, "So you know you did wrong. What did you do about it?"

"I ignored the conviction for some stupid reason, and just tried to blow it off," he sighed.

In a flash I received the complete interpretation. The bee represented honey, which represented the woman. Proverbs 5:3 says, "For the lips of an immoral woman drip honey" (NKJV). In the dream, this bee went up Brian's nose and tickled his senses. She appealed to his pleasure senses through flirting and through her indecent acts. When he tried to blow his nose, it represented his blowing the whole incident off. Brian is the keeper of his senses. His eyes, his nose, and his heart, and sin—or this bee—won't simply just go away. You cannot just blow off sin like it didn't happen. Instead, you must confess it and unload this type of burden from the heart and soul. This is the process of repenting and guarding your heart with all diligence.

I felt like the Lord sent him this dream to warn him of his current condition as well as for future protection. I sensed the Lord was saying that spiritual warfare is at hand.

Brian was flabbergasted by the whole incident, from the actual occurrence to the dream and its interpretation. But more importantly, he was in awe of God's graciousness towards him. We were both crying as we prayed together. He confessed this sin and willingly gave it to God. Needless to say, there have been no more interruptions during his sleep.

January 25, 2010. Last night I had another dream about fear. Yes, God has indeed unveiled yet another layer to this onion of fear that needs to be peeled away.

I was sitting at a table with a group of people when this woman approached me with this beautiful, gold Egyptian bracelet. It just glimmered with radiant jewels. It was so appealing to the eyes. It was stunning. I watched her twist and manipulate this bracelet three times and then place it on my wrist.

Shortly after that, another Egyptian woman, whom I knew to be the girl's mother, came up to me and said, "Before you can wear that bracelet, you must accept and vow to our 'rite of ownership.'" She then proceeded to play this Egyptian music from a ghetto blaster that was right beside me on the floor. As this music played—the same kind of music you see playing when they charm snakes to rise out of a container—this bracelet started to tighten like a snake coiling its body around its victim. I instantly shouted, "No, I will not vow and accept your god, nor will I worship him." I ripped the bracelet off my wrist and threw it across the floor.

Immediately the ghetto blaster began to contort and morph into fingers trying to grab me. I then shouted, "The blood of Jesus washes me. The blood of Jesus cleanses me. The blood of Jesus protects me." Instantaneously the music and contortions ceased, and the Egyptians were gone. I looked around the table to see who was sitting with me. I took a quick survey in my heart of who may be judging or criticizing me, but there was no one.

I woke up with this interpretation: The Egyptians represented those who enslaved, and they wanted to enslave me. The bracelet was symbolic of fear, a fear demon/god. In this dream, the fear was my fear of confrontation. What silences me from confrontation? What is the root? Fear of failure? Fear of rejection? Fear of what other people think of me? Am I afraid that I might look like a fool?

The beautiful bracelet was symbolic of fear's disguise. It comes to convince you of its beauty. Symbolically, fear has many "jewels." I had accepted the lie that if I wore those jewels, I would be safe. If I don't confront I won't fail. If I don't face I won't be rejected. If I don't confront others can't have an *opinion of me. This bracelet represented the many facets of fear and the underlying jewels that accompany it. In this dream, fear came at me disguised as this beautiful, radiant bracelet, and I had to choose whether to accept and wear it or refuse and reject it.*

The Egyptian mother who said I had to vow to a right of ownership signified my choice to be enslaved to it or not. Fear is a choice. I am not a victim to it, even though it may feel like it at times. It does not control me, though it often feels like it does. She was alluring me to worship her god, which was fear. The Lord revealed that when I shouted, "The blood of Jesus washes me," it signified my position; I am a child of God who sent His Son to wash me of all my fears. He owns me. That explained the first twisting of the bracelet. When I shouted, "The blood of Jesus cleanses me," it signified my freedom—freedom to choose to be free from fear and from enslavement to sin. I am cleansed of all fear and cleansed of all sin. That explained the second twisting of the bracelet. Finally, when I shouted, "The blood of Jesus protects me," that signified the truth of where my safety is: in Him. That explained the third twisting of the bracelet.

Fear cannot have a hold on me! Perfect love casts our fear. In this dream, God has revealed His love for me. I do not have to fear, fear itself or fear confrontation. I must face fear dead on with these three truths:

1. *I am a child of God, washed of all my fears.*
2. *I am free from fear, cleansed of all my sins.*
3. *I am safe no matter what I confront because My God protects me.*

Day 35

Testing the Spirits Regarding Visions and Dreams

Beloved, do not believe every spirit, but test the spirits to see whether they are from God.

—1 John 4:1, ESV

Not all visions or dreams are of God. Like any message we believe to be from the Lord, we must judge the vision/dream based on our knowledge of Scripture and the character and nature of God. Each of the tests by which we can evaluate other prophetic words applies to visions and dreams as well. We simply must trust that when we seek His truth, God will reveal to us what is of Him, what is of the enemy, and what is simply from our own mind.

Some dreams are just from too much sugar the night before, which creates an overactive imagination. Other dreams are from our own hearts and souls. They are like a mirror, reflecting back to us what we are thinking and how we are feeling. Nighttime is the perfect time for a natural filtering process of our hearts and souls to take place. It is a means by which our emotions of fear, anxiety, stress, sadness, confusion, as well as joy, anticipation, and exhilaration can express themselves. These types of dreams are usually fragmented and make no sense at all at first. However, don't toss them aside as invaluable. Our dreams from the heart or soul can be valuable assets to understanding our joys, concerns, stresses, hurts, and pain.

Soulish dreams can also be used as a healing tool to better understand ourselves. They can reveal to us our emotions, lies and deceptions we may have believed, and even bitter roots that have taken hold in our lives (Prov. 14:10). Proverbs 4:23 says, "Keep your heart with all diligence, for out of it spring the issues of life" (NKJV). Our hearts carry everything we have been through. In fact, Psalm 16:7 says that our hearts can instruct us "even at night." These types of dreams—though they are not directly from God in the sense that they do not carry His message—can confirm that

God cares about bringing us to a place of healing and well-being. In this way they are from Him to enable us to find resolve.

In Job 4:12–21 we find the only example in Scripture of an evil spirit speaking to someone in a dream. In this passage Eliphaz tells Job that a word was secretly brought to him (Eliphaz) "in a disturbing vision at night" (v. 13). He explained that fear came upon him. He trembled, and it made all his bones shake. He went on to share that a spirit passed before his face, but he could not discern its appearance. It is doubtful that this was God speaking to him for many reasons. First, as we have seen, God is not the author of fear but of perfect love, which casts out fear. (See 1 John 4:18.) Second, the message Eliphaz received through this dream did not line up with other words from the Lord, and its fruit was not consistent with the positive, life-giving fruit of a message from God. In fact, in Job 42:7, God criticized Eliphaz for misrepresenting Him.

Throughout Scripture we read about the Lord defending Himself and revealing that a "dreamer of dreams" had given a false or lying dream that was not from God. Therefore, when you have a vision or dream, just ask yourself if what is being shown godly. Does it edify? Is it lining up with the character, nature, and ways of God? Does it bear witness with you or the person you are instructed to give it to? Does it draw you closer to the Lord or turn you away from Him? Does it have purpose and meaning? Is it for good or evil? And has God given the interpretation? God always interprets.

Be open to God, and do not fear. He has equipped us both to hear His voice and to test the spirits.

Reflect

1. Think about an instance in which you had a dream that was not of the Lord but seemed to come from your subconscious thoughts or feelings. How did you know that it was not of the Lord? Was there any redeeming quality or message in it that God used to help bring peace or healing, even though the message itself was not from Him?

_____
_____
_____
_____

2. Have you ever had a dream that seemed to be from the enemy? How did you identify the source of that dream? What were the signs and indicators that it was not of God?

_____
_____
_____
_____

3. When we are first learning to hear the voice of the Lord—in whatever form it may come to us—it is sometimes challenging to build confidence testing the spirits and judging the words, visions, or dreams we may receive. Consider the different tools and questions we have discussed as effective methods of evaluating the source of any prophetic download we think we have heard or seen. Are they roughly the same for each type of message (quickening, word, vision, or dream), or are they different? Does this encourage you that honing your ability to test the spirits may not take as long as you originally thought?

_____
_____
_____
_____

Pray

Heavenly Father, thank You for equipping me with various means of processing the world around me, including emotions and dreams. Help me not to be afraid to receive divine dreams and visions from You. Allow Your perfect love to cast out any and all fear I have about hearing from You in this way. I choose to believe that when You speak to me in my dreams or in a vision I will know if it is from You and will confidently receive the interpretation. Thank You for loving me so well and communicating to me so faithfully. In Jesus's name. I pray. Amen.

Exercise

Listen to a worship song. Let the song become your prayer to God. While the worship music is playing, ask God to meet with you in any way that He chooses. Write down any thoughts, words, or images that came to mind as you listened to the music. Journal your thoughts about their meaning.

Lesson Eight

Actions That Block Us from Hearing God

Day 36

Distractions

Do not worry, saying, "What shall we eat?" or "What shall we drink?" or "What shall we wear?" For the pagans run after all these things, and your heavenly Father knows that you need them. But seek first his kingdom and his righteousness, and all these things will be given to you as well.

—Matthew 6:31–33, NIV

It is easy to become distracted with the busyness of life. We have things to do, people to see, and places to go. The infamous story of Martha in the Gospels will be our model for the pitfalls that come with being distracted by many things. From her story and interaction with Christ we can learn much about the way distractions can keep us from hearing God effectively and how to counteract the pressure to go, go, go in a world that seems to demand our time and attention.

In Luke 10:38 we see Martha welcome Jesus into her home. She started off right; she invited Jesus in. We can liken this part of the story to our prayer life. We invite Jesus in. But then what do we do next?

The Gospel writer tells us that Martha had a sister named Mary. While Martha was busy serving Jesus (probably making something to eat, possibly cleaning up, maybe putting on some coffee), it was Mary who took the time and postured herself in prayer by sitting at His feet to talk and listen to Jesus. She was still, attentive, and waiting for Him to speak. Martha, angry with Mary for not helping her, stormed into the room and said to the Lord, "Lord, doesn't it seem unfair to you that my sister just sits here while I do all the work? Tell her to come and help me" (v. 40). We too can get caught up in life: work, business, cleaning, cooking, watching TV and movies, hobbies, and even, like Martha, doing many good things serving the Lord. When this happens it is easy to take our focus off of serving the Lord and instead become fixated on our schedule and the obligations on our calendar.

Jesus's response to Martha was this: "My dear Martha, you are worried and upset over all these details! There is only one thing worth being concerned about. Mary has discovered it, and it will not be taken away from her" (vv. 41–42). It wasn't that what Martha was doing was wrong so much as she made a choice in a very significant moment to shift her focus from knowing Christ (relationship) to doing things for Him (works). Martha chose at that very moment to be busy and worried about many things, whereas Mary opted to sit at Jesus's feet while He visited them.

I remember when the Lord gave me a personal revelation of this very story. I had gone to this conference by myself, and when it was time to be released for lunch a woman sitting beside me invited me to her house for lunch. I thought, "How very kind and generous. I'm always up for meeting new people." So off we went. As soon as we arrived at her home she seated me at the table and proceeded to make some lunch. It was a closed-concept layout, so we weren't able to chat back and forth while she prepared the food. I offered to help, but she graciously refused. When lunch was ready, she brought over one plate, set it down in front of me, and proceeded toward the bathroom, saying, "I am so glad you haven't asked to use the washroom yet, as I am sure it is a mess. I am going to give it a quick clean." I replied, "I am sure it is fine. Aren't you going to come and eat with me?" "Maybe in a few minutes," she shouted, "but I want to clean up first." One bite, two bites, three bites, and before I knew it I was left alone to myself with my omelette.

To say I felt awkward is an understatement. This woman was cleaning her house while I sat at the table eating my eggs—in silence. We barely exchanged any words as she ran up the stairs and down the stairs with laundry in her hands the first time, then a broom in hand the second time. One space after another was gaining all her attention. I learned nothing of her, and she learned nothing of me. I was a guest in her home, but instead of visiting together she preferred to serve me and then clean her house so I wouldn't think it was a mess. She was worried about many things. When we went back to the conference I honestly could relate to how Jesus could have felt in Martha's home. It wasn't an experience I'd ever forget.

We too can be so busy with life that we don't take time to pray, to sit at His feet, and be still to hear Him speak. Perhaps we believe we are getting by with the time we spend with the Lord, even though we pray only while we work, while we drive, or while we are busy doing stuff. It is easy to justify it or, worse yet, believe that our circumstances are to blame. How busy is our life? How scheduled is our day? How much time have we given to God? To the TV? To a hobby? To sleep? To everyday matters? None of these activities and obligations are wrong or bad in and of themselves, and it is even biblical to communicate with God all day long as we go about our day. However, we need to be still at times to fully experience the benefits of our intimacy with God. God wants for us to give Him some of our time, and not just when it is convenient for us. We all can decide and choose to set some time aside for God. There are no excuses. Every one of us has the same amount of time in a day.

Take a few moments to write out your schedule on a typical day. Then convert the activities in a twenty-four hour period to a pie grid, like the figure below. In this chart, include a typical day with hours spent watching TV, working, and obligations (for example, everyday household chores, shopping, working outside, working on vehicles, serving at church, etc.). Also add sleeping, leisure activities, exercise, and finally time with God, which includes dedicated prayer, worship, and Bible time. (For a more detailed accounting of your time, you can do this activity after journaling your hours every day for a week to truly see where your time is spent.) Be honest.

My Schedule

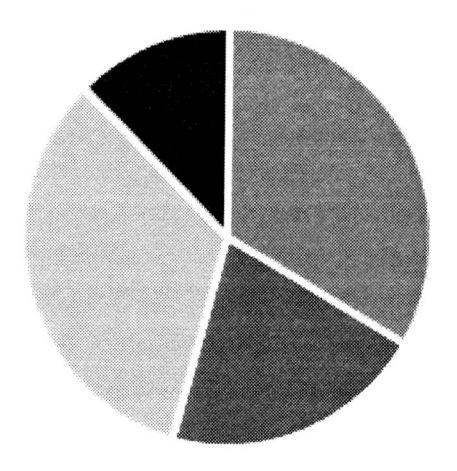

- work
- exercise, TV, leisure
- sleep
- obligations

    If we are honest, the chart above is most likely reflective of the typical day for almost every American and Canadian. It is probably even slightly off, because most people spend their evenings just watching TV or going out and having fun (leisure). Others may have a chart that is skewed more toward obligations at home, at church, or following their children's extracurricular activities. But if you notice, there is no time for God—except for maybe on Sunday for one hour. If we were to include an intimate and focused fifteen mins to one hour with God daily, that would mean giving something up and adjusting our schedule, and many people are not willing to make that change.

    Maybe shifting from a Martha mentality to a Mary one means getting up earlier or cutting something out of our schedule, or better time management. Saying you're tired is also not an excuse. There is strength in the Lord! I encourage you: Do whatever it takes. Learning to hear God takes time, practice, effort, and at first, discipline, but it is fun. Enjoy it! He desires to show you great and mighty things. Perspective is everything. Being with God has benefits, and time spent with Him is glorious.

Making time for God also just makes sense from a practical standpoint. God can give us strategy, wisdom, and insight that can help us work smarter and not harder. What would take us all day to accomplish, God can perform immediately. What could take us years to figure out on our own, God can reveal in one prayer time. What could take us years to study and learn, God could give wisdom for in one prayer time. And sometimes, we just need to hear God tell us how much He loves us, give us an encouraging word, or remind us He is with us. God can speak into every area where we may be in bondage to wrong thinking and set us free.

God is a God of exchange. If you are too tired, that is the best time to seek God, because He can give you strength, energy, power, and a refreshing of His Spirit. If you are sorrowful, God can give you joy. If there is a spirit of heaviness, God could grant you a heart of gladness.

The fact is, we can all blame other things in our lives that take away from our time with God. But the truth remains that we all have control over our time, and each of us can choose our priorities. The harsh reality for each of us is that what we desire, we make a priority. What we cherish, we make time for.

Discipline yourself to make time alone with God a priority. Pray. Read and study the Word. And most importantly, take the time to hear Him speak. Be still and listen. If you have no desire for this at this point, then simply pray and be honest: "God, I confess I have no desire to pray or read Your Word. Give me these desires, and in obedience to Your Word, I will follow through." One powerful tool at our disposal is praying in tongues. It stirs us up as we pray God's will, and it edifies us. Start with what you can, whether it be five minutes, ten minutes, twenty minutes, or a ten-minute block twice a day. You choose. The point is, just start.

Don't be surprised if you find that when you sit down to pray that suddenly your mind starts wandering. Instantly it is thinking about the laundry that's piled up or the car that needs to be fixed or, oh yeah, you were supposed to phone that someone back. Perhaps you may even find yourself daydreaming, and before you know it, you get up and leave, never giving God a chance to speak. Don't be discouraged by these setbacks. This happens to all of us. Waiting on God takes diligence and practice. It takes time—our time—and it takes discipline at first.

Don't beat yourself up if all you can manage at first is five or ten minutes. That's a start. You are in training. Every temperament is different. Some personalities can handle sitting for extended periods of time, while others get restless quite quickly. Resist the urge to compare yourself to "those Christians" who get up at four o'clock in the morning and sit in God's presence for hours on end or "those Christians" who have memorized the entire Word of God so when they pray it's like they have the Bible right in front of them. And then there are "those Christians" who have visions and dreams and encounters with God more than you can count. It does you no good to fixate on what your relationship with God looks like in comparison to these people or anyone else. Start where you are by learning who you are and what works for you. Some people need to start with worship. Others start with the Word. Still others may need to be surrounded with flowers or candles. Whatever enables you to get excited to be with God, do that![36] I can promise this: Once you experience God, then you will hunger for Him, and you will be excited to spend time with Him.

Jeremiah 29:13 says, "And you will seek Me and find Me when *you search for Me with all your heart*" (NKJV, emphasis added). Jesus often slipped away in solitude to pray and to dialogue with the Father quietly and privately. He also instructed His disciples to do the same thing. I am not saying that we cannot pray while working, running, driving, etc., but the benefits of setting aside time in our day to spend in quiet solitude, focused on giving God our full attention, are innumerable. When we behold our God and sit in His presence we are changed into the One we are beholding. It is a supernatural exchange, another benefit of an intimate relationship with a God who speaks.

Reflect

1. Write down the distractions that keep you from sitting at the feet of God daily, whether it be scheduling obligations, your to-do list, or thoughts. Make a plan for when you will find time for God. Make sure that your goal is reasonable and attainable. A "go big or go home" goal of an hour or more a day may be hard to sustain at first if you are accustomed to staying very busy with other things and haven't been making it a practice of spending time with the Lord. The important thing is scheduling a block of time—even if it is ten minutes at first—and sticking with it.

_____
_____
_____
_____

2. When you made your list and then pie chart of your daily activities, did you notice anything you would like to change aside from the amount of time you spend with the Lord? If your job takes up an exorbitant amount of your time and leaves you stressed, should you take that area of your life to the Lord to ask for His leading about how to handle it? Is your time spent on hobbies versus with family appropriate?

_____
_____
_____
_____

3. Take a few moments to think about this statement: When we behold our God and sit in His presence we are changed into the One we are beholding. In what ways would you like to see yourself become more like the Father? Honestly take stock of who you are now and consider how you could become more like Him and what it would take to develop those qualities.

_____
_____
_____
_____

Pray

Heavenly Father, I confess that I can be easily distracted. I haven't always practiced listening to Your voice or making time with You a priority. But I desire for that to change. I ask You Lord to empower me by Your Spirit to recognize when I am getting distracted, when I am watching too much TV, or spending too much time on any activity. Help me not only to serve You but to spend time with You. I pray this in Jesus's name. Amen.

Listen

Look at your list from the first question above. Repent for making these other things in your life a greater priority than your time with God and ask God to show you how to reorder your life in light of your understanding of the proper order. Spend a few minutes silently and expectantly awaiting a response.

Day 37

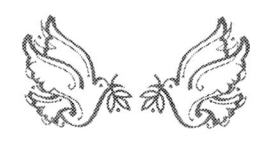

Lack of Rest

Be still, and know that I am God!

—Psalm 46:10

As we saw in the last session, it is easy to overschedule our lives to such a degree that we leave no time for intimate communication with the God who is speaking to us today. Many of us schedule ourselves to the point of distractedness but still get enough sleep and rest. Many others, however, find ourselves struggling even to find time to rest and recharge. As a result, our thoughts become chaotic, and our spirits become overwhelmed. Being chronically tired or weary can wear out our strength, energy, and zeal, leading to exhaustion and frustration. If we do not rest, relax, or learn to limit or let go of certain activities as well as wrong thinking, then the result is burnout. This state of mental turmoil is dangerous for our spirit, soul, and body.

Being tired, weary, burnt out, or oppressed can certainly hinder not only our ability to hear God, but it also affects the accuracy of what we are hearing. Our wearied feelings can cloud our perspective of God, what we think He is saying, and confuse the truth.

This struggle is nothing new. The Bible offers plenty of examples of biblical figures who loved the Lord and served Him but nonetheless had to take a step back once in a while to repent of the constant barrage of activities and obligations that they had allowed to cloud their schedules, impeded their rest, and troubled their hearts.

When Moses was judging the people, he would do it from morning until evening. (See Exodus 18:13–22.) When his father-in-law, Jethro, noticed all that he did for the people, he asked Moses, "What is this thing that you are doing for the people? Why do you alone sit, and all the people stand before you from morning until evening?" (v. 14, NKJV). In the next verse we read that Moses responded, "Because the people come to me to inquire of God. When they have difficulty, they come to me, and I judge between one and another; and I make known the statutes of God and His laws" (NKJV). This seems right in that Moses was serving God and being available for service, but Jethro discerned that it was not good. He knew that both the people and Moses would eventually wear themselves out, for this was too much for one person to take on. So Jethro instructed Moses to select God-fearing men to be "leaders over groups of one thousand, one hundred, fifty, and ten" to be "available to solve the people's common disputes" so that Moses could focus on "the major cases" (vv. 21–22). In this way, they would bear the burden with Moses and he could begin to get some much-needed rest. Jethro understood that Moses could not serve God or the people of God when he was overtired and overwhelmed by responsibilities.

The prophet Elijah was a fearless leader. He successfully and confidently confronted four hundred and fifty prophets of Baal and four hundred prophets of Asherah. So what made him flee from a woman, one woman, when she threatened to take his life? Emotional burnout. When God's people serve Him without replenishing themselves—especially when we fail to realize that significant victories can sometimes leave us open to spiritual attacks from the enemy—it can lead to emotional turmoil of all sorts. Elijah suffered from fear, paranoia, discouragement, exhaustion, self-pity, depression, and even called out to God to kill him! (See 1 Kings 19.)

Just as He did with Elijah, God will guide us through busy times if we press into Him for rest and refreshment. As we discussed in the last session, it may seem counterintuitive to make time to be still before the Lord when we have so much vying for our time, but time spent with God is worth every minute lost to the other obligations that are clouding and wearying our minds and spirits and tearing apart our bodies. He will redeem the time for us, and the benefits we will reap from that rest will transform our lives.

Reflect

1. Take a few minutes to be still before the Lord and examine your heart to see if you are in turmoil over a lack of rest. Maybe the answer will be obvious to you, but it is also possible that you have become so accustomed to the busyness of your schedule that mental and emotional chaos have become your new normal. If you find that you are, indeed, overtired, take time to repent of not observing God's commandment to rest and make a commitment to surrender your time to the Lord.

_____
_____
_____
_____

2. Sometimes in our natural thinking it is hard to see where and how to make time for rest in our busy lives. Ask the Lord to reveal to you how to incorporate intentional times of rest and relaxation into your schedule so that you can recharge spiritually, mentally, and physically.

_____
_____
_____
_____

Pray

Heavenly Father, I come to You with an open heart. I ask You to search me. Reveal to me how I can incorporate intentional times of rest and relaxation into my schedule so that I can recharge spiritually, mentally, and physically. Show me what that looks like, Lord. Help me to self-care so that I don't get burnt out. I am no good to anyone if I am weary and tired. Help me also to incorporate fun into my life. There are times when life gets so serious that I often forget to play. I pray this in Jesus's name. Amen.

Listen

Put on some deep worship music, and ask the Lord to quiet your mind and fill you with His peace that passes understanding. Spend a few minutes silently meditating on Him instead of carrying your regular mental load.

My Story

The Energizer Bunny Running on Empty

It all started in October of 2014. I had been working toward getting my doctor of philosophy of clinical Christian counseling. For over a year I had been studying day-in and day-out at our lovely kitchen table. Some days I had peace and quiet; other days were loud and chaotic as my family was coming and going.

At the time we had no office or other space for me to study at, so I had no choice but to do the best I could with what little I had. This included holding practicums with individuals to whom I counseled in the evenings, after studying all day, wherever a room wasn't being utilized. One time I was left to meet with someone in our small laundry room. But I made do.

To make matters worse, we still had my husband's business, for which I was and still am the office manager in charge of payroll, budget, and other secretarial duties. Though it was not all-consuming, it was one more thing on my ever-growing to-do list that couldn't be eliminated. Add to this list the suppers I needed to make, laundry to clean, and other household obligations that also needed my attention. I was running on empty most days yet burning the midnight oil most nights. Eventually, my prayer life started waning and my body started breaking down.

Nighttime was the worst. I would be lying there in my bed, and at first my breathing would be short and shallow. My stomach felt heavy, gassy, and uncomfortable. I would get these adrenaline-like surges or electric shock sensations under my skin down my arms, legs, and feet. It felt like tingling after the surge—or like acid sizzling in my legs and sides of my feet. Then I would get this sudden gush of heat that would come from my gut and rise to my head, just like that night I called out to God. Only this time, there was no alcohol or drugs involved. While I was experiencing these odd bodily manifestations my legs would start to twitch and my muscles would start contracting or pulsating. It would last anywhere from twenty-five to forty-five minutes at a time. Dizziness and light-headedness would follow. Panic would set in.

Questions arose in the silence of my mind. What is this? Why is this happening? What is wrong with me? Some nights it would get so bad that I would have to go to the hospital, only to have them tell me I was perimenopausal and get sent home. Perimenopausal? Really? It was frustrating to say the least and draining to no end. But I had no choice; I had to keep plugging along.

Month after month, blood test after blood test, nothing showed up. It was so disheartening not having any answers. Perimenopause was still the suspected culprit. I was consumed with school, obligations, ill health, and trying to function as best I could. My mind was focused on education during the day but tormented come bedtime.

Prayer time with God was quick. At times all I could muster up were two simple words— "Help me"—because of the fear of the unknown symptoms. It felt like God was far, far away. He wasn't. He was there with me the whole time. But in my state of mind and the busyness of the season I was in, I was tired and distracted, full of fear, and overwhelmed.

At first, instead of turning to God I kept going like the Energizer bunny running on empty. Finally, I realized school could wait. Laundry could wait. The business could wait. Everything could be put on hold while I sought quality time with God about my situation. And that is precisely what I did. In my weariness and tiredness I cried out to God. I sought Him for His wisdom. His counsel. His guidance for my health. I didn't feel like it, nor did I have the energy, but I knew too many months had gone by without intentional intimacy with God. And I had let it happen.

I opened the Bible and sat there waiting for Him to show up and wanting Him to speak. I needed hope. I needed comfort. I longed for His embrace. Finally, Isaiah 43:1–2 spoke sincerely to my heart: "But now, this is what the L*ord says—he who created you, Jacob, he who formed you, Israel: 'Do not fear, for I have redeemed you; I have summoned you by name; you are mine. When you pass through the waters, I will be with you; and when you pass through the rivers, they will not sweep over you. When you walk through the fire, you will not be burned; the flames will not set you ablaze'" (*NIV*). As I pondered these words and conversed with the Lord, I felt He was saying that I would not be instantly healed or delivered. This was something I was to go through, yet God was with me. And when I asked Him to bring peace to my mind because of the fear I had, He spoke Isaiah 41:10, 13 to me. "So, do not fear, for I am with you; do not be dismayed, for I am your God. I will strengthen you and help you; I will uphold you with my righteous right hand. … For I am the* L*ord your God who takes hold of your right hand and says to you, Do not fear; I will help you" (*NIV*). So, every time the enemy would come with his fearmongering I would begin to quote this scripture as I lay there in my bed, body manifesting.*

In the presence of God and the stillness of my heart, the Lord also revealed to me that my ill health was all stress based and grief based. I had a mini vision, if you will, and I could see these words: stress, dehydration, constipation, acid indigestion. *Each have their own symptoms—and I manifested almost all of them! It had a rippling effect. These in turn triggered fear and anxiety, because I had no idea what was going on. Who knew that stress and grief could cause so much dysfunction in the body? I was so very out of tune with myself. I wasn't even aware of what anxiety was or what it felt like. But man, it is horrible! Needless to say, I began to care for myself and implemented a stress management plan. I also changed my diet and began drinking plenty of water. My healing was progressive as I implemented self-care and heeded the principles of God's Word. Shortly after that, my next textbook to study contained detailed descriptions of stress and anxiety. Coincidence? I think not!*

By June 2015 God had spoken a new weapon of warfare to me, Jeremiah 30:17: "But I will restore you to health and heal your wounds" (NIV). Every time Satan would attack I would counterattack by repeating, "The Lord is restoring health to me and healing my wounds." Then the Lord led me to confess healing scriptures over myself. Even though the symptoms were still raging, God's Word would settle my heart and silence the fear.

By November 2016 I started to feel so much better. I can honestly say that God is faithful to His Word, as Jeremiah 30:17 entirely came to pass by June 2017. Praise God! I am back to my regular health. I am healed!

Day 38

Disobedience and Sin

Catch us the foxes, the little foxes that spoil the vines, for our vines have tender grapes.

—Song of Solomon 2:15, NKJV

As believers, true believers, we possess a noticeable desire to please God our Father. Because of our new spirits, which we received upon salvation, we are no longer enslaved to the flesh (though, if enticed and if we yield to it, we can sin). Our renewed spirits long to please God and remain in a state of right-standing with Him. We may, even after salvation, find our flesh struggling with addictions—whether chemical dependencies or otherwise—but if our hearts have not been hardened we should experience remorse and regret when we stumble and fall and fail to live up to the standard of righteousness for which we were created. This is because though our spirits have been made new, our flesh remains weak and can be tainted by the temptation to sin. Unless we are diligent to renew our minds to the Spirit of truth and guard our hearts from the whispers of the enemy, we will find ourselves in danger of falling into disobedience and entertaining sins that can overtake us and develop into habits and lifestyles that will keep us from hearing the Holy Spirit's voice and lead us far from the Lord.

Our enemy, Satan, is well acquainted with these truths. He knows how to subtly appeal to our flesh to tempt us to disobey and sin in increasing measure. We may not even realize the severity of our actions until our decisions have escalated to the degree that we have separated ourselves from our relationship with the Father. How does this happen? Satan understands that disobedience of any kind can cause us to entertain sin so that we think about it over and over again. This leads us to tolerate sin, as our hearts become hardened to it. When this happens, we begin to justify sin. At this point we are in danger of allowing ourselves to sin and stay in sin. We may even get to the point at which we fail to see these destructive actions and behaviors as sin at all. When this happens we are in danger of becoming enslaved again to the very sin that Jesus freed us from at Calvary.

> An evil man is held captive by his own sins; they are ropes that catch and hold him.
> He will die for lack of self-control; he will be lost because of his great foolishness.

—Proverbs 5:22–23

Regardless of our perception of it and in whatever form it manifests (for example, disobedience, delay, impure thoughts, unforgiveness, etc.), sin hardens our hearts to God's voice. (See Isaiah 5:18–19; 2 Timothy 3:1–9; 4:3–4.) Disobedience to the voice of God—whether spoken through the Bible or through the inner witness; the still, small voice of the Spirit; a prophet; our circumstances; or visions and dreams—is always serious and always sin. Even delayed obedience is a form of disobedience that can lead to serious and negative consequences in our walk with the Lord and ability to hear from Him.

For example, let's say we hear the still, small voice tell us to read the Word. But we have a million things to do, so we tell ourselves, "I will do it later." As time goes on, we forget, and before we know it, it is bedtime. The next day, the same thing happens, and so on and so on. The more we delay heeding the voice of the Spirit, the easier it is to ignore Him, which then grieves and quenches Him and His leading in our lives. If it goes on long enough, it could give the enemy a foothold to lead us into other, more destructive types of sin.

The grace of God does not permit us to sin. Fleeing from sin is for our protection. Obedience to God's commands is for our benefit. Heeding the voice of God is for our prosperity in all things, and we know God takes pleasure in the prosperity of His servants. When we are faithful to obey God, we can count on Him to respond to our prayers and to grant us the very things our heart desires, beginning with more of Himself.

> Delight yourself also in the LORD, and He shall give you the desires of your heart.

—Psalm 37:4, NKJV

Reflect

1. Take an honest look at your heart, thought life, and actions. Are there any areas in which Satan has begun to convince you to compromise, convincing you to entertain, tolerate, or justify sin? If so, what is it? Exposing these areas and repenting of them—and, in some cases, seeking help and

healing from a trusted Christian mentor and accountability partner—is the only way to free yourself from the pull of that sin and walk in renewed relationship with God.

2. Have you been guilty of delaying obedience to the voice of God or Word of God? Consider what reason you gave for justifying the delay and identify if there may be a pattern of prioritizing this activity/relationship/etc. over the Lord. Repent and ask the Lord to help you to make obeying His voice more important than whatever has been getting your attention.

Pray

Heavenly Father, I don't want to do anything that would keep me from hearing You. I long to please You and to walk in unbroken fellowship with You, communicating with you each and every day. Lord, give me a heart of obedience so that I can avoid the pitfalls of sin and temptation and stay on the path You have ordained for me. Alert me to when I begin to step out of obedience and warn me when I delay in responding to a word or dictate from You so that I can make a change right away. I want to serve You fully and faithfully all the days of my life. In Jesus's name, I pray. Amen.

Listen

Ask the Lord to show you the true desire of your heart, whether Him or something else. Spend a few minutes silently and expectantly awaiting a response. If it is not Him, repent and ask the Lord to take His place at the helm of your life.

Day 39

Exalting Human Reasoning Over the Wisdom of God

> "My thoughts are nothing like your thoughts," says the LORD. "And my ways are far beyond anything you could imagine. For just as the heavens are higher than the earth, so my ways are higher than your ways and my thoughts higher than your thoughts."
>
> —Isaiah 55:8–9

Our human logic and reasoning can get in the way of hearing God and lead to double-mindedness. When it does, we open ourselves up to a variety of pitfalls and sinful thought patterns.

God gave us our analytical minds to use for figuring things out, but our logic can reason against what God is trying to say or what He is trying to show us, therefore hindering whatever it is that God is trying to do in and through us. Our human reasoning can eventually become an idol if we consistently allow it to thwart God's Word and choose our understanding instead of God's wisdom. Further, when we use this logic to discredit what God is doing or what His Word says, then we are yielding to the temptation of questioning God and walking in pride.

Reasoning within ourselves can also be what justifies our sin and leads us to doubt the truth of God's Word or who He says He is. That's because God's Word requires faith in things that are not seen, things that seem impossible, things that we cannot make sense of. Often the Lord will give us a word that goes against what seems logical, but faith calls upon us to trust in Him anyway and believe that He has our best interests in mind.

The Book of James warns us of the consequences of not coupling godly wisdom with faith:

> If you need wisdom, ask our generous God, and he will give it to you. He will not rebuke you for asking. But when you ask him, be sure that your faith is in God

alone. Do not waver, for a person with divided loyalty is as unsettled as a wave of the sea that is blown and tossed by the wind. Such people should not expect to receive anything from the Lord. Their loyalty is divided between God and the world, and they are unstable in everything they do.

—James 1:5–8

God's wisdom is not like our wisdom. That's why it requires faith and also why the payoff for trusting Him is so great. Have you ever asked yourself why James would warn us ahead of time to believe and not doubt God's wisdom when He gives it? It is because God's answer or way of doing things will more than likely seem impossible, illogical, and not at all how we would do it. It may even go against the very laws of nature. Remember when God told Moses to part the Red Sea and lead the people of Israel across? How about when Jesus bid Peter to step out and walk on water? The fishermen who had fished all night long and caught nothing until Jesus simply told them to throw their nets on the other side? We read story after story in the Scriptures of how God's wisdom seemed to make no sense, and yet when people stepped out in faith and took Him at His word, miracles happened.

Miracles require faith not only to receive them but to believe in them. How many times do we read in the Word where Jesus did miracles and some didn't believe? Perhaps we have seen a miracle firsthand and reasoned it away? Our logic tosses us back and forth. It will try and talk us right out of God's way of doing things. If we exalt our human reasoning over the wisdom of God, we "should not expect to receive anything from the Lord" (v. 7). Instead, we need to learn to differentiate between man's wisdom and God's. Get so acquainted with Abba and His Word that your logic gets excited when it discerns, "I know that didn't come from me!"

Reflect

1. Read James 1:5–8 again. Reflect on a recent request you made of the Lord in light of this scripture. Did you place "your faith … in God alone," or did you allow human reasoning to cause you to "waver"?

_____
_____
_____
_____

2. Is there a miracle you have always longed to see God perform? What is it, and is it in line with His Word, character, and nature? What would it take for you to believe and not doubt that God could perform that miracle?

_____
_____
_____
_____

Pray

Dear God, I am so glad to serve You. You are omnipotent, omnipresent, and omniscient—all-powerful, all-present, and all-knowing. Your wisdom is so much greater than anything my mind can fathom. Lord, I defer to Your wisdom. Help me not to assume I, Your creation, could ever comprehend Your matchless wisdom. I rely on You to share Your wisdom with me; without it, I would perish. Give me the humility to seek your wisdom always and the faith to receive what You share with me. In Jesus's name, I pray. Amen.

Listen

Ask the Lord for a word of knowledge about a person or situation and for an accompanying word of wisdom. Spend a few minutes silently and expectantly awaiting a response. Then pray (and act, if necessary) in accordance with that word of wisdom.

Day 40

Ignorance to How or What God Is Speaking

For God speaks again and again, though people do not recognize it.

—Job 33:14

By now we should be confident that God desires to know and communicate with us intimately and freely. He is speaking to our hearts using a variety of modes and longs for us to hear Him and respond. As believers, we must understand that if we are still not hearing God it is not because of a lack of effort or desire on His part. Just as creation itself testifies to the existence and glory of God so that there is "no excuse for not knowing" Him (Rom. 1:20), if we believe God is speaking and we still do not perceive His voice, we must accept our role and responsibility in hearing God speak.

In this lesson we have looked at various actions that can serve as obstacles to hearing from God, and in the next we will examine attitudes of our heart that can hinder our spiritual ears from hearing His voice. However, it is possible to gain and amass knowledge about how to hear from the Lord but remain so caught up in the theory that we never actually allow ourselves to practice. When we try to hear God speaking, we second-guess ourselves to such a degree that we are not attuned to Him; we are intensely focused on our own actions and thoughts and too intent on judging the source of the word before the word ever comes. If this is the case, we will likely not be aware that God is speaking to us, or we will struggle to perceive His voice over the din of our own internal monologue.

Be aware of your thoughts. Let your emotions—the fruit of your thoughts—be your barometer in detecting which thoughts you are entertaining and focusing on. Our feelings can be an indication of who we are hearing (God, self, or Satan) and what we believe to be true. If your feelings as it relates to hearing the Spirit speak to your spirit are frustrated and tied up in your struggles to hear His voice, it could be an indicator that your thoughts are speaking so loudly that your spirit cannot hear. In that case, you must learn to quiet your thoughts and be still before the Lord. If you detect only painful feelings when you listen for God to speak to you, it could be an indicator that thoughts, lies, or temptations from Satan are crowding out your mental space to such a degree that the still, small voice of God gets lost in the noise. When we struggle with this, we need to immediately pray, telling God that we desire with all our heart to submit to Him and resist the devil, and then seek healing for those hurts that are so present in our heart and mind. This will teach us to cast down those thoughts and replace them with the truth so that God can speak His truth into our heart, making it a revelation to us.

God is faithful to keep trying to speak to us when we desire to hear His voice, but we cannot expect Him in every instance to call us by name and say, "Go and phone Phyllis," or whomever. Remember, the voice of God can sound like it is just us having those thoughts or impressions, promptings, or urgings. This means you may perceive the unction of God as the thought that, "I should phone Phyllis." This is not to say, however, that God won't call your name and that instead of the quickening coming as a first-person idea He won't speak in second person. (Remember Samuel?) My point is simply that you are not going to hear, "Thus sayeth the Lord: Go call Phyllis." If this is what we expect we will continue to miss the word of the Lord for us.

Persistent difficulty hearing God speak to us can also mean we do not know enough of God's character, His nature, or His way of doing things. It is our responsibility to press in to God through study of His Word and pursuit of His presence. If we are not hearing God speak it may indicate that there is a need for us to increase our study of the Word and our time being still and silent in prayer time with God. How do we detect a fake hundred dollar bill? By studying the real thing.

Finally, we may think we are missing the voice of God when in reality we hear the message but just do not fully understand or believe the word that is being spoken. The seed is sown in our hearts, but Satan comes and steals it from us. (See Matthew 13:19.) Sometimes the enemy may use others to convince us that what we are hearing could not possibly be from the Lord. The Book of Job provides us with a great example of this. After Job's three friends had all visited him and spent time telling him all their analyses of the reasons for Job's distresses, it says that the Lord answered Job out of the whirlwind, and said, "Who is this who darkens counsel by words without knowledge?" (Job 38:1–2, NKJV). It is important to make sure that we are placing our faith in God and surrounding ourselves with faith-filled friends who want to hear the Lord speak as much as we do.

Whatever your struggle, do not grow tired in trying. Remember, the Word promises this for those who are persistent in their pursuit of God:

> Keep on asking and it will be given you; keep on seeking and you will find; keep on knocking [reverently] and [the door] will be opened to you. For everyone who keeps on asking receives; and he who keeps on seeking finds; and to him who keeps on knocking, [the door] will be opened.
>
> —Matthew 7:7–12, AMPC

This is God's promise to those who love Him and desire to hear Him speak to them. This is His promise to you.

Reflect

1. Now is an excellent time to take stock of your growth since the start of this study. Are you experiencing the Holy Spirit speaking to you with greater frequency and clarity than you did before? Have you learned to hear His voice in new ways? If so, congratulations and keep up the good work. If not, which of the pitfalls discussed in this section most resonates with you? Consider approaching a pastor or trusted mentor to see if they can help you determine any other areas that may be blocking you from hearing the Lord in your life.

___

2. Which of the actions in this lesson is your greatest struggle? What is your plan for overcoming this obstacle and making a change in your actions in order to start hearing from the Lord more clearly and effectively?

___

3. What does Matthew 7:7–12 tell us about the nature of God and His love for us?

___

Pray

Heavenly Father, I come to You, in Jesus's name, asking persistently, seeking constantly, and knocking faithfully on the door of heaven. I know that You will answer, appear to me, and open the door so that I may enter into deep fellowship with You. I acknowledge my responsibility in our relationship to pursue You with my whole heart and apply my faith to believe that I can and will hear from You clearly. Continue to speak to me, for I am listening. Amen.

Exercise

Sit quietly for a moment. Ask God to reveal any actions that may be hindering you from hearing God in your life now. Listen. Take time to confess this to God.

Next, partner up. Pray with someone, asking God what He wants to speak to your partner. Then speak it! You may receive a scripture or pictures or a clear message of what to say. Test the spirits, but do not try to analyze it or reject it if it seems too simple to you. It may very well be exactly what they need to hear. Also, you may not hear anything at all, but by faith open your mouth and trust as well as believe that God will speak through you for them.

If you are doing this activity independently, select a person to pray for. Ask God what He wants to say to them and write down what He says, whether it be a scripture, picture, or a clear message. As with the group activity, test the spirits, but do not try to analyze it. Make a commitment to share that word with them in the next week.

Lesson Nine

Attitudes That Block Us from Hearing God

Day 41

Pride and a Rebellious Spirit

"What sorrow awaits my rebellious children," says the Lord. "You make plans that are contrary to mine. You make alliances not directed by my Spirit, thus piling up your sins."

—Isaiah 30:1

Pride is boastful, crediting its own strength and how good it is at something; therefore, it tells us there is no need for God. It is often the precursor to a rebellious attitude, which tells us that there is no need to submit to God with our heart or actions. Rebellion leads to disobedience or defiance against God, His Word, or His instructions, either generally or personally. It is knowing what we need to be doing and refusing to do it, or knowing what we should not be doing and doing it anyway. Repeatedly, story after story in the Bible, we read how humanity rebelled against God, refused to heed His word, and instead, "did whatever seemed right in their own eyes" (Judg. 17:6). The results are always catastrophic. First Samuel 12:15 declares, "However, if you do not obey the voice of the Lord, but rebel against the commandment of the Lord, then the hand of the Lord will be against you, as it was against your fathers" (NKJV). Psalm 106:43 says, "Again and again he [God] rescued them, but they chose to rebel against him, and they were finally destroyed by their sin."

Pride and a rebellious spirit both refuse to seek the counsel of God and thus cause us to depend on our strength and own wisdom. These attitudes keep us from hearing God by preventing us from receiving the word of the Lord or even causing us to reject it all together.

A biblical example of the danger of harboring pride is David's wife Michal, who allowed pride to get in the way of her relationship with the Lord. She valued her image and reputation more than she valued God. In 2 Samuel 6:14 we read how "David danced before the Lord with all his might." He leaped and twirled before the Lord in the priestly garments, and it says that Michal "despised him in her heart" (v. 16, NKJV). Later Michal commented to David how he shamelessly uncovered himself. David's response demonstrated humility and a right spirit before God. He said, "I was dancing before the LORD … I celebrate before the LORD. Yes, and I am willing to look even more foolish than this, even to be humiliated in my own eyes!" (vv. 21–22). David was not ashamed to openly express his love and appreciation toward His God. Michal, on the other hand, worried about her image and wanted to guard her family's sophisticated reputation. Her pride cost her the chance to walk with God as intimately as David did and left her barren. (See 2 Samuel 6:23.)

Another biblical example of this is Samson, who, filled with pride, boasted about killing one thousand Philistines with the jawbone of a donkey. (See Judges 15:14–18.) The Word of God says, "Have no confidence in the flesh" (Phil, 3:3, NKJV), but Samson came to trust in his own strength more than he trusted in God, who gave him that strength to begin with. God received no glory, while Samson credited himself. This attitude led to outright rebellion of God's commandments. (See Judges 16:1.) In all actuality it was the Spirit of God who gave him the power over his enemies. Ultimately Samson's reliance on his own strength caused him to lack the discernment that would have saved him from Delilah's manipulations and trickery. (See Judges 16:4–31.) When the Philistines cut his hair, God removed His hand of blessing and anointing from Samson, stripping him of his strength. Had he credited God with his strength and power, Samson might have avoided enslavement, torture, and eventual death.

Pride can also lead to scoffing or idolatry. Remember, idols can be anything or anyone that takes priority over God or turns us away from God. Pride exalts its own reasoning above the sovereignty of God, and a rebellious spirit sets itself on the throne. When we choose to walk in these attitudes, we are the ones distancing ourselves from God. Neither is compatible with a healthy, thriving, intimate relationship with the living God, who wants to be the only Lord of our hearts. (See Hosea 13:6; Zephaniah 2:10.)

These attitudes cause us to give ourselves over to and follow wrong thinking, wrong feelings, or wrong desires and opens a door for Satan to tempt us through the weakness of our flesh and our unrenewed mind. Satan will always tempt you to rebel against God and His ways, but maintaining a thankful and humble heart will remind us we are a new creation; old nature is dead! Therefore, we do not listen to Satan.

Deuteronomy 8:10–11 tells us the antidote for pride and a rebellious spirit:

> When you have eaten your fill, *be sure to praise the LORD your God* for the good land he has given you. But that is the time to be careful! Beware that in your plenty you do not forget the LORD your God and disobey his commands, regulations, and decrees that I am giving you today.
>
> —emphasis added

To counteract the damage of a prideful and rebellious heart, we must give praise to God and humble ourselves before Him. Pride says, "My way is better or right," but humility says, "God knows best. His ways are better and right, and He is deserving of my praise and thanksgiving." When we ask, seek, and knock with humility, gratefulness, and repentance, the door will be opened unto us. (See Matthew 7:7–12.) God promises that if we call Him, He will answer and show us great and mighty things that we do not know. (See Jeremiah 29:11–14; 33:3.)

Confess and repent where pride and a rebellious attitude exist in your life and remember you are a new creation in Christ who desires to obey God. When the enemy whispers to you with a spirit of rebellion and says, "I don't want to," or, "I can't," reject the thought immediately and replace it with the battle cry of the obedient heart: "Not my will, Lord, but Thy will be done." When we refuse to listen to Satan, who will always tempt you to act independently of God, the ears of our hearts will remain open to hear the inner witness and still, small voice speaking to our spirits.

Reflect

1. Has there ever been a time when your pride or desire to do something on your own, without God's approval or help, caused you to fail or make a mistake? What was the result? What might have been different if you had heeded the voice of the Lord?

_____
_____
_____
_____

2. Consider your heart carefully and honestly. Is there any area of your life in which pride and a rebellious attitude have taken root? If so, stop, repent, and praise the Lord for the work He has done in you and in your life. Humble yourself before Him and ask Him to show you the root of these attitudes so that you can avoid falling into their trap again.

_____
_____
_____
_____

Pray

Great and holy, strong and mighty, beautiful and sovereign Lord, I come to You with a humble heart seeking Your continual grace and mercy. Without You, without Your salvation and favor, I am ruined, heavenly Father. It is in You that I live and move and have being, and it is by Your Word and words to me that I am sustained. Show me where there may be pride or rebellion in my heart threatening to dethrone You from Your rightful place so that I can repent and return to proper fellowship with You. I'm sorry if I have knowingly or unknowingly exalted myself above You. I choose to walk forward from this day with You in Your rightful place at the helm of my life's course. In Jesus's name, I pray. Amen.

Listen

Think of an instance in which you submitted to God instead of rebelling or choosing your own way. Ask the Lord to show you how your obedience made Him feel. Spend a few minutes silently and expectantly awaiting a response.

Day 42

Unforgiveness and Bitterness

> If another believer sins, rebuke that person; then if there is repentance, forgive. Even if that person wrongs you seven times a day and each time turns again and asks forgiveness, you must forgive.
>
> —Luke 17:3–4

Offense, anger, bitterness, wrath, resentment, clamor, and evil speaking are all fruit from the tree of unforgiveness. When we feel offended, angry, hurt, and even victimized by others, we tend to feel vindicated in holding on to that pain. It is like we justify in our hearts and rationalize in our minds that it is our right to stay in unforgiveness. The only problem is that when unforgiveness takes root in our hearts, the love within us begins to grow cold. Consequently, our hearts become hardened. A hardened heart is a heart that is like rock, insensitive and unyielding to God's voice within and even to God's Word. It is like a callus that builds up over time from repetitive actions, in this case the wrongdoing done to us that we mull over in our minds.

The Word of God makes it evident that we are to keep our hearts free from allowing these painful emotions to fester.

> Let all bitterness, wrath, anger, clamor, and evil speaking be put away from you, with all malice. And be kind to one another, tenderhearted, forgiving one another, even as God in Christ forgave you.
>
> —Ephesians 4:31–32, NKJV

Now this does not mean, however, that we suppress painful emotions, bury them, ignore them, or get busy and deny them. It also does not mean that we despise ourselves because we feel these kinds of emotions or try not to feel them. The reality is, God created us as emotional beings, and our feelings have a purpose. Our emotions talk! Feelings alert us to danger, injustice, pain, and a problem that needs to be solved. They are also a barometer to our safety, sense of justice, and level of contentment. Even painful feelings are often a catalyst revealing a wound, injustice, or a grave concern to/for something or someone. It is OK to feel emotions, both comfortable ones and uncomfortable ones.

I personally do not call emotions positive or negative, good or bad, as it implies one is more favorable than the other or that one should be felt, while the other one should be packed away. Feelings are feelings, and they are neither right nor wrong. Each needs to be felt and explored. In fact, our health and overall well-being are dependent on healthy expression of our feelings.

The problem with emotions begins when we want to dwell on them for too long or allow ourselves to be led by them. Should we express them in godly ways? Yes. Feel them? Yes. Grieve the loss? Yes. Tell God about them? Yes. We must learn to understand what they are trying to say to us, then solve the problem in ways conducive to Scripture and pleasing to God. Painful emotions can alert us to a problem that needs to be solved. If it can't be solved, then one needs to come to a place of acceptance and let go. When we sulk or drip in self-pity, nothing gets accomplished, and we set ourselves up for unforgiveness and bitterness to take root in our heart. By dwelling or stewing in anger instead of getting in tune with why we are angry, we give place to the devil (Eph. 4:27, NKJV). Holding on to bitterness, wrath, anger, clamor, and evil speaking both tears us apart from the inside and grieves the Holy Spirit. (The next lesson includes a more in-depth study of what it means to grieve the Holy Spirit, as well as its consequences.)

Colossians 3:12–14 tells us how to balance our emotions with a godly perspective:

> Since God chose you to be the holy people he loves, you must clothe yourselves with tenderhearted mercy, kindness, humility, gentleness, and patience. Make allowance for each other's faults, and forgive anyone who offends you. Remember, the Lord forgave you, so you must forgive others. Above all, clothe yourselves with love, which binds us all together in perfect harmony.
>
> —Colossians 3:12–14

Make allowance for people's faults. Recognize that people are not perfect. They have weaknesses, flaws, failures, and imperfections; just as we all do. We get locked in unforgiveness and bitterness when we fail to accept that people will fail us. We are not entitled to perfect treatment. This is the key to forgiveness and letting go of bitterness. By walking in forgiveness instead of allowing our feelings to rule us and create a root of unforgiveness and bitterness in our lives, we remain tender-hearted. To stay tender-hearted is to put on love. Love is what "binds us all together in perfect harmony." It is the perfect posture from which to hear God.

Reflect

1. Why do you think God gave us emotions, knowing they could lead us away from Him?

_____
_____
_____
_____

2. Forgiveness is a choice. Consider your heart and ask God to reveal to you if you are harboring any unforgiveness or bitterness toward anyone (including Him) or about any situation in the past or currently. If you discover these roots, take your pain to God in prayer. Release it to Him. You may even want to go one step further and seek a Christian counselor, someone gifted who can get to the root of the beliefs, lies, distortions, and strongholds associated with that unforgiveness and bitterness through healing, restorative prayer.

_____
_____
_____
_____

Pray

Heavenly Father, thank You for the freedom You offer me through Your Son. I want to walk in the fullness of that liberty, and I know that I cannot do that if I am harboring bitterness and unforgiveness against others. Lord, show me how to release those against whom I have held a grudge, and turn my anger and hurt to godly love. Help me to express the feelings I have appropriately so that they don't fester within me. Give me a tender heart to serve You and others. I pray this in Jesus's name. Amen.

Listen

Ask the Lord if there are any emotions that you have given too much reign in your life and, if so, how to correct that imbalance. Spend a few minutes silently and expectantly awaiting a response.

Day 43

Doubt

> The one who doubts is like a wave of the sea, blown and tossed by the wind. That person should not expect to receive anything from the Lord.
>
> —James 1:6–7, NIV

Remember what I said earlier about how man's logic can't comprehend God's wisdom because God operates in the realm of faith, whereas man works in the realm of his physical senses—what he can see, hear, and feel in the natural? When we rely on our own logic instead of allowing God to renew our minds and show us how to walk by faith, it leads to doubt. Doubt causes us to disbelieve God's power, His love, or His provision to perform His instructions or His word in our lives. Doubt produces in us an attitude of self-preservation because it causes us to rely on ourselves, others, or things of this world to meet our needs instead of believing God and waiting for Him and His timing. It will make it hard for us to hear God or receive "anything from the Lord" (James 1:7, NIV). Left unchecked, it can lead to pride and rebellion, as well as unrest, which we have seen the consequences of already. (See Hebrews 3:12, 19.)

Let's look at the fruit doubt bore in Eve's life. Eve doubted God when she chose to believe Satan's lie that she and Adam would not die if they ate of the tree of the knowledge of good and evil the Garden. She doubted that God would really mete out consequences for disobeying His word not to eat from the tree, but more than that, she doubted God's provision. If He were really good and really wanted them to enjoy all good things, why would He make the tree off-limits? If He really wanted to take care of them, why would He prevent them from having the knowledge of good and evil? Instead of placing her faith in God's goodness and His love for them, which would have led to obedience, Eve's doubt led her to covet the one tree that was forbidden and, ultimately, to disobey His instruction. She heeded Satan, who tempted the weakness of her flesh, instead of placing her faith in God, who gave Adam and Eve the rule about not eating from the tree in order to protect and preserve their relationship with Him. By entertaining doubt, Eve opened the door to Satan's influence so that she was enticed by her desires, idolizing self and falling into sin.

Whatever is not of faith is sin, so doubt not only leads to sin; it is sin.[37] And sin keeps us from hearing and obeying God. We can justify doubt ("If God really wanted me to believe in Him, He wouldn't have let that happen") and deny doubt ("It isn't that I don't believe, it's just that …"), but the bottom line is that doubt of any kind will cause us to draw away from God and harden our hearts. It will hinder our ability to hear God. It's like having ear wax built up so thick in our ears that we can no longer hear Him.

Don't let that scare you. We all can doubt. The good news is there is a quick and easy remedy: confession. Confession of sin, including doubt, slams the door on Satan and reopens our heart to receive all that God has to say to us. It keeps us humble before God and keeps our hearts soft, pliable, and teachable, because through confession we are acknowledging our dependence on God and what He has already done for us. When we show God we know we need Him in our lives and recognize that we would be lost without Jesus's work on the cross for us, there is no more room for doubt. Faith will fill our hearts, and our fellowship with Him will be restored.

Reflect

1. Are there any areas of doubt in your life that you need to confess to the Lord? If so, repent and share your doubts with God. He is faithful to respond and will show you His love and provision for you in the area of your doubt.

_____
_____
_____
_____

2. Think about your life before you met Christ and made Him your Lord and Savior. What role did doubt play in your life? What fruit did it bear? How did your life change when your spirit was renewed to the things of God and faith replaced that doubt? How did it feel to know God was everything He promised and everything you would ever need?

_____
_____
_____
_____

Pray

Dear God, like the father of the boy seeking Jesus for healing in Mark 9:23–25, I come begging You, "I believe; help my unbelief!" I admit that sometimes it is hard to trust in all of Your promises for me because they are so great and incredible that my natural mind struggles to believe it. When I waver or begin to rely more on my own reason than on my faith, please correct my thinking, Lord. Cause Your perfect love to so fill up my heart that any hint of doubt is immediately dispelled. I want to know You so intimately that there is no room for unbelief of any kind. Thank You that You desire to know me too. Amen.

Listen

Ask the Lord to share with you the name of someone you know who isn't a follower of Christ. Spend a few minutes silently and expectantly awaiting a response and then pray that he or she would come to know, trust, and love God with their whole heart and mind.

Day 44

Depression

The Lord is close to the brokenhearted; he rescues those whose spirits are crushed. The righteous person faces many troubles, but the Lord comes to the rescue each time.

—Psalm 34:18–19

Emotions are there for a reason. God created us with emotions, so it is only natural that we will feel anger, sadness, and even deep sorrow when someone dies, our circumstances are grim, or when an injustice has been committed. Grief is a normal human response to sad situations or losses we have suffered. It is okay to feel this way. Grieving in a healthy way for a healthy period is one strategy with which God has equipped us for processing the circumstances of our life and healing from our hurts. When we grieve, it is best to seek God in prayer. Anger, sadness, and grief become a problem when they are rising without just cause or lasting longer than what should be considered healthy. They can lead to depression, which is a type of oppression.

Depression is a persistent state of feeling down, sad, or weak in mind and body. It manifests as hopelessness and difficulty focusing or concentrating and can lead to physical inactivity. When we remain depressed, we enter into a state of oppression. To be oppressed means "to press upon or against; crush; to weigh down, as sleep or weariness does; to burden with cruel or unjust impositions or restraints; subject to a burdensome or harsh exercise of authority or power."[38] We may find ourselves oppressed by emotions and circumstances that seem to be out of our control, people abusing their power or authority, as well as from demonic entities. (See Isaiah 3:5; Acts 10:38.)

We must recognize that persistent feelings of anger, sadness, and grief may be signs that the emotions have not be dealt with or that Satan is whispering in your ear. These powerful emotions, coupled with the confusing and tormenting voice of the enemy, can drown out the voice of God.

When sadness and grief are allowed to progress to a state of depression and oppression, we develop a blockage from hearing God. We may feel too down to even go to God.

Depression's grip is so powerful because it is a multifaceted problem that affects the spirit, soul, and body. Dr. Neil Anderson and Joanne Anderson put it this way:

> Depression affects the whole person, and a complete cure requires a wholistic answer. No human problem manifesting in one dimension of reality can be isolated from the rest of reality. Like any other sickness of the body and soul, depression is a whole-life problem that requires a whole-life answer. Depression is related to our physical health, what we believe, how we perceive ourselves, our relationship with God, our relationships with others, the circumstances of life, and finally, it may have something to do with Satan, who is the god of this world. You cannot successfully treat depression without taking into account all related factors. We have a whole God who is the creator of all reality, and He relates to us as whole people.[39]

We can begin to counteract the effects of depression and oppression in our lives by first seeking medical advice. It is always a good idea to seek a professional. Yet, it would be unfortunate to stop there. Medicine can help, but there is far more going on than can be addressed chemically. I encourage you to seek a professional Christian counselor who will help with understanding the roots to your pain and working through them, since addressing our beliefs and thought life is paramount to overcoming depression. Christian counselors can also help solve spiritual conflicts and spiritual issues. They can help you identify as well as understand the losses in your life and help you let go. Going to God in prayer is also critical. He alone is our Strong Tower amidst any storm. And last, we must renew our mind to the truth of God's Word. Then, when the enemy, through our flesh, tries to remind us of the pain that led us to this state, we need to remind ourselves instead of the promises of God for us:

> Do not be afraid or discouraged, for the Lord will personally go ahead of you. He will be with you; he will neither fail you nor abandon you.
>
> —Deuteronomy 31:8

> O Lord, you are my lamp. The Lord lights up my darkness.
>
> —2 Samuel 22:9

The Lord is a shelter for the oppressed, a refuge in times of trouble.

—Psalm 9:9

Anyone who is among the living has hope.

—Ecclesiastes 9:4, NIV

May the God of hope fill you with all joy and peace as you trust in him, so that you may overflow with hope by the power of the Holy Spirit.

—Romans 15:13, NIV

God's will is to see the depressed and oppressed walk in freedom and fellowship with Him. When we submit to God and resist the devil (that is, refuse and reject what he is tempting us to do, lying to us about, or accusing us of) he must flee!

If you have dealt with or are currently dealing with depression, you are not alone. I understand all too well the devastating effects of depression, as I have battled it myself. All throughout Scripture we find many who also felt the pangs of depression. All one has to do is read the Book of Psalms to see David's numerous bouts with depression. I in no way am minimizing anyone who finds themselves suffering with depression, and I realize addressing it isn't as simple in practice as it may sound in these paragraphs. However, if you are feeling any of these feelings, know that God has made a way of escape. God has provided pastors, the body of Christ, doctors, and professional counselors who are equipped to help you overcome depression and oppression. These struggles are not a death sentence for your relationship with God. If they have been blocking you from hearing God speak to you, you can rest on God's promises that healing will come and you can—and will—begin to hear Him again!

Reflect

1. Read Psalm 143:7–8. What does David's prayer in this scripture tell us about God's desire for us to approach Him with all our troubles? Now read Psalm 34:18–19 and Psalm 145:14, which was also written by David. What do these passages tell us about God's answer to David's prayer in the midst of his depressed state?

_____
_____
_____
_____

2. Many people dealing with depression and oppression feel trapped by shame over their emotions or their lack of energy. Read Romans 8:1 (NKJV). What does this verse tell us about God's heart for His people? What does it imply about the "walk" of every believer who has been made new in Christ, even those who are battling these strongholds?

_____
_____
_____
_____

3. If you are struggling with depression and oppression, stop now and ask the Lord to give you the strength to submit to Him and resist the devil. Then make a plan for practical next steps, such as making an appointment with a Christian counselor, therapist, or psychiatrist, as well as seeking healing and deliverance.

_____
_____
_____
_____

Pray

Heavenly Father, thank You that Your will is for me to walk in freedom and experience the joy and peace only You can bring. Lord, I turn my emotions over to You and submit them to Your will. Where there is profound hurt or grief, allow the Comforter to rise up within my spirit to bind those wounds. Where there is oppression or a stronghold of depression, flood me with Your healing grace and break the bonds of those chains. Where I need the courage to take the next step to visit a doctor or find a Christian counselor, rise up within me to make me brave in You so that I can begin to walk the path back to experiencing the freedom You bought for me through Christ's sacrifice on the cross. Heal me, Lord, so that I may turn to others and be a conduit for Your hand on and in their lives. In Jesus's name, I pray. Amen.

Listen

Ask the Lord to share with you the name of someone you know who needs a word of encouragement today. Spend a few minutes silently and expectantly awaiting a response. Make a commitment to share that encouragement with him or her promptly.

Day 45

Worry and Fearfulness

Anxiety in the heart of man causes depression, but a good word makes it glad.

—Proverbs 12:25, NKJV

Satan whispers untruth. He exaggerates it. He sows doubt by causing us to doubt God's provision, His willingness, and His ability. When doubt alone doesn't accomplish the purposes Satan set out to accomplish, he plants the related seeds of worry, anxiety, and fear that will wreak havoc on our peace and drown out the voice of God in our lives. Once anxiety and fear have taken root, they spread quickly and can infect every thought that crosses our mind and every circumstance we encounter. Even once-positive experiences can become cause for worry or an opportunity for us to dwell on the potential negative outcomes.

I once heard an acronym about fear that said fearful thoughts are really just:

F*alse*
E*xaggerations*
A*ppearing*
R*eal*

For people trapped in a state of worry and fearfulness, however, those thoughts can seem very real indeed. Satan is a tormentor. He knows that these strong emotions can throw us into a constant state of distress, alarm, and terror that will torment our minds, manifest negative symptoms in our body, and prevent us from communing with God spirit to Spirit. When this happens, these painful emotions hijack our God-ordained response to real danger, triggering adrenaline—the same response you would have if, say, you encountered a bear on your path as you were walking along a wilderness trail. However, unlike in that scenario, in which your adrenaline would subside after the danger goes away, imagined fear or fear of potential future unknowns doesn't just wander off the wilderness path; instead, imagined fear triggers and creates a cycle of emotional and physical responses that become self-perpetuating. Sometimes this can cause us to make assumptions and jump to conclusions. These are cognitive distortions, inaccurate thoughts that nonetheless can seem very real and trigger very real feelings of anxiety and fear that are hard to dispel.

The people of Israel were no strangers to fear. Though they had seen the Lord provide for them over and over—from God bringing them out of slavery in Egypt with all the riches of the Egyptian people, to a miracle that allowed them to walk across the Red Sea on dry land, to supernatural provision of food and clothes that never wore out, to the literal presence of God following them in the form of a cloud by day and a pillar of fire by night—they consistently worried that death, doom, and destruction were around the next mountain. Their cries and complaints to their leaders and to God directly show the way in which the spirit of fear was both all-consuming and catching, spreading through their camp like wildfire.

In Numbers 13, we read that God gave Moses instructions that after generations wandering in the desert His people finally were ready to explore the Promised Land He had set aside for them. Moses called the leaders of each tribe together and gave them specific instructions about how they were "to spy out the land of Canaan" and what they were to look for (v. 17, NKJV). He told them, "See what the land is like, and find out whether the people living there are strong or weak, few or many. See what kind of land they live in … Do their towns have walls, or are they unprotected like open camps? … Do your best to bring back samples of the crops you see" (vv. 18–20). When they got to the Valley of Eschol they cut down a single cluster of grapes so large that two men had to carry it together. It was obvious that this was, indeed, a land of promise and prosperity.

Unfortunately, it was also occupied by powerful people who had built fortified towns. The team of Israelite scouts had even seen giants walking in the land among the people. In spite of the fact that God had promised them that land, and in spite of the fact that "it truly flow[ed] with milk and honey," the men were consumed by fear. "Next to them we felt like grasshoppers, and that's what they thought too," they exclaimed (v. 33). Out of a team of twelve men, the best of their tribes, Caleb alone had the faith to take the land. The others cowered in fear, refused to act, and spread lies among the people of Israel about the land. Their cycle of worry and fear continued into the next generation.

We need to regularly recall all that God does for us so that circumstances don't blind our perspective of God. As children, of God, we cannot allow our physical senses, situations, and feelings determine the outcome or what is the truth. The truth is what God says, what is written in His Word, regardless of what we see or feel. We walk by faith and not sight. When we recognize fearful thoughts, anxious emotions, or worry, it is a sign that the evil one is influencing us and whispering in our ear. Instead of fixating—which is a type of meditating—on lies of the enemy or those things we cannot control, we must make a choice to meditate on what is pure, good, and of good report. We must make a choice to meditate on the One who can control our situation and perfect that which concerns us. (See Philippians 4:6–8; Psalm 138:8.)

Worry causes one to be anxious or uneasy, annoyed or bothered. In fact, worry is meditating on something that you cannot control, so if you are going to expend energy meditating, why not meditate on the One who can control your situation, the One who can perfect that which concerns you? (See Psalm 138:8, NKJV.)

I don't in any way mean to imply that the strongholds of anxiety and fear can be overcome in one prayer session by simply choosing to change our focus. These blockages are real and have strong roots. They must be dealt with seriously and, usually, over time before healing is achieved. Renewing our minds to meditate on the Spirit of truth is the first in a multi-step process to overcoming chronic worry and fear. As with the stronghold of depression, do not hesitate to call upon the help of pastors, doctors, and professional Christian counselors to aid you in your fight for freedom. Remember that God sacrificed His only Son so that you could take hold of complete and total freedom and walk in relationship with Him, hearing His voice daily. As you gather a team of trusted counselors to stand alongside you in your fight to overcome these attitudes, do not forget that God is your "strength and shield" (Ps. 28:7). He "will personally go ahead of you. He will be with you; he will neither fail you nor abandon you" (Deut. 28:7), so fear not!

Reflect

1. Oftentimes people who struggle with anxiety and fear were raised by parents or loved ones who also dealt with these same strongholds. They grow up learning that worry is good and helpful, like a protective sixth sense that allows them to control circumstances and avoid danger or pain. Other times, fear is rooted in adverse childhood trauma. In these instances, it is likely that the individual has never learned how to deactivate the body's response to fearful situations, so now in the present the body, when triggered, instantly responds in anxiety. Examine your heart. If this is part of your testimony, recognize it, own it, and seek a professional, but also repent of allowing fearfulness and worry to develop a stronghold. Make a plan for how you will begin the journey to walking in wholeness and freedom.

_____
_____
_____
_____

2. Why is it that fear spreads so quickly when it is shared with others? Can you think of a Bible verse or another passage of Scripture that supports your answer or demonstrates the "catching" nature of worry and fear?

_____
_____
_____
_____

3. Which of the attitudes in this lesson is your greatest struggle? What is your plan for overcoming this obstacle and making a change in your attitude in order to start hearing from the Lord more clearly and effectively?

_____
_____
_____
_____

Pray

Dear God, thank You that Your plan for me is good and that You had worked out all the details of my life long before I was even born. Nothing surprises You, Father, and there is no obstacle or circumstance in my life that will ever be too great for You to overcome. Lord, become more real to me than the fears over which I worry. When I experience anxiety, prompt me through Your Holy Spirit to meditate on Scripture or to turn to You in prayer to experience relief in the moment. Show me what I may do to break out of the cycle of worry and fearfulness so that I can experience Your peace, which passes understanding. If I need the help of a pastor, doctor, or Christian counselor, lead me to a professional who is rooted and grounded in You and will develop a plan of action that has Your plan for me in mind. In Jesus's name, I pray. Amen.

Exercise

Ask the Lord to reveal to you any fears or anxieties you are currently struggling with. List them. Perhaps some come to mind immediately? Do you have a fear of failure, rejection, financial instability, or confrontation? Are you feeling anxious about the future? Is there pain in your body that is causing you to feel afraid or anxious? Whatever fears you are feeling, write them all down.

Next, tell God how these fears and anxieties affect you. Be honest with Him. Do they control you in any way? Are they inhibiting you from taking necessary risks or participating in life? Do they cause your body to suffer, tremor, or to respond in some other uncomfortable way?

Then ask God if there are any lies or deceptions attached to these worries and fears. Now listen, and journal what He says. Spend a few minutes silently and expectantly awaiting a response.

Finally, pray:

Heavenly Father, thank You for revealing these worries and fears to me. Thank You for Your love and affection toward me. I confess that I have allowed these worries and fears to control me. I have often made decisions based on these fears. I repent for agreeing with worry and fear. Thank You, Lord, for Your forgiveness and love. I recognize that You have not given me a spirit of fear, but of power, love, and a sound mind (2 Tim. 1:7). In the name of Jesus, I renounce any spirit of fear that is harassing me or operating in my life in any way. I desire to receive Your perfect love that casts out fear.

Now, one by one, begin to confess and renounce your fears and anxieties:

Father, I renounce the fear of _____, the fear of _____, and the fear of _____. (If you have more fears, then repeat).

Today, I choose to live and walk by faith in You. Help me to trust in You. I pray this in Jesus's name. Amen.

My Story
Death to Self Brings Life

March 19, 2008. Fear in all forms has been my deepest struggle thus far in my walk as a Christian and even before I was a Christian. I at times have felt like an onion when it comes to fear: Just when I think I have been healed and delivered of it, God unveils or peels another layer off, only to expose another layer that needs to be dealt with. One particular fear that has paralyzed me is the fear of winter driving. The root of that fear goes back to an incident/accident that happened on icy roads almost twelve years ago.

A couple of nights ago the Lord gave me a dream. I usually don't remember my dreams, but when I do, they are significant. In this dream, I saw a huge cross. I started walking toward it. As I got closer, I saw Jesus standing beside/in front of it. I drew near to Him, and once we were face to face He asked me, "Are you willing to die for Me?"

"Yes, Lord," I said.

Then Jesus asked again, "Are you willing to die for Me?"

I looked at Him a bit confused and said again, "Yes, Lord, I am."

Then He looked at me again and asked emphatically, "No. Are you willing to die for Me?"

"Yes," I cried.

Then I raised my hand up, facing the cross, and I saw the nail go into my hand. I raised my other hand, and a second nail pierced through my hand. There I was, arms up in complete surrender. Finally, my feet were pierced, and I was in total submission. I did not feel pain or fear, for Christ Jesus was right beside me.

I knew the interpretation of the dream: I had not surrendered to Christ and what He already accomplished on the cross. I was instead yielding to fear. But in this dream I was nailed to the cross as a symbolic act of surrender—surrender to Him and His lordship over my life as He stood right in front of me face to face. I realized that the fear that gripped me was fear of death. The root of fear is death, whether it is physical death, spiritual death, or death to self. For me, I believe I was fearful of all three, but in that vision I realized that any fear is about self-preservation.

I woke up feeling release. I felt free, overwhelmed, and very much repentant. I was so overwhelmed by the dream because it felt like it transcended time and emotion.

It was so real, and its impact was so lasting that I decided I needed to share it with a friend I was already scheduled to meet with. As I began to share my experience with her, I noticed she was holding a cross that was attached to her keychain. Her eyes were looking at me intently, but I felt that she wasn't listening to me. I could see her blank stare, so I asked her what was going on. I was right. She revealed to me that, that morning as she was preparing to leave the thought of giving me a keychain with a cross on it just dropped in her mind. It was a thought inspired by God, but she reasoned against it for two reasons:

1. She only bought six of them, and I wasn't one of the ones to whom she wanted to give it.
2. If it were God speaking to her, then she would wait until Easter to give it to me, because in her mind it would be more meaningful.

She apologized first to the Lord for reasoning against His instructions, and then she apologized to me because she realized that God had indeed spoken to her about giving me the keychain with a cross on it. Both of us saw the significance of that gift. The cross would remind me of complete surrender, of spiritual death and death to self, as well as self-preservation. And the fact that it was a keychain attached to my keys would be another reminder that even in a car Jesus is with me face to face. I do not have to fear death. Jesus is in complete control.

Lesson Ten

Grieving and Quenching the Holy Spirit

Day 46

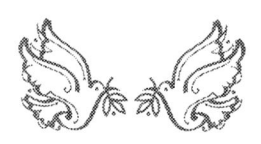

Grieving the Spirit of God

Do not bring sorrow to God's Holy Spirit by the way you live.

—Ephesians 4:30

We know that all sin is rebellion, but did you know that sin grieves the Holy Spirit in us? Isaiah 63:10 says, "But they rebelled and grieved His Holy Spirit" (NKJV). Because the Holy Spirit is a Person, He can be grieved just like you and me.

We grieve the Spirit of God when we willingly choose to sin or voluntarily stay in sin—any sin. The enemy knows and understands that when we rebel we have just rejected God's goodness, God's blessings, and God's hand of protection on our lives. Satan rejoices when we ignore God's presence, inner voice, or leading, because he knows that the Word says that "if … [we] live according to the flesh … [we] will die" spiritually speaking (Rom. 8:13, NKJV, see also vv. 5–17). His goal is to see us lost, separated from God,[40] and deaf to His voice speaking to us. Intentional and habitual sin accomplishes each of these purposes in our life.

We can also grieve the Spirit through unwholesome talk and through hurting one another. Ephesians 4:29–31 directly connects the words we speak with the state of our relationship with God:

> Don't use foul or abusive language. Let everything you say be good and helpful, so that your words will be an encouragement to those who hear them … Do not bring sorrow to God's Holy Spirit by the way you life … Get rid of all bitterness, rage, anger [all of which can lead to], harsh words, and slander.

Why are our words important to God? How could what we say bring grief and sorrow to His Spirit? Because God loves all people;. He cares for all His children, those who are Christians and those who are not. When we are hurtful or hateful to one another—whether we think it is justified or not—this causes Him grief because it goes against who He is, love. That is why we are instructed in Ephesians 4:32 to, "Be kind and compassionate to one another, forgiving each other, just as in Christ God forgave you" (NIV).

When we choose to sin and do not confess our wrongdoing and when we hurt others with unwholesome and damaging words, we are walking contrary to what God has spoken directly to us in His Word. Our renewed, regenerated spirit knows this, and it alerts us to wrongdoing, giving us a chance to repent and change our ways. This conviction of sin is powerful to produce change in our hearts and keep us from living in sin. However, if we ignore conviction and choose instead to walk in unrepentant sin, this helpful conviction will turn sour in our spirits, causing chronic guilt, mental anguish, and emotional turmoil. It will also lead to a hardened heart. (More on that in the next session). What's more, unrepentant sin, habitual or not, and harmful speech also give Satan legal access to wreak havoc in our lives.

For our conscience's sake, and for our own heart's sake, when we do sin, we need to confess quickly. When we fail to confess and repent (i.e., acknowledge, admit, and change our minds and turn from doing wrong behavior), our conscience gets seared. In other words, it becomes desensitized towards sin. The more we sin, the easier it is to sin some more. And the more we sin, the more our hearts become hardened. (See Ephesians 4:18–19.) However, if we humble ourselves and show our dependency upon God, we remain sensitive toward God, maintain a clean heart before Him, and our hearts stay soft and pliable.

Reflect

1. Read Ephesians 4:21–31 (NKJV). In your own words, what is the central message of this passage? What do these scriptures tell us about God?

_____
_____
_____
_____

2. Read Luke 6:45. What does this tell us about the source of hurtful words and how we can cut them off at the root so that our words speak life instead of death?

_____
_____
_____
_____

3. Are there any areas of your life in which you could be grieving the Spirit of God? Consider your heart and your actions. If you have hurt others with your words, confess it and repent. If you have unconfessed sin, confess it and repent. If you are walking in habitual sin, confess it, repent, and

make a plan for change so that you will be able to resist the pull of that behavior and maintain a clean heart.

___

Pray

Heavenly Father, I am in awe of Your profound grace and mercy toward me. Thank You for sending Jesus to redeem me from the curse and make a way for me to be reconciled back into right relationship with You. Lord, help me not to take that for granted by willfully choosing to sin or, when I do, failing to confess and truly repent. Keep my heart clean, soft, and pliable so that I can walk in unbroken fellowship with You. In the name of Jesus, I pray. Amen.

Listen

Ask the Lord to give you a fresh revelation of Jesus's sacrifice on the cross for you. Spend a few minutes silently and expectantly awaiting a response. Conclude your time of listening with praise.

My Story

Letting Go of Others, Holding on to God

Here I sit again recognizing I have grieved the Spirit of God. I have lost my peace. When will I learn? When will I realize far more quickly and understand that it is better to seek God and to have Him deal with my emotions and heal them rather than to remain in my feelings and stew? The latter is always worse. Plus, I know the latter grieves Him. I can feel it. How can I tell? Because I feel heavy, weighed down, grieved, and overwhelmed by my anger.

I haven't been ready to deal with this pain, and I indeed am not prepared to forgive. This pain is drawing me deeper and deeper into the abyss of darkness. Pressure pushes on my chest. Instead of recognizing that I was grieving the Spirit of God and willingly walking toward unrest, I have continued to complain. I have continued to murmur. I have continued to be self-focused and feel justified in my behaviors. I have told anyone who would listen what was done to me. As far as I have been concerned, my perpetrator deserved my wrath, deserved exposure. How dare this injustice be done to me! It can be so unfair. Why is it OK that I go to God while my villain goes left unpunished? Why should I forgive yet again while nothing changes? In fact, it appears that the person who did this to me continues to prosper while still drawing away from God.

I still feel unloved, rejected, and invisible. I feel that I have been put last, that I am an afterthought, only to be appeased. I also feel angry, resentful, irritated, insulted, and put down, and it drives me crazy how my feelings are constantly minimized. I feel aggravated, annoyed, bitter, and full of momentary hatred.

I paused here to cry, to allow myself to feel my pain of what was done to me, and to allow God to minister to my hurts and reveal any lies. I then confessed and repented of my sins. After I did this, I was ready to pray.

Father, why is it sometimes so hard to do what I know is right? Instead, I hang on to this hurt. I hang on to this pain, knowing that I am suffering because of it. I hang on to unforgiveness and bitterness, and all the while I know this is grieving Your Spirit. Lord, I am seething on the inside, and I realize I am creating a callous in my heart. My heart is hardening toward You and my perpetrator. I am rationalizing in my mind reasons to stay in this place of grief and self-pity, then anger, and even rage.

But I know this will hold me captive. I know that as long as I stay in this place of sorrow and bondage to bitterness my path will only become darker and darker. So, I come to You, Father, and I am ready to deal with this pain. I am prepared to forgive. I know forgiveness is a choice and not a feeling, so I will move toward You. Lord Jesus, I choose to forgive in spite of my feelings. Lord, what do You want to say to me?

I paused again to listen for God's voice. This was His reply:

My child, I will refresh you and replenish your sorrowful soul.[41] Be still, and know that I am God.[42] I love you. You are not unloved, rejected, and invisible. You are accepted in the Beloved. You are My beloved.[43] I rejoice over you with gladness. I will quiet you with My love. I will rejoice over you with singing.[44]

I responded:

Father, I can sense Your peace, and it is sweet to me. Father, I release this situation and all people involved to You. I place them on Your lap. I choose not to hold on to this pain or any resentment and unforgiveness. I let go of vengeance. I ask that You deal with them, because being mad is only hurting me. Open my heart, Lord, and heal my damaged emotions. Fill me to overflowing with Your love, Your light, and Your life. Help me to see them the way You see them. Help me to walk in the fruit of Your Spirit again. Fill me, Lord, with peace, hope, and self-control. Every time Satan comes again to tempt me to remember others' faults, quicken me by Your Spirit to take those thoughts captive. I ask You, Father, to bless them, in Jesus's name. Amen.

When I was finished, I felt such peace. There was a stillness in my soul. The Spirit of God was no longer grieved within me, and I left the prayer room feeling as though the weight of the world had been lifted.

Day 47

What Is a Hardened Heart?

> Do not give the devil a foothold. … Do not bring sorrow to God's Holy Spirit by the way you live.
>
> —Ephesians 4:27, NIV

To walk in the Spirit means to hear Him and obey Him. We are led by the Spirit when we obey Him the moment He prompts, quickens leads, directs, or warns us of impending danger, regardless of how we feel. When we decide to sin, then we are walking in the flesh. To walk in the flesh means to hear Satan and obey him, regardless of the conviction we may feel in our spirit.

> I say then: Walk in the Spirit, and you shall not fulfill the lust of the flesh. For the flesh lusts against the Spirit, and the Spirit against the flesh; and these are contrary to one another, so that you do not do the things that you wish.
>
> —Galatians 5:16–17, NKJV

Walking in the flesh gives place to the devil to wreak havoc in our lives. Though God's Spirit is grieved through these actions, we are the ones who suffer needlessly, especially because God has made a way of escape for us through confession and repentance. If the cares, lures, and desires of this world become a higher priority than the realities and desires of God's kingdom and purposes, then we will gradually cease to recognize and experience intimacy or fellowship with God. We're still saved but hardened. We may still go to church, fellowship with other believers, but we are not growing or being discipled. Over time, we become desensitized to sin and our heart becomes hardened to the things of God.

A hardened heart is a heart that is like rock, insensitive and unyielding to God's voice within and God's Word. It is like a callus that has built up over time from repetitive actions or ear wax that has clogged up the ear. That's because whatever we neglect, we become hardened to. Whatever we focus our hearts upon, whatever we delight in, we become sensitive to at the exclusion of other voices.

In Mark 4:19 Jesus cautioned us to be careful what we are focusing on and where our heart is. He said, "The cares of this world, the deceitfulness of riches, and the desires for other things entering in choke the word, and it becomes unfruitful" (NKJV). When we are concerned more about the natural realm and the cares of this life, it chokes out the Word of God in our lives, whether it is the Holy Spirit speaking within or what has been planted in our hearts by the Bible.

We can have many things that we focus on—hobbies, TV, work, even ministry—but if our hearts are not sensitive to the Spirit of God, these things can begin to take first place in our hearts. The more priority we give to other things, the less we will be able to discern, detect, and be intimate with God. The more our focus is off of God and on the flesh, the harder our hearts will become and the farther we will fall from the Father. Jesus said in Luke 12:34, "For where your treasure is, there your heart will be also" (NKJV). If our treasure is with things far from God, our heart will be separated from Him too.

Habitual, unrepentant sin is the most obvious way our heart becomes hardened to the things of God. There are other ways in which our hearts become hardened, however:

- *By ignoring or disobeying the promptings or voice of the Holy Spirit:* Hebrews 3:15 says, "Today if you will hear His voice, do not harden your hearts as in the rebellion" (NKJV). Whether God speaks to us within through a prompting or knowing; through the still, small voice; another person or circumstances; in visions or in dreams; or through His word, we need to be quick to heed His voice so that our hearts remain soft and we do not grieve Him. We must not be like Pharaoh, whose willful disobedience to God's instructions through Moses hardened his heart. (See Exodus 4:21.)
- *When we choose to complain and murmur instead of praising, trusting, and remembering all that God has done and what He promises to do*: Trials and tests will come, but we need to deal with why we are complaining. We have to face it, change it if we can, and accept what we can't. We go to God and complain to Him. We unload our pains, sorrows, griefs, and murmurings onto God and then choose to praise, trust, and remember all that God has already done for us. He will not fail us. He is the Shepherd who promises to lead us to green pastures, sit us beside still waters, comfort us when we mourn, and bless us to be a blessing. The promises go on and on. When difficult times beset us, we must focus on His word, spoken or written, and what He says, as opposed to what we see or feel.

For He is our God, and we are the people of His pasture, and the sheep of His hand. Today, if you will hear His voice: "Do not harden your hearts, as in the rebellion, as in the day of trial in the wilderness, when your fathers tested Me; they tried Me, though they saw My work. For forty years I was grieved with that generation, and said, 'It is a people who go astray in their hearts, and they do not know My ways.'"

—Psalm 95:7–10, NKJV

- *Ignoring emotions, such as anger, fear, rage, sadness, and the like*: It does not glorify God or honor Him when we pretend to be stoic and press down our emotions. Neither do I encourage pretending they are not there. This too causes a hardened heart. Instead, tune in to God and your feelings. Tell God exactly how you are feeling. Don't feel ashamed for being emotional. Instead, ask yourself, why am I feeling this way? What is the root? After all, God created us to be emotional beings. He is not angry that we feel. We can unload these feelings to God and allow Him to comfort us, speak into them, bring truth and clarity to the situation, as well as bring healing to our damaged emotions.

In each of these situations we have to be aware of pride. Pride will keep you from recognizing and acknowledging your weaknesses. It is like trying to see yourself in a mirror but standing too close to the glass. If you are trying to see what you look like, you cannot stand in front of a mirror with your nose pressed to the glass. Your vision will be blurred because your eyes cannot focus, and even then, your frame of vision will be too short to perceive much of anything at all. To gaze at your whole face or body, you must step back a bit so that you can see the entire picture. Pride causes us to become so hyper-focused on ourselves that our vision is blurred and we lose the ability to see past our own noses, as the old adage goes. Don't let pride cause you to miss the signs of a hardening heart and be your fall.

Reflect

1. How is it possible to be a churchgoer and still develop a hardened heart?

_____
_____
_____
_____

2. Reread Luke 12:34. Ask yourself, where is your treasure? Is it 100 percent in God, or have you made earthly relationships, hobbies, work, church activities, or something else part of your treasure? Based on this, where is your heart?

_____
_____
_____
_____

3. Take a look into the mirror of your heart. What do you see there? Take a few moments to pray and ask God what He sees in you. Listen for His response. If there is pride, repent of it and ask Him to help you submit to Him fully.

___

Pray

Heavenly Father, it is my sincere desire to communicate with You intimately and regularly. I want to speak to You and to hear Your respond; I long to hear Your thoughts and to become acquainted with the various ways You choose to speak to Your people. Lord, help me not to do anything that would harden my heart toward You or Your voice. When my actions, attitudes, and attentions stray from You and Your will for me, correct me so I can adjust my behavior and ensure that nothing impedes our fellowship. I delight in You and serving You above all else, Lord. In Jesus's name. Amen.

Listen

Ask the Lord to give you a vision of the state of your spiritual heart or to tell you its condition by some other means. Spend a few minutes silently and expectantly awaiting a response. Respond accordingly.

Day 48

The Road to a Hardened Heart

Do not be deceived, God is not mocked; for whatever a man sows, that he will also reap. For he who sows to his flesh will of the flesh reap corruption, but he who sows to the Spirit will of the Spirit reap everlasting life.

—Galatians 6:7–8, NKJV

Romans 1:21–25, 28–32 gives us a step-by-step explanation of the progression of spiritual rebellion and moral corruption that will lead to a hardened heart.

> Yes, they knew God, but they *wouldn't worship him* as God or even give him thanks. And they *began to think up foolish ideas* of what God was like. [The New King James Version says they "became futile in their thoughts."] As a result, *their minds became dark and confused.* ["Their foolish hearts were darkened," NKJV.] Claiming to be wise, they instead became utter fools. And instead of worshiping the glorious, ever-living God, *they worshiped idols made to look like mere people and birds and animals and reptiles.* So *God abandoned them to do whatever shameful things their hearts desired.* As a result, they did vile and degrading things with each other's bodies. They traded the truth about God for a lie. So they worshiped and served the things God created instead of the Creator himself, who is worthy of eternal praise! Amen. ... Since they thought it foolish to acknowledge *God, he abandoned them to their foolish thinking* ["God gave them over to a depraved mind," NIV] and let them do things that should never be done. *Their lives became full of every kind of wickedness, sin,* greed, hate, envy, murder, quarreling, deception, malicious behavior, and gossip. They are backstabbers, haters of God, insolent, proud, and boastful. They invent new ways of sinning, and they disobey their parents. They refuse to understand, break their promises, are heartless, and have no

mercy. They know God's justice requires that those who do these things deserve to die, yet they do them anyway. Worse yet, they encourage others to do them, too.

—emphasis added

First, this passage tells us that "they knew God," but instead of worshiping or praising Him, they refused to give Him thanks (v. 21). This mental shift away from gratefulness to God and worship of His name and nature began to change their thought life. Their thinking "became futile" (v. 21, NKJV), and they developed "foolish ideas of what God was like" (v. 21). This tells us that they were no longer listening to or hearing the voice of God, whether spoken or through His Word, since to hear and heed God's voice is to know Him. The more they lost track of who God is, the "darker" (NKJV) and harder their hearts became. Eventually they began to follow other gods, idolizing the creation instead of the Creator. (See v. 23.) Verse 25 says, "They traded the truth about God for a lie." As a result, "God gave them over to a depraved mind" (v. 28, NIV) to do what ought not to be done. This is what is known as quenching the Spirit. (More on that in the next lesson.) In the end, they were "filled with every kind of wickedness, evil, greed, and depravity" (v. 29, NIV).

We should not interpret verse 28 here to mean that God wants us to fail or that He will forsake us. Nor does He allow bad things into our lives so that we learn from evil. Instead, this passage shows us that we choose to give evil full reign in our lives when we pursue Satan's temptations and disobedience to the Spirit's leading or convictions. This is the spiritual law of sowing and reaping that was set in place since the beginning of creation. Galatians 6:7–8 confirms this truth: "Do not be deceived: God cannot be mocked. A man reaps what he sows. Whoever sows to please their flesh, from the flesh will reap destruction; whoever sows to please the Spirit, from the Spirit will reap eternal life" (NIV). We have been given free will, the ability and freedom to choose. When we do not heed the principles of God's Word, there are consequences to those choices. Now, we will never be so far from God that He cannot draw us back to Himself, but the process of softening a hardened heart is often long and requires total reliance on the Father and His leading.

Reflect

1. Like Romans 1:21–25, 28–32, Ephesians 4:17–19 explains the progression of rebellion and corruption that results in a hardened heart. Read Ephesians 4:17–19, and write out the progression in those verses, just as we did with the passage in Romans.

_____
_____
_____
_____

2. How do you prevent a hardened heart? Back your response up with Scripture.

_____
_____
_____
_____

3. Even though our free will can allow us to make choices that lead us away from the Lord, it is nonetheless a gift from a loving God who desires authentic relationship with us. Why is it important that God was willing to give us free will? How does that gift make it possible for us to have an intimate relationship with Him?

_____
_____
_____
_____

Pray

Heavenly Father, thank You for your matchless mercies, which are new every morning. Thank You that Your passionate pursuit of my heart and a relationship with me took You as far as the cross of Calvary. Lord, help me never to take that for granted. As I study Paul's warning to believers in Romans 1 and Ephesians 4 I am sobered by the thought of what it would look be like to live a life separated from You because of my choices and actions. God, may that never be so. May my heart be ever increasingly softened toward You and Your guidance. May the consequences of my choices only lead me into deeper fellowship with You. In Jesus name, I pray. Amen

Listen

Ask the Lord to reveal to you if there are any desires you want more than Him. Spend a few minutes silently and expectantly awaiting a response. Respond accordingly.

Day 49

Quenching the Spirit of God

> Do not quench the Spirit. Do not despise prophecies. Test all things; hold fast what is good. Abstain from every form of evil.
>
> —1 Thessalonians 5:19–22, NKJV

Constant and repeated disobedience and failure to respond to the Spirit's voice and leading will eventually cause such hardness of heart that we become resistant and unresponsive to God. As a result, His fire is put out, and we quench Him. (See 1 Thessalonians 5:19–22.) *To quench* means "stop the natural flow." One dictionary says it is "to subdue or destroy; overcome; quell; to put out or extinguish."[45] What does this mean for the believer? It means that our hearts get so hard and unresponsive that He stops speaking. This is not because God ceases to love us but because we have chosen to harden our hearts. As we saw in the last session, this is nothing more or less than the law of sowing and reaping in effect.

We see from 1 Thessalonians 5:20 that "despising prophecies" is related to quenching the Spirit. This scripture is addressing the quieting of the Lord's voice in a corporate setting. While our individual sin and hardness of heart can cause God to be silent in our lives and removes His hand of blessing from us, a similar effect can take place in churches and other ministry settings when the Holy Spirit's voice is restricted and limited. If church or organizational leadership does not support the operation of the prophetic, the Spirit will be quenched in that body. Putting out the fire of the Holy Spirit means nothing less than the loss of His activity and His supernatural gifts among His people. Individual members who are seeking to hear the voice of the Lord will continue to receive individually, but general words, visions, dreams, or other manifestations of God's Spirit in corporate settings will cease.

This is tragic and unnecessary. Paul summarizes his instructions to the church at Corinth in 1 Corinthians 14:26–40. His final words in that chapter are: "My dear brothers and sisters, be eager to prophesy, and don't forbid speaking in tongues. But be sure that everything is done properly and in order." There is no reason to restrict the flow of the Holy Spirit in our corporate worship. It is possible to allow Him free reign to move in our midst and still ensure that "everything ... [is] done in a fitting and orderly way" (v. 40, NIV).

The Holy Spirit desires to speak to us as individuals and as the body of Christ in corporate worship. His heart, which longs for intimacy with us, His creation, is grieved when our actions reap a harvest that keeps us from hearing His voice speak words of encouragement, direction, and love. Once we recognize the hardness of our heart and identify that His Spirit has been quenched, it is essential that we take immediate action to reverse the effects of our sin and cry out for fellowship to be restored with Him.

Reflect

1. What is the difference between how the Spirit is quenched in the life of the individual believer versus in a church or other ministry organization? Is the process the same, or is it different?

_____
_____
_____
_____

2. How can we be sure not to quench the Spirit of God? Back your response up with Scripture.

_____
_____
_____
_____

Pray

Dear God, thank You for Your relentless pursuit of me. Thank You that even if I stray from You, You will never stop wanting to engage in intimate fellowship with me. Lord, I don't want to quench Your Spirit. I want to reap life and intimacy with You, and I want to be a part of a church that is doing the same. I pray for the leadership of my church and the other members. I pray that they would fully embrace the move of Your Spirit so that You are not quenched but allowed to move and speak to the corporate body, as well as individuals. I pray this in Jesus's name. Amen.

Listen

Ask the Lord to give you a word of encouragement for your pastor or another ministry leader. Spend a few minutes silently and expectantly awaiting a response. Make a commitment to share that encouragement with him or her promptly.

Day 50

Softening a Hardened Heart

> And I will give you a new heart, and I will put a new spirit in you. I will take out your stony, stubborn heart and give you a tender, responsive heart.
>
> —Ezekiel 36:26

The Holy Spirit desires that we be led by Him and not by the weakness of our flesh, because our flesh has been crucified. It no longer has power over us. His power in us equips us to walk in victory. (See Romans 6:12–14; 13:12–14.) In other words, we have no excuse to sin. Most of our weaknesses are the result of basic human God-given needs not getting met conducive to Scripture and in ways pleasing to God. When these needs go unmet, we become weak and vulnerable. Thus, Satan comes to tempt us to get those needs met perversely. As we have seen over and over again, however, the fact of our salvation alone is not enough to keep us from sinning. None of us is without sin. First John 1:8 tells it like it is: "If we claim we have no sin, we are only fooling ourselves and not living in the truth." If we allow our hearts to become hardened and quench the Spirit of God, we will reap the consequences, which is death, according to Romans 8:6.

Once the Spirit has been quenched, only God knows how long He will remain silent. We can be sure of this, however: God longs to communicate with us, regardless of what we have done and how far from Him we may have strayed. There is a road that will lead us back to fellowship with God through softening our hearts and unquenching the Spirit. It may take time, but total restoration is possible, and we can be sure that the Helper and Comforter will assist us in our journey. It often means aligning ourselves back with the Word of God.

We know that the first steps to softening our hardened hearts and un-quenching the Spirit are confession and repentance. That is, we must admit to our specific sins and then make a commitment to turn away from the actions and behaviors that separated us from fellowship with God. First Thessalonians 5:16–24 sums up the rest of the process perfectly:

> Rejoice always, pray without ceasing, in everything give thanks; for this is the will of God in Christ Jesus for you. Do not quench the Spirit. Do not despise prophecies. Test all things; hold fast what is good. Abstain from every form of evil. Now may the God of peace Himself sanctify you completely; and may your whole spirit, soul, and body be preserved blameless at the coming of our Lord Jesus Christ. He who calls you is faithful, who also will do it.
>
> —NKJV

In these verses Paul articulates six distinct steps that will carry us along the road back to intimate communication with God: praise, a strong prayer life, thanksgiving, the active pursuit of God's voice, discernment, and a commitment to abstain from unrepentant and habitual sin.

Paul's admonition to "rejoice always" (v. 16) means to praise Him. Our hearts will soften when we are willing to be undignified like David and express our highest praise to Him. Don't be ashamed of Him. Love on Him lavishly! Tell Him repeatedly how much you love Him and honor Him. Show Him how much you love Him by prioritizing His praise over your own pride.

The next step is a strong prayer life. "Pray[ing] without ceasing" (v. 17) means we must stay in constant fellowship and communication with God throughout our day, both in times of solitude and stillness and during the busyness of everyday life. There is nothing that is too big or too small for us to take to God. He cares about all things in our life, and developing the habit of approaching Him in prayer is a crucial step to restoring open and unimpeded communication with Him.

It should come as no surprise that thanksgiving is the next crucial component in this process. Remember that the road to a hardened heart (as we saw in Romans 1:21–25, 28–32) begins with a refusal to glorify God or give Him thanks. While praise is glorifying God for who He is, thanksgiving is showing gratitude to God for what He has done for us. When Paul admonishes us to "be thankful in all circumstances" (v. 18), it is an instruction to shift our focus from our sin or our failure to measure up and instead look to Him and what He has already done in our lives. The truth is that we have good news: Christ "measured up" for us. We do not need to concern ourselves with our past mistakes or even our current circumstances, because that will cause us to give priority to our physical senses instead of the state of our spirit. When we find ourselves frustrated or beset by sin, we need only ask ourselves, What does God's Word say about us? Who are we in Him? If you need to look up the answers in the Word, do it. Then give thanks to God for the answers to those questions.

It may seem counterintuitive that the next step to unquenching the Spirit so that we can hear God's voice would be pursuing His Word and words to us, but it really makes perfect sense. Just as athletes train for years to develop muscle memory so that when everything is on the line their bodies know exactly what to do, heeding Paul's command not to "despise prophecies" will position our spirits to receive from the Lord in whatever form His message to us may come, whenever He chooses to speak. We should seek His voice in the Word of God, actively listening for wisdom in the form of *logos* and *rhema* words. We should be still before Him in prayer, patiently expecting to receive from the inner witness; the still, small voice; a vision or dream; or a revelation about our circumstances. We should also be receptive to prophetic words from prophets, those anointed with the gift of prophecy, and trusted believers.

Lest we forget to "test all things; hold fast what is good" (v. 21), Paul reminds us of this crucial practice in this next step to softening our hearts. Remember, when you do receive teaching that provides you with a *rhema* word; get or give a prophetic word, visions, or dreams; or hear an instruction, warning, quickening, or other message, test it! Consult the chart in Session 5 of Lesson 5 in this book to help you determine if what you are hearing or what has been spoken of you is, indeed, of God or if it is from your thoughts or the enemy. This will help keep you from falling back into error.

The final step to restoring our fellowship with the Spirit of God is perhaps the most obvious. When Paul admonishes us to "abstain from every form of evil" (v. 22), he means that we must resist the devil. Give him no place. Walk in the Spirit and not in the flesh. This is more than simply repenting. Remaining pure and maintaining a godly thought life is what closes the door to Satan and his tactics. Recognize him, his voice, his temptations and accusations, and his lies. Satan's neverending desire is to tempt us to act independently of God and go against His word, whether spoken or written in the pages of Scripture. The truth is, God's Word is life. It is an extension of Himself, teaching us and equipping us with wisdom. When we run to it, we will run away from the enemy.

The rest of this passage in 1 Thessalonians 5 contains a powerful promise to those desperate to establish or re-establish intimacy with God and hear Him speak to them: "Now may the God of peace Himself sanctify you completely; and may your whole spirit, soul, and body be preserved blameless at the coming of our Lord Jesus Christ. He who calls you is faithful, who also will do it" (vv. 23–24, NKJV). Even when we are estranged from Him because of the consequences of our sin, God is a God of peace, not a God of wrath. Because of Christ's substitutionary work on the cross, God's wrath against our sin was poured out on Jesus. He who knew no sin became sin for us so that we could enjoy God's mercy, love, and affection toward us. (See 1 Thessalonians 1:10; Romans 5:21.) As soon as we turn from the evil, the door is shut on Satan and the door to God's grace is opened before us!

This grace is essential to our relationship with the Father. God does not expect us to be perfect, whether we have had a hardened heart or not. He knows we are not as long as we live on this earth where Satan has free reign. Yet, accepting grace and walking in obedience means we cannot use our imperfections or the weaknesses of our flesh as an excuse to justify our actions and behaviors. Why? Because sin has no power over us anymore. It is our choice as to who we will listen to: the

Holy Spirit or the enemy. Our goal should be this: to "be imitators of God, therefore, as dearly loved children and live a life of love, just as Christ loved us and gave himself up for us as a fragrant offering and sacrifice to God" (Eph. 5:1–2, NIV). In our pursuit of this goal, we will fail at times, but it is our responsibility to confess our sins right away, repent, receive His forgiveness, and then declare we are the righteousness of God with the Holy Spirit living on the inside of us. It is He who empowers us to do what is right and not fall again into the snare of the evil one's temptation to gratify our flesh. If we don't do this, our hearts will remain hardened, and we will continue to yield to Satan and his whispers.

We must train ourselves to form new habits. This can be hard work, but we "can do all things through Christ who strengthens" us (Phil. 4:13, NKJV). If we find that we are struggling with a sin that we just cannot seem to let go of, then we need to pray and ask God to deliver us from this bondage. We may also need to seek others help by way of openly confessing this sin that has a stronghold over us. Often, when our secret is out in the open, the power that Satan has over us because of the shame, guilt, and condemnation is broken, and we are then healed. (See James 5:16.) This sort of persistent sin may also signal a deeper root issue that needs the healing power of Jesus. For this, I recommend seeking out someone who is equipped to help you listen in prayer and wait for the Lord to reveal the true root of the sin, whether emotional or spiritual in nature. Remember, there is wisdom in the multitude of counselors, and the Counselor Himself is living inside of you.

Beloved, our God is a good God. The fact may be that the storm is happening all around, but His truth is that He will take us through it and even calm it for us! He is with us, and He will never forsake us. He longs to communicate His heart towards you. There are mysteries He wants to reveal and strategies He wants to share to help you overcome obstacles. He wants to give you wisdom for every difficult situation, comfort when you are feeling down, and joy to give you hope. He speaks love over us if we would just stop and listen. He is the ultimate Provider; our intimate Protector; the Waymaker when there is no way; and the One who sees all things, knows all things, and can stop the devil in his tracks! He is speaking to you now, so sit a while and listen.

Reflect

1. In your own words, summarize the steps to softening a hardened heart and unquenching the Spirit. How might these steps be a helpful guide to anyone who desires to hear God speak, even if their heart is not hardened?

_____
_____
_____
_____

2. What is the difference between praise and thanksgiving? Why is this distinction important to our relationship with God?

_____
_____
_____
_____

3. What does grace mean for us? What does grace not mean?

_____
_____
_____
_____

Pray

Heavenly Father, thank You that You don't expect perfection. Thank You that I can come to You just as I am. I praise You for Your grace and for Your mercy. I ask that You search my heart. Show me, Lord, if my heart has been hardened. Reveal to me the roots, if any.

Wait. Be still and see if He shows you anything before you continue:

I desire to be teachable, humble, and easily led by You. Sanctify me completely, and may my whole spirit, soul, and body be preserved blameless at the coming of our Lord Jesus Christ. I pray this in Jesus's name. Amen.

Exercise

We have arrived at Day 50 of our journey together with God. Ask Him what He wants to speak over you. Ask Him what He wants to say or show you. Spend a few minutes silently and expectantly awaiting a response. Conclude your time of listening with praise and thanksgiving. You may also want to make a list of all that you are thankful for.

My prayer for you;

Father, I thank You for every person who has taken this journey with me to hear You speak. I ask You Father to bless them and keep them. Shine Your face upon them Lord, and be gracious. Let Your peace be their portion. Continue Father to draw them ever so close to You. Reveal Yourself to them in a way that they have never experienced before. Increase in them a hearing ear and heighten their spiritual senses. Let them be fruitful for Your Kingdom and propel them into Your destiny. I pray this in Jesus name, Amen.

Appendix A

How to Troubleshoot Problems with Hearing God

But it was to us that God revealed these things by his Spirit. For his Spirit searches out everything and shows us God's deep secrets. No one can know a person's thoughts except that person's own spirit, and no one can know God's thoughts except God's own Spirit. And we have received God's Spirit (not the world's spirit), so we can know the wonderful things God has freely given us. When we tell you these things, we do not use words that come from human wisdom. Instead, we speak words given to us by the Spirit, using the Spirit's words to explain spiritual truths. But people who aren't spiritual can't receive these truths from God's Spirit. It all sounds foolish to them and they can't understand it, for only those who are spiritual can understand what the Spirit means. Those who are spiritual can evaluate all things, but they themselves cannot be evaluated by others.

—1 Corinthians 2:10–15

1. Ask God for a hearing ear. Isaiah 50:4–5 says, "The Lord God has given Me the tongue of the learned, that I should know how to speak a word in season to him who is weary. He awakens Me morning by morning, He awakens My ear to hear as the learned. The Lord God has opened My ear; and I was not rebellious, nor did I turn away" (NKJV). Each of us is unique in our ability to hear God. Some are seers (they see visions and dreams), some are hearers (they hear God quite acutely), some are knowers (they are perceivers), some are feelers (they sense/feel God's presence or what He is saying through feeling it in their bodies), and some operate in more than one way. Don't despise or reject how you hear God. We often find ourselves comparing ourselves to others because of the way God has gifted them to hear Him or how He has chosen to speak to them. Whether you are a seer, hearer, knower/perceiver, feeler or a combination, accept it and appreciate God's design in

you. On the other hand, there is no reason to deny yourself from asking that God speak to you in other ways.

2. Learn to be still. Practice sitting at the feet of Jesus quietly and without busyness or distractions. Psalm 46:10 says, "Be still, and know that I am God."

3. Meditate on a passage of Scripture—not a chapter but a passage. Ponder it repeatedly. Then ask the Lord to speak to you regarding the verse. Ask Him to enlighten the eyes of your understanding that you may hear Him talk to you. Always invite Him into the practice of meditating on His Word, for He is the one who gives revelation. As you continue this practice you will be like David, who wrote in Psalm 119:103–104, "How sweet are Your words to my taste, sweeter than honey to my mouth! Through Your precepts I get understanding; therefore I hate every false way" (NKJV).

4. Ask God if your heart has been hardened. Has life beat you up? Do you need healing? Do you need His comfort? Perhaps He has spoken, and you didn't respond. Ask Him if He has spoken to you before and you have unknowingly or willingly disobeyed His prompting. Ask Him to reveal His specific request or your last act of disobedience, for when God speaks; we must learn to obey. The Scriptures warn us, "Today, when you hear his voice, don't harden your hearts" (Heb. 4:7).

5. Sin hinders us from hearing God. It is not that sin separates us from Him, for Christ has forgiven us from all sin: the past, present, and future; therefore we can come boldly to God by His Spirit. However, sin hardens our hearts and makes us less sensitive to His voice, usually because we are seething with offense, hurt, wounds, anger, or some other painful emotion that consumes our thoughts. Hebrews 3:12–13 cautions us, "Beware, brethren, lest there be in any of you an evil heart of unbelief in departing from the living God; but exhort one another daily, while it is called 'Today,' lest any of you be hardened through the deceitfulness of sin" (NKJV). When sin is exposed, do not justify it, do not entertain it, do not tolerate it, do not rationalize it, and do not ignore or deny it. Confess it. Admit that you did wrong (or that you are feeling wounded or are angry) and talk to God about it. Tell God who or what the problem is, how it made you feel, and ask God to heal your damaged emotions. Be specific. Then repent. Turn from it. Ask God to help you have victory in that area. And know that you are already forgiven, so thank Him for His mercy. Confession and repentance are part of sanctification as well as keeping our hearts soft and pliable.

6. Is there anyone you need to forgive? Do business with God.

7. Wait with expectancy. Expect God to speak. Be patient. It takes practice and discernment. While you wait, get acquainted with Scripture. Believe that God is an interactive God. He wants to

communicate with you. Psalm 62:5 says, "My soul, wait silently for God alone, for my expectation is from Him" (NKJV).

8. Trust Him. There are times and seasons. There is a time to speak and a time to be silent, and God has that right. There are times when we may have questions or concerns, but God chooses to be silent. We may be going through something, and we don't immediately hear from God. Don't lose sight that God has our good in mind. He may be calling us to press in deeper, to fast and pray. Seek Him.

9. You may need to fast and pray. Jesus is our ultimate model, and there were times when Jesus would leave the crowds to go fast and pray. However, the Old Testament is also full of wonderful examples of how people would fast and pray to seek God and hear Him more clearly. In those times of solitude, and without food, we are more spiritually attuned. (See Luke 4:1–14; Isaiah 58:6–12; Ezra 8:21–23.)

Appendix B

Learning to Judge and Test What You Hear

Do not scoff at prophecies, but test everything that is said. Hold on to what is good. Stay away from every kind of evil.

—1 Thessalonians 5:20–22

The Word is clear that we are to test the spirits and judge any word that we hear from the Holy Spirit for ourselves or for others. Below is a checklist of questions and activities that will help you discern the real source of any word.

1. Learn to journal. Ask yourself, what is the subject or topic of what you heard? What message did it contain? A word of edification? Exhortation? Comfort? Direction? Instruction? Wisdom? Counsel? (See 1 Corinthians 14:3; James 3:17.)

2. Is the content in agreement with God's Word? Remember, the Spirit of God is always in agreement or harmony with the Word of God. Whatever He speaks, it will never contradict God's Word. (See 1 John 5:6–11; 1 Timothy 6:3–5; 2 Timothy 3:16–17.)

3. Does it line up with God's character, nature, and personality? (See 1 John 4:1–6; Galatians 5:22–23.)

4. Does it draw you closer to God or draw you away from God? Does it cause you to grow in the process of sanctification or lead you to sin? (See Deuteronomy 13:1–5; James 1:13–15.)

5. What "fruit" or emotion did it produce in you? The Word of God declares we will know people and words by their fruit, whether good or bad. (See Matthew 7:16–17.) The Spirit of God always

speaks truth; always produces life; and never speaks death, bondage, fear, condemnation, or legalism. Nor does it leave us in confusion or having to guess at His purpose. (See Galatians 5:1, 13, 22–23; 1 Corinthians 14:33; Romans 8:14–16; 2 Corinthians 3:6; John 16:13.)

6. If it is the future, it must come to pass. (See Deuteronomy 18:21–22.) There are some exceptions. If the prophecy has a condition attached it must be followed, or it will not be fulfilled. One must respond in obedience. (Leviticus 26 is one example among many scriptures that support this exception.) Another exception is that sometimes the word given needs someone to contend for it. In the story of Hezekiah, we see that prophecy of his death was given, but because Hezekiah cried out to God in distress God changed the course of action and added fifteen more years to his life. (See also 1 Timothy 1:18.)

7. If you are still unsure about the source of a word, there is safety in a multitude of counselors. Ask spiritual advisors, leaders, or friends who know the Word of God better than you do and who you know hear from God. They can assist you in discerning if what you are hearing sounds biblical and can bring confirmation or correction to what you have heard. (See Proverbs 11:14.) Remember to be humble with a teachable spirit.

Notes

1. Is this biblical? Can Jesus reveal Himself in this way? Yes, He can. John 1:4–5 says, "In Him was life, and the life was the light of men. And the light shines in the darkness, and the darkness did not comprehend it" (NKJV).
2. Dictionary.com, s.v. "religion," http://www.dictionary.com/browse/religion?s=t.
3. Ibid., s.v. "relationship," http://www.dictionary.com/browse/relationship?s=t.
4. See Romans 7:15–20.
5. See Matthew 1:18–20.
6. See Hebrews 2:17–18; 4:14–15.
7. See Luke 4:17–19, 21.
8. See Romans 10:4.
9. This metaphor appears so often in Scripture that the Book of Hebrews even refers to Christ as "the great Shepherd of the sheep" (Heb. 13:20).
10. Mark Batterson, *The Circle Maker* (Grand Rapids, MI: Zondervan, 2016), 115.
11. BlueLetterBible.org, s.v. "*eidō*," https://www.blueletterbible.org/lang/lexicon/lexicon.cfm?Strongs=G1492&t=KJV.
12. Mark and Patti Virkler, *How to Hear God's Voice* (Shippensburg, PA: Destiny Image, 2006), 48–49.
13. BlueLetterBible.org, s.v. "*ginōskō*," https://www.blueletterbible.org/lang/lexicon/lexicon.cfm?Strongs=G1097&t=KJV.
14. David Watson, *I Believe in the Church* (Grand Rapids, MI: Eerdmans, 1979).
15. Ibid.
16. BlueLetterBible.org, s.v. "*ruwach*," https://www.blueletterbible.org/lang/lexicon/lexicon.cfm?Strongs=H7307&t=KJV.
17. Ibid., s.v. "*uwr*," https://www.blueletterbible.org/lang/lexicon/lexicon.cfm?Strongs=H5782&t=KJV.
18. Merriam-Webster Online Dictionary, s.v. "perceive," https://www.merriam-webster.com/dictionary/perceive.
19. In three of these examples we see God blocking the perception of people instead of granting it. Since it is His Spirit alone who gives us the anointing to perceive, and in His Sovereignty, the Lord can both give and take away this gift.
20. BlueLetterBible.org, s.v. "*apokalyptō*," https://www.blueletterbible.org/lang/lexicon/lexicon.cfm?Strongs=G601&t=KJV.
21. *The New American Standard New Testament Greek Lexicon*, Bible Study Tools, s.v. "*paraklesis*," https://www.biblestudytools.com/lexicons/greek/nas/parakletos.html.
22. BlueLetterBible.org, s.v. "*parakletos*," https://www.biblestudytools.com/lexicons/greek/nas/parakletos.html.

23 Frederick Dale Bruner, *The Gospel of John: A Commentary* (Grand Rapids, MI: Wm. B. Eerdmans, 2012), 610.
24 One example is the Scriptures' description of God as both the lion of Judah—powerful, ferocious, and untamed—and the Lamb of God, who is gentle and meek and willing to lay down His life as a sacrifice.
25 Neil T. Anderson, *Who I Am in Christ* (Ada, MI: Bethany House, 2001).
26 Andrew Wommack, *Spirit, Soul, and Body* (Tulsa, OK: Harrison House, 2010), 51.
27 Elmer Towns, *Fasting for Spiritual Breakthrough* (Ventura, CA: Regal, 1996).
28 Ibid., 81.
29 Dictionary.com, s.v., "exhort," http://www.dictionary.com/browse/exhort?s=t.
30 Graham Cooke, *Developing Your Prophetic Gifting* (Ada, MI: Chosen, 2003), 170.
31 Ibid., 166.
32 Ibid., 167.
33 When learning or considering how God uses circumstances to speak to us, we also need to understand that just as much as God can and does use circumstances to guide us into His will, circumstances are not always a sign that God is speaking or that it is an indication that God is leading us. Discernment will be key. Circumstances alone should not be a litmus test to determine if it is God speaking.
34 Another excellent example of God speaking through a vision and the recipient pressing in to receive the interpretation may be found in Zechariah 1:8–10, 18–21; 2:1–2; 6:1–8.
35 *Life Application Study Bible* (Grand Rapids, MI: Zondervan, 2011), s.v., Acts 10:15–16.
36 It is extremely helpful to know your God-given temperament. If you do not know your disposition, then I suggest you find yourself a certified temperament counselor like myself, because understanding who you are and how God created you to specifically relate to Him will give you a sense of freedom and confidence to be yourself. Though I agree there are times and seasons to establish various disciplines in prayer, in reading the Word of God, in meditation of the Holy Scriptures to deepen our relationship with God that may not be natural to our temperaments, seeking God conducive to our temperaments is most efficient and far less stressful.
37 Romans 14:23 says, "But whoever has doubts is condemned if they eat, because their eating is not from faith; and everything that does not come from faith is sin" (NIV).
38 Dictionary.com, s.v., "oppressed," http://www.dictionary.com/browse/oppressed?s=t.
39 Neil T. Anderson and Joanne Anderson, *Overcoming Depression* (Ada, MI: Bethany House, 2004), 10.
40 Before becoming born again we are separated from God spiritually. After being born again, sin does not separate us from God, though we often distance ourselves from him.
41 See Jeremiah 31:25.
42 See Psalm 46:10.
43 See Ephesians 1:6.
44 Zephaniah 3:17.
45 Dictionary.com, s.v. "quench," http://www.dictionary.com/browse/quench?s=t.